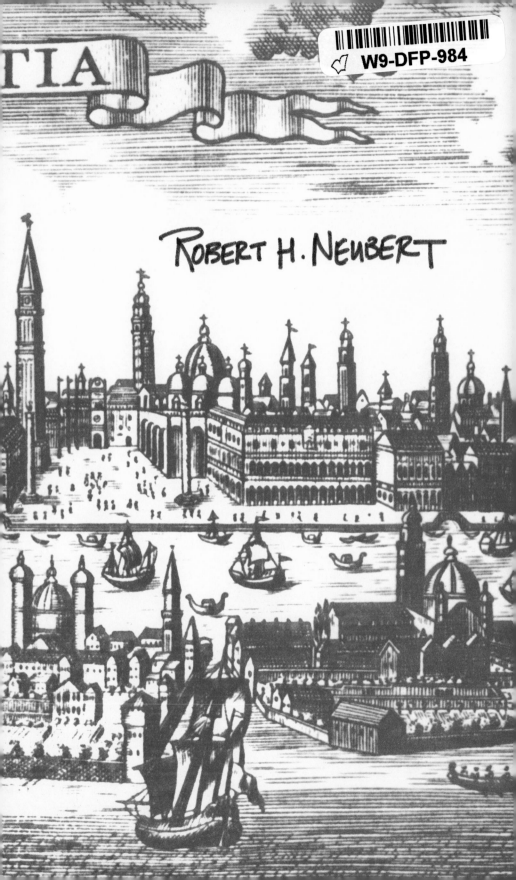

VENETIAN COOKING

VENETIAN COOKING

200 Authentic Recipes from a Great Regional Cuisine Adapted for American Cooks

H. F. BRUNING, JR.
AND
CAV. UMBERTO BULLO

Macmillan Publishing Co., Inc. • New York
Collier Macmillian Publishers • London

Preceding page: View of Santa Maria della Salute from Accademia Bridge over Grand Canal.

The photographs in this book were taken by H. F. Bruning, Jr.; Leslie Davidson; and Photo Renard, Venice.

Macmillan Publishing Co., Inc.
866 Third Avenue, New York, N.Y. 10022
Collier-Macmillan Canada Ltd., Toronto, Ontario

Library of Congress Catalog Card Number: 72-12454
First Printing 1973

Printed in the United States of America

TO LESLIE & MARIA

CONTENTS

Foreword

FIRST OF ALL I want to bring to the attention of the readers or those consulting this collection of recipes that I am not pretending to have discovered or invented anything new in the culinary art. Many cookbooks have been written about Italian cuisine and there are many publications devoted to the art of eating well in general that point out the foods most appealing to the connoiseur. I am not a professional cook; neither do I pretend to be a good enough teacher to point out which dishes are best suited for satisfying the more demanding palates. I am simply a man who likes to eat well and who will prepare the meals that give me the most satisfaction.

The origin of this collection is the preparation of Venetian cuisine as it is done in our homes. In this small book we have collected the various recipes most enjoyed by Venetians, and although they are simple, they are most appetizing.

To this end, the art of eating well even in a simple manner and deriving therefrom the greatest pleasure, one should keep in mind the following ten commandments:

. . . that in order to eat well the preparation of the food must be done with the greatest care, at best almost religiously, at least with patience and willingness.

. . . that the starting materials, meat, fish, or whatever, be fresh and of the first quality.

. . . that foods for their perfect enjoyment must be cooked neither too long nor too short a time.

. . . that foods do not need to be excessively seasoned or sauced, but that seasonings and sauces used in moderation will enhance the flavor without overtaxing the digestion.

. . . that it is necessary to pay attention to one of the principle condiments, namely salt; easy to add if need be, but impossible to remove.

. . . that to properly enjoy a meal it is indispensable that one arrive at the table with appetite, which is to say with the stomach well prepared, and that to so stimulate the appetite a simple but good *aperitif* may be taken beforehand.

. . . that everything turns out better when one prepares foods of his own liking.

. . . that it is an intelligent and healthful practice not to eat hurriedly, so as to better savor the flavor and to digest meals more easily.

. . . that the stomach has its demands, but also the eye wants its part, which is to say that the presentation as well as the preparation should be done with care.

. . . that, finally, the simplest fare becomes a feast when taken in the company of loved ones, good friends, or congenial acquaintances, while the most elaborate banquet gives no satisfaction if little sympathy exists among those present.

I would like to close with a Venetian proverb: *A tavola non s'invecchia mai.* At the table one never grows old. With that thought in mind I wish you the very best, hope you will enjoy this collection and . . . *buon appetito!*

UMBERTO BULLO

Winged lion, symbol of St. Mark, patron saint of Venice.

Introduction

A NUMBER OF PEOPLE have asked us what is so special about the Venetian kitchen that merits a book devoted exclusively to the subject. What they are really asking is, "With all the Italian cookbooks around, why bother with another?"

A comprehensive answer would take too much space, probably be insulting to the people and cuisine of whole regions of Italy, and conceivably be interpreted as a mixture of Venetian chauvinism and sour grapes. Therefore, we shall be as brief and unoffensive as possible.

Italy has an area only about three-quarters that of the state of California and although it is difficult for Americans to grasp, differences from one region to another are enormous. For example, a Sicilian who speaks only Sicilian dialect and a Venetian who speaks only Venetian cannot converse intelligently even if they should want to. Just as the language changes from region to region, so too do customs, including the preparation of food. One has only to go the 115 miles from Venice to Bologna to appreciate how great this change can be. The Bolognese kitchen, one of the most renowned, is noted for its heartiness. What then is the hallmark of Venetian cooking?

Venetian cooking is more delicate, more subtle, and lighter than that of other regions.

With that statement we have most likely offended 98 percent of the Italian and Italian-American populations. Nevertheless we believe it is true since there are three ingredients which account for most of the sins of the Italian kitchen in general: garlic, olive oil, and tomato. Sins include the excessive and often indiscriminate use of spices and herbs.

Venetians tend toward moderation. Specifically, garlic is normally browned in a small amount of olive oil and then discarded before other ingredients are added. This gives a slight perfume to the oil but chunks of garlic do not wind up in the finished dish. Tomato sauce is measured in tablespoonfuls, not cupfuls, and herbs and spices are used discreetly. In short, most Venetian dishes are designed to retain and complement the flavor of the principal ingredient rather than to mask it.

The recipes we give are for the most part simple and flexible. They are simple enough so that even the greenest novice in the kitchen should have few problems preparing the most complicated. They are flexible just because they are so simple and not ritualistic. If one is making a soufflé he had better follow the ritual reasonably closely if he wants to avoid a culinary disaster. Not necessarily so with Venetian cooking where there is latitude. For example, one of the authors prefers more anchovies in his *bigoli in salsa*, spaghetti with anchovy sauce, than the other, while some people even add some tuna and capers. It still comes out to be *bigoli in salsa*, and it is still Venetian. The point is that the recipes as they stand are honest and we believe excellent, but if you wish to add or subtract a little bit, go ahead. Think of what will bring the greatest pleasure to you and to those whom you wish to please.

EQUIPMENT

Most Venetian cooking is done on top of the stove and much of it requires simmering. We have no particular preference when it comes to pots and pans beyond the fact that the thicker the bottoms the easier it is to obtain even heat, the important factor in simmering. As to the number of pots and pans, the more the better. Some recipes call for three saucepans, but certainly a pot or even a frying pan may often be substituted. Most people even moderately interested in cooking will have at least the minimum requirements in this area.

For anyone deeply interested in any kind of Italian cooking a cheese grater of some sort is a necessity since freshly grated cheese is far superior in flavor to pregrated. We use a very simple curved one which is also useful as a rolling surface in the making of *gnocchi*, page 105. Other more efficient types are available.

Wire whips, spatulas, wooden spoons, a skimming device, poultry shears, and a baster are all so useful that most people probably already have them. Items that are helpful but sometimes not found in home kitchens include a food mill and a potato ricer. They are not absolutely necessary but will make things easier for a couple of the recipes.

INGREDIENTS

If you can, try to find Italian rice, pasta, *prosciutto*, and Parmesan cheese. If not available substitute the best domestic qualities.

Excellent materials for the majority of other ingredients are readily available in most parts of America. A few, we know, will be difficult to find anywhere (squid, octopus, and razor clams, for example), but recipes calling for hard-to-find ingredients represent a minuscule part of the book.

QUANTITIES

The recipes state how many they will serve. Keep in mind, though, that they are designed to be parts of a typical Venetian meal, which means two courses at least. If you plan to serve them as a one-course meal, all the quantities should be increased substantially. We have noted in the recipes when a dish is exceptionally heavy and in some cases have made suggestions for a suitable accompanying course.

RECIPE TITLES AND INTRODUCTIONS

The recipe titles are given first in Venetian, then in Italian, and finally in English. The italicized parts before the recipes are general comments by the Venetian coauthor, while the rest of the introductions are the American coauthor's explanations of procedures which might seem strange or points which he feels may be of interest.

Antipasto

MODERATION should be the keynote in dealing with *antipasti*. The cook is tempted to prepare too much and the diner to eat it all. *Anti* means before and *pasto* means meal, and an *antipasto* should not interfere with the meal itself. Rather, it should whet a lagging appetite and calm an overzealous one. It should bring the diner to a point where subsequent courses may be thoroughly enjoyed.

More than any other course *antipasto* requires planning if you wish to serve a combination of several things, which is often done. This makes it all the easier to fall into the trap of preparing too great quantities. Certain *antipasti*, though, are more appreciated when accompanied by other things. For example, sardines or tuna go well with pickled vegetables. Baked mussels, baked scallops, and raw oysters, on the other hand, all seem better by themselves. Or so it seems to us. There are no set rules; it depends wholly upon one's own personal preferences.

All but two of the recipes in this section are for seafood, which should tell you something about Venetians. We also refer to recipes to be found in other parts of the book, those that are occasionally served as *antipasti* but are more often eaten as a second course or as a vegetable course. Finally, you will find a list of things that require no recipe and can be prepared with the aid of a can opener, vegetable peeler, or a meat slicer.

The Squero, *or gondola yard, one of the few remaining in Venice.*

ANGUELE IN SALSA
ANGUELLE O LATTERINI IN
SALSA DI ACETO
Marinated Whitebait

These little fish when treated as indicated below result in a most appetizing antipasto.

The word "minnow" describes them very well, but a minnow is a fresh-water fish and the ones we are after come from salt water. The term "whitebait" is safer since it is the generic term for very small edible fish, any of which will work for this recipe. Call them what you like, they still look like minnows: silver-sided, dark along the back, and an inch or a little more in length.

Whitebait may be used as one part of a mixed fish fry and the leftovers marinated as in this recipe.

FOR 4 TO 6 ANTIPASTI:

1 pound anguele, *whitebait*
Cooking oil
Flour
Salt
2 cloves garlic, peeled
White wine vinegar

1. Simply wash the fish. They put away people who try to eviscerate and scale whitebait. Allow them to drain well on a slanted surface.

2. Please read the general instructions for frying fish, page 114. Fill a deep fryer or a saucepan about half full of cooking oil and bring it to 375 degrees.

3. Dust the whitebait with flour and throw one into the oil to see that the temperature is right. The fish should start to bubble immediately but not too violently. When the temperature seems to be correct, fry the fish 10 or 12 at a time, cooking them until the boiling has subsided substantially and the fish are lightly browned. This should take 3 minutes or so. Remove them and place on paper towels to drain and cool.

4. Lightly salt the fish and align them in a fairly steep-sided ceramic or glass dish. Place the garlic with the fish and pour over enough good

white wine vinegar to barely cover. Most of the vinegar will be absorbed by the flour crust, giving the fish a strange soggy appearance. This is as it should be.

5. Marinate the fish a minimum of 2 hours before serving. They will remain good for 2 or 3 days if refrigerated. Eat everything except the head. Serve with fresh Italian or French bread or with cold *polenta* (page 221).

CAPE SANTE AL FORNO
CONCHIGLIE DEI PELLEGRINI
AL FORNO
Baked Scallops

The scallop is a mollusk with a special shell, the lid of which is in the form of an open fan, quite lovely and interesting. More important for our purposes here is the inhabitant of the shell. Baked, scallops become da lecarsi i dei, *as the Venetians say, or* de leccarsi le dita, *in Italian. Italian, Venetian, or English, it all means so good that you will want to lick your fingers to get that last little bit.*

This excellent recipe presents certain problems, not related so much to the cooking as to the quantities of the ingredients.

First of all, scallops so prepared may be served as either an *antipasto* or as a main course. As a main course allow 2 to 2½ times as much as for an *antipasto*. As an *antipasto* 2 large scallops with their coral—the reddish-orange-colored part attached to the white muscle of the scallop—make one serving. The white of the scallops run between 1 and 1½ inches in diameter while the shells themselves are about 5 inches at their widest point. In the United States, where scallops are generally sold already shucked and with the coral removed, it is better to think in terms of weight. Allow a scant quarter pound of scallops per serving as an *antipasto* and a generous half pound as a main course.

OPENING AND CLEANING SCALLOPS:

Often, if scallops are allowed to rest on their curved shell side for a half hour or so, they will open wide enough that a knife may be slipped in before the scallop realizes what hit him. Use a rather large sharp knife and cut the scallop away from the flat top shell. Spring the lid and discard it.

If the scallops do not open voluntarily, work the blade of a kitchen knife between the shells, being careful neither to cut yourself nor to break the shell.

If still unsuccessful, place the scallop in a shallow baking dish in an oven preheated to 350 degrees. After a couple of minutes the shell will pop open. Remove immediately from the oven and cool the scallop under running water.

By whatever means the scallop has been opened (surprise attack, sheer force, or heat), it presents at this point a pretty dismal picture. Nevertheless, cut the scallop away from the bottom shell, working carefully, trying to remove it in one entire piece. With the aid of a sharp pointed knife gradually cut and/or pull away all the extraneous parts of the scallop; be sure to discard the black part connected to the coral, but try not to disconnect the coral from the white. All that should remain is the white and the coral, about 15 percent of the starting weight. Wash well with running water. When you believe the scallop to be clean, wash again, because they are quite often very sandy. Set the scallops aside.

Clean the bottom scallop shells inside and out. Steel wool works nicely.

All this being done, we are now ready to proceed to the recipe.

FOR 4 SERVINGS AS AN ANTIPASTO:

Butter
About 1 pound cleaned scallops
1 clove garlic, peeled and cut in half
½ cup bread crumbs
¼ cup parsley, finely chopped
(⅛ cup grated Parmesan cheese)
4 tablespoons olive oil
8 teaspoons butter
8 teaspoons cognac

1. Preheat the oven to 375 degrees.

2. Butter 4 scallop shells or 4 small individual baking dishes. Divide the scallops among the shells as evenly as possible.

3. Rub the inside of a small mixing bowl with the garlic. Put the bread crumbs, parsley, and cheese (optional) into the bowl. Mix well.

4. For each shell place 2 tablespoons or more of the bread-crumb

mixture over the scallops. Pour about 1 tablespoon of olive oil over the bread crumbs and place a 2 teaspoons piece of butter near the hinge of the shell. As the scallops bake the butter will run down underneath and bubble up through the crumbs.

5. Place the shells on a cookie sheet or in a shallow pan and put into the preheated oven. Cook for 8 minutes. Remove from the oven and for each shell pour 2 teaspoons of cognac over the crumbs. Return to the oven and cook for another 10 to 14 minutes, the time depending upon the size of the scallops.

6. If at the end of the cooking time the bread crumbs still have not browned slightly, place the shells under the broiler for a minute or two. Serve immediately.

(Save the shells. They may be used for any number of dishes, but particularly for seafood cocktails and Newburgs.)

FOLPETI LESSI
POLIPI ALESSI
Boiled Octopus

An octopus of the first quality, properly prepared, makes one of the truly appetizing antipasti. It should, however, be eaten sparingly, particularly in the evening, because of its limited digestibility.

The complaint most often heard about octopus (aside from its appearance) is its toughness, which lends credence to its reputation for indigestibility. If you have ever handled uncooked octopus you know that raw it is very tender. When placed in boiling water, though, it almost immediately becomes tough. The object is to cook it until it becomes tender again. But overcooking a poor quality octopus will not make it more tender; in fact, all that happens is that it loses its flavor.

Octopus is best when cooked in sea water. Desiccants in household salt change the flavor and some say make the octopus more chewy.

There are differences of opinion as to the optimum size octopus. We prefer those of about 5 ounces, while others like those of 2 ounces. In the South of Italy octopi may run up to several pounds. The most flavorful part is the body and heavier octopi seem to have bodies that are larger in proportion to the size of the tentacles. We could be wrong about this.

Without doubt, though, smaller octopi are more adapted than large ones for the recipe after this one.

For those not practiced in eating octopus perhaps a few words about technique are in order. The whole thing is edible except for the eyes and mouth. The eyes look like beebee shot when cooked and are gritty when chewed. The mouth is extremely tough. Both the eyes and the mouth may be removed before cooking if you wish. Otherwise (and much easier) slice the cooked octopus in half lengthwise and you will immediately be able to spot the mouth. Cut it away and discard. The eyes are a little more difficult to find, but once found can easily be popped out by poking around with a table knife.

If small, a half octopus makes a single bite. Larger ones are cut into several pieces. A 5-ounce octopus is a bit too large for an *antipasto* for 1 person and too small for 2. Figure about three-quarters of an octopus per serving in this case. You may wish to sprinkle on a bit of pepper and perhaps some salt if you used too little during cooking.

FOR 4 ANTIPASTI:

4 quarts water
6 tablespoons salt
About 1 pound octopus as discussed above

1. Bring the salted water to a boil.
2. While the water is coming to a boil, prepare the octopus. Wash the tentacles, making sure to remove all the dirt from the suction cups. Hold the body in one hand, the mouth of the octopus facing up, and place under the faucet. Squeeze gently. You will notice that some ink comes out of the body openings (not the mouth but the system of openings through which the octopus brings in and forces out water, his propulsion mechanism). Release the pressure on the body so that water can re-enter. Squeeze gently again. Continue this process until the water comes out clean.
3. Pick up an octopus and hold it mouth side up. Smooth the tentacles down along the body. Slowly lower the octopus into the boiling water, holding it until the tentacles curl up. If you simply throw the octopus into the water the tentacles will remain straight, a dead giveaway that the cook is a novice when it comes to octopus. Partially cover the pot when all of the octopi have been added.
4. Cook until the octopus is tender. Test for tenderness by poking it

with a table fork, in the area where the tentacles are joined to the body. How long will it take to cook them? This depends upon the type of octopus as well as the size. A 2-ounce octopus may take as little as 15 minutes while a 5-ounce octopus may take as long as 45 or 50 minutes. The only rule is practice.

5. When tender, remove the pot from the heat but leave the octopus immersed in the cooking water. If removed from the water the tentacles in particular become dry and rubbery. Octopus is usually eaten tepid or cold and may be accompanied by fresh Italian or French bread.

FOLPETI CONSI
POLIPI CONDITI
Octopus Salad

For those who enjoy both octopus and celery, there is no better dish than this.

Prepare boiled octopus by following the preceding recipe. Cut the octopus into small bite-size pieces. Dice fairly finely a half rib of white celery per serving and mix with the octopus. Dress with olive oil, vinegar or lemon juice, and salt and pepper to taste. Serve with fresh Italian or French bread.

GAMBARETI, SCHIE O SCHILE,
GAMBARI E GAMBARONI
GAMBERETTI, GAMBERI DELLA SABBIA
O GAMBERETTI GRIGI, GAMBERI,
E GAMBERONI
Shrimp and Prawns

Shrimp are among the simplest of seafoods to prepare and the resulting antipasti *are delicious. But it is imperative that the shrimp be absolutely fresh. Otherwise they will have an ammoniacal flavor.*

From the above titles you can see that shrimp and prawns are going to present a few problems. To many people a shrimp is a prawn and a prawn a *scampo* and a *scampo* a shrimp. We are discouraged by some cookbooks which give a recipe calling for *scampi* and then say to start with a pound of shrimp. *Scampi* are a different branch of the family and look more like mini-lobsters than shrimp or prawns. They will not be discussed here since in Venice they are not eaten very often as *antipasto*. (See page 79 for *risoto di scampi* and the sections on fried and broiled fish, pages 114 and 116. In Venice these are the three most popular ways of preparing *scampi*.)

Going back to shrimp and prawns, there is so much confusion in the nomenclature of these crustaceans that we shall stick to the terms small, medium, and large or jumbo to describe them. We probably should point out that *schie*, gray shrimp, are about as far removed from their cousins as the *scampo* is, but because *schie* look so much like *gambareti* (small pink shrimp), are cooked in the same way, and are eaten as an *antipasto*, we have included them here.

FOR 4 ANTIPASTI OF SMALL SHRIMP:

> Salted water, 3 tablespoons salt per quart of water
> 1 to 1¼ pounds small shrimp with heads, total length of the shrimp
>   2 inches or less

1. Bring the salted water to a boil.
2. Wash the shrimp under running water and add them to the boiling water. When the water returns to a rolling boil the shrimp are done. Drain them.
3. Shell the shrimp and dress them with the following mixture.

Dressing:

> Olive oil
> Lemon juice or vinegar
> Pepper
> (Finely chopped parsley)

Dress to taste. A good ratio for a start is 5 parts olive oil to 1 part lemon juice or vinegar.

(A particularly popular way of treating *schie*, gray shrimp, is to marinate them in their shells and have the diners clean them, using fingers, at the table. Pour a generous amount of olive oil over the cooked, unshelled shrimp. Split a clove or two of garlic in half and place with the shrimp. Sprinkle on quite a bit of pepper, mix well, and allow to marinate for 2 or 3 hours, stirring occasionally. Serve with an extra napkin.)

FOR 4 ANTIPASTI OF MEDIUM SHRIMP:

> 6 or 7 shrimp per serving, about ¾ pound of 2 inch headless shrimp
> Cold water
> Salt, 3 tablespoons per quart of water

1. Wash the shrimp under running water and place them in a pot. Add enough water to cover and a little more. Add salt.

2. Place the pot over a high flame and bring the water to a boil. Start timing when a rolling boil is reached and cook for 4 or 5 minutes. Pour the shrimp into a colander and allow to cool.

3. Shell the shrimp and vein them if you wish. Venetians do not unless the veins are black and ugly.

4. Dress the shrimp in the same way as for small shrimp above.

Large or jumbo shrimp, body length about 4 inches:

We find these both ways, with or without the head. Four make a good large *antipasto*. Minus the heads, allow about a pound of shrimp for 4 servings; with the heads you will need 1¾ to 2 pounds.

Cook large shrimp following the procedure for medium shrimp except longer, 8 or 9 minutes. Shell and vein the shrimp. They may be dressed in the same way as small and medium shrimp or simply served with mayonnaise and lemon juice.

GARUSOLI
MURICE
Boiled Sea Snails

This delicacy is best during hot weather when the snails are more plump and of fuller flavor.

The snail used is *L. murex brandaris*, a variety of whelk about 2½ inches in length at maturity. A certain amount of care should be exercised for these snails die easily and spoil rapidly, even after cooking, so eat only those cooked the same day.

The snails are cooked in their shells and served either hot or cold. The diners then try to remove the meat from the shell. This is done by taking two snails and with the pointed end of one digging into the hard part at the foot of the other and trying with a twisting motion to pull out all the meat. This will happen about once in 20 times. Usually the foot breaks away from the tasty tender part. When this happens one holds the shell in his hand (the pointed end of the shell pointing down) and he then bangs the heel of the hand several times on the table. With luck, the meaty part of the snail will pop out onto the tablecloth instead of the floor.

Do not eat the hard part of the foot. It is difficult to chew and even more difficult to digest.

Whelks are probably impossible to find in stores in the United States. If you live near a seacoast, though, you might like to read Euell Gibbons's *Stalking the Blue-Eyed Scallop* (David McKay Company, Inc.), for whelking instructions. The whelks he finds are larger than the Adriatic variety, but their young might be well adapted for this recipe.

FOR 4 ANTIPASTI:

> *2 pounds whelks*
> *Cold water*
> *Salt, 3 tablespoons per quart of water*

1. Wash the whelks well, removing any marine life that may have attached itself to the shell. Check carefully to be sure that they are still alive. Do this by pulling on the foot and releasing. If the whelk snaps back into its shell, it is all right.

2. Place the whelks in a pot and cover with cold water. Add the salt. Place the pot over a high flame and cook for 6 minutes from the time the water reaches a rolling boil.

3. Drain well and serve immediately or, if you wish, allow them to cool.

GRANSEOLE E GRANZI
MAIE O GRANCEVOLE
Sea Spiders or Thornback or Spiny Crabs

With a piece of fresh bread this antipasto *can become a complete meal.*
The Latin name of these crabs is *Maja squinada,* but we shall stick
with the Venetian. *Granseole* are fairly large spiny crabs and are the
female of the species. They are eaten in spring and early summer when
they contain coral, the roe. The *granzio,* the male, is best in late winter
and early spring. The males are usually a little larger than the females,
but it is an unusual crab that has a shell larger than 8 inches at its widest
point. Male or female, the meat is delicious and one of the great delicacies
of the Adriatic.

Normally the crabs arrive in the market alive. When they die the
price drops about 50 percent, but they may still be eaten. If you ask how
long the crab has been dead the fishmonger will probably say, "He's
dead? He was alive five minutes ago." On the chance that he may be
bending the truth a bit, it is better to pay the extra for a live one.

One average *granseola* is enough for two abundant servings as an
antipasto or for one as a main course.

The cleaning of crabs is pretty much the same for all varieties. If you
are lucky enough to live near waters where edible crabs are available, the
description of how to clean them may prove useful, since any good crab
will make an excellent *antipasto.*

THE COOKING:

An average granseola *or* granzio, *1¼ to 1½ pounds*
Salted water, 3 tablespoons salt per quart of water

1. Rinse the crab under the faucet. If alive, place in a pot and cover
with cold water. Salt the water. Place the pot over a high flame and bring
the water to a boil. Start timing when the water reaches a rolling boil.
Cook for 15 to 20 minutes depending upon the size. If the crab is dead,
first bring the salted water to a boil, then add the crab and cook 15 to
20 minutes from the time the water returns to a rolling boil.

2. Drain off the water. Holding the crab with a towel, make 2 or 3
holes near the head with a sharp, pointed instrument. Place the crab in a

position to allow any water trapped inside to drain out through the holes. Cool to room temperature.

CLEANING THE CRAB:

1. Tear off the legs. Crack them with a small hammer or a nut-cracker. Extract the meat from the large parts of the legs. Set the meat aside.

2. Turn the crab onto its back. There will be a flap on the bottom which should be carefully lifted and pulled back until it breaks off. On the male crab a vein will be attached to the body end of the flap. Pull gently and the vein will come out of the body. It contains sand and dirt and is not terribly appetizing, but it will not hurt you.

3. Hold the crab in your left hand, palm up. The crab should be topside up and facing right so that you get a side view of it. With your left hand grasp the crab where the legs were attached. With your right hand take hold of the top shell directly above the point where the rear legs had been and lift up and to the right. You should now have two pieces.

4. Clean the top shell, that part in your right hand. Remove the tough skinlike material, but save the coral (if any) and the brown pasty substance. Using a hammer again, break away the head part from the rest of the shell. (This is difficult to explain but should become obvious when you are confronted with the crab.) Use this shell as a dish and place the crab meat in it.

5. From the part of the crab that was in the left hand, remove and discard the lungs. The lungs are gray and spongelike and you should have no trouble spotting them. Once they are removed everything else, except the shell, is edible. Break the shell into pieces and pick out the meat, adding it to the other meat. When all the meat has been collected, dress it.

The dressing:

Olive oil
Pepper (and salt)
Lemon juice or vinegar

1. Pour enough olive oil over the meat to moisten it thoroughly. If you used enough salt in the cooking water you should not need to add

any now. Sprinkle on some pepper and lemon juice or vinegar to taste. Mix well and serve.

2. Bread sticks are nice with this when served as an *antipasto*. When served as a main course, accompany it with fresh Italian or French bread.

MAZANETE LESSE
CARCINI RIPARI, O GRANCHI
COMUNI, ALESSI
Common Shore Crabs, Green Shore Crabs,
or Harry Crabs, Boiled

It is time-consuming to eat these small crabs, but for the patient diner there are great rewards, for both the meat and coral are exceptionally flavorful.

As with *granseole* in the preceding recipe, there are various names for this crab. The Latin is *Carcinides moenas* or *Carcinus moenas*. They are small as eating crabs go, usually about 2 inches across at the widest point. In Venetian they are called *mazanete* up until the time they molt and become soft-shell crabs, *moleche*. *Moleche* are excellent when fried.

It is interesting how these crabs are caught in the Venetian lagoon. In the fall the female crabs are filled with eggs which they want to lay in the deep water of the canals of the lagoon. The fishermen set out two nets at right angles, having the origin on the side of a deep canal. As the crab starts toward the canal she encounters the net and follows it, always heading for deeper water, until she reaches the canal and falls into a conveniently placed trap.

The fisherman with *mazanete* in his trap has a business decision to make. *Mazanete* sell for a quarter or a third of the price of *moleche*. If the fisherman keeps them in the trap they will eventually shed their shells and he can pick up the extra money. But they must be culled daily by hand, time-consuming work, and they must be delivered to market promptly.

Mazanete may simply be boiled and eaten like any other crab. Were it not for the coral, however, they would not be worth the effort.

They may also be boiled and dressed, and we include two recipes, one similar to the other, but differing enough to merit their own space.

The starting point for both is the recipe that immediately follows, *mazanete lesse.*

FOR 4 ANTIPASTI:

> 2 *pounds live* mazanete
> Cold salted water, 3 tablespoons salt
> *per quart of water*

1. Wash the *mazanete* well with running water. If they are particularly dirty, scrub them with a brush. Handle them carefully. Their pinch is not dangerous but it is annoying.

2. Place the crabs in a pot and cover them with cold water. Add salt and place the pot over a high flame. Depending upon the size of the crabs, cook for 12 to 15 minutes from the time the water reaches a rolling boil.

3. Drain and allow to cool. Clean the crabs following the procedure in the preceding recipe, except that the legs should be discarded because they contain so little meat. Serve them as they are or prepare one of the following recipes.

Mazanete in Salata
Crab "Salad"

1. Cook and clean the *mazanete* as discussed above and place the meat and coral in a dish or bowl. Do not worry too much about small pieces of shell. It is impossible to separate the meat and shell perfectly.

2. *Olive oil*
   Vinegar
   Pepper
   1 or 2 cloves of garlic, peeled

Add enough olive oil to moisten the crab meat thoroughly. Then add vinegar and pepper to taste, along with a peeled clove or two of garlic. Test for salt. Allow the crab meat to marinate for 2 hours.

3. Remove the garlic and serve the crab "salad" with fresh Italian or French bread.

Mazanete a la Furlana
Crabs Furlana

1. Cook the crabs as before but do not clean them. Remove only the legs and the flap from the bottom of the crab.

2. *Olive oil*
   1 or 2 cloves of garlic, peeled
   Pepper

Place the crabs in a bowl and add quite a bit of olive oil. It is not necessary to cover them, but they should be well moistened. Add a peeled clove or two of garlic and rather a lot of pepper. Allow the crabs to marinate 3 or 4 hours. During marinating stir the crabs occasionally so that they will be well soaked with the oil.

3. Serve with a piece of Italian or French bread. The diners, using their fingers, clean the crabs at the table.

CAPE E OSTREGHE
LAMELLIBRANCHI
Clams and Oysters

Clams and oysters, whether raw or cooked, are among those foods most preferred by Venetians.

As a rule, if it has a shell and comes from the sea, Venetians like it. Clams and oysters are not exceptions.

The Venetian lagoon is rich in clams from the standpoints of quality, quantity, and variety. Regardless of size they are all fair game.

Clams are, we believe, best when eaten raw and without sauce. Many people sprinkle on a few grains of pepper and a squirt of lemon juice. Clams may also be prepared as a soup (page 35), a pasta sauce (page 54), or a *risotto* (page 76).

Oysters are only eaten raw, again with a little pepper and lemon juice perhaps. We have no recipes for cooked oysters.

PEOCI AL FORNO
COZZE AL FORNO
Baked Mussels

This juicy mollusk can be served as an excellent antipasto that arouses the appetite and also the thirst for a good dry white wine. They are eaten preferably during the hot months when plumper and of pleasing flavor.

Wash the mussels well, and then one at a time open them in such a manner as to leave all the contents in one of the shells. They are aligned on top of an iron plate or slab that will enter the oven. In opening the mussels take care that they do not lose their own salty water.

Prepare a mixture of bread crumbs with a little parsley and cheese, pepper, and a whiff of garlic. About a teaspoonful of this mixture is placed on each mussel, then a dot of butter and several drops of olive oil. Everything into the oven and after little more than 10 minutes the mussels will be ready to resuscitate a flagging appetite!

The proportions of bread crumbs, parsley, and grated cheese vary widely from cook to cook. The important thing is not to overdo it. Some people go so far as to add ground meat or sausage or tomato sauce and in such quantities that one has the impression of eating a meatball on the half shell instead of a mussel.

The season has everything to do with how much meat is found inside the mussel and how flavorful it is. Mussels in Venice are at their best from May to September, while in other locations there may be little change from one season to another. If the mussels are lean, put two on one shell.

The number needed for a serving depends upon the size of the mussels. Six mussels 3 inches in length make a medium serving, as do 8 of 2½ inches or 10 of 2 inches.

For further information about mussels, consult Euell Gibbons's *Stalking the Blue-Eyed Scallop* (David McKay Company, Inc.).

The bread-crumb mixture:

1 clove garlic, peeled and cut in half
½ cup bread crumbs
¼ cup grated Parmesan cheese
¼ cup finely chopped parsley
Pepper to taste

Rub the inside of a small mixing bowl with the garlic. Place the other ingredients in the bowl and mix thoroughly.

PREPARING THE MUSSELS FOR BAKING:

Allow about ½ pound of mussels in the shell for each serving.

The cleaning and opening of mussels is time-consuming and a bit difficult at first, but the results are well worth the effort.

Wash the mussels and scrub them with a stiff brush to remove any marine life that may have attached itself to the shell. With a table knife remove the beard. (The beard is the material to which the mussel anchors itself.) Pull the beard in the direction away from the hinged end of the shell. Insert the knife blade between the shells at the point where the beard had been, being sure to hold the mussel horizontally to avoid losing too much juice. Normally, if a little pressure is exerted by the thumb on the top shell, one can slide it enough so that the knife blade may be easily inserted. Do this step over a soup dish or a pan in order to catch the juices. Slide the knife blade around the end of the mussel opposite the hinge. As the shells separate, scrape the meat from the top one. With the knife loosen the meat from the bottom shell, but leave it in the shell.

BAKING THE MUSSELS:

The opened mussels
The bread-crumb mixture
Butter
Olive oil
The juice from opening the mussels

1. Preheat the oven to 425 degrees.
2. Place the mussels in a shallow baking dish. Do this in such a way as to lose as little of the juice as possible. Sprinkle a generous teaspoonful of the bread-crumb mixture on top of each mussel. Dot with butter and add four or five drops of olive oil. Baste with the juice from opening the mussels. Bake in the preheated oven for 12 to 15 minutes or until the crumbs begin to brown. If after 15 minutes the crumbs still have not browned, place under the broiler for a minute or two. Serve immediately.

A second, easier version of the recipe may be used when large numbers of mussels are to be prepared.

PREPARING THE MUSSELS FOR BAKING:

1. Wash the mussels as before and remove the beards.
2. Coat the bottom of a large frying pan with olive oil. The pan must have a cover.
3. Place the pan over a fairly high flame. When the oil is hot add all the mussels at once and cover the pan immediately. Be careful not to

be splashed by the hot oil. After two or three minutes the mussels will open. Remove the pan from the fire.

4. Arrange the mussels in their shells in a shallow baking dish and spoon the juices over them. Proceed with the bread-crumb mixture, dotting with butter, basting, and baking as in the first method. It is not necessary to add more olive oil, the amount used in opening the mussels being sufficient.

PESCE IN SAOR
PESCE FRITTO CON SALSA
Marinated Fried Fish

The period most propitious for this dish is from spring until the middle of summer. It is used particularly by the Venetians at the time of the Feast of the Redeemer.

As an antipasto *it is a dish that is a little heavy, but very delicious. It may be eaten with a piece of bread, but many prefer it with cold* polenta.

This recipe provides an excellent way of preserving leftover fried fish. The fish most adapted are fresh sardines, and soles and flounders up to about 8 inches in length.

Pesce in saor may be eaten either as an *antipasto* or as a main course. It improves with marinating and remains good for several days.

FOR 4 GENEROUS SERVINGS AS AN ANTIPASTO:

1½ pounds fresh fish as discussed above
Cooking oil
Flour
1 pound onions
1½ cups olive oil
(⅓ cup good dry white wine)
½ cup vinegar or more, to taste

1. Clean and scale the fish, washing them well with running water. If sardines are used, cut off the heads. Place the cleaned fish on a slanted surface and allow to drain well.

2. See page 114 for detailed instructions for frying fish. Heat cooking oil to 375 degrees in a half-filled deep frier or a saucepan.

3. Coat the fish lightly with flour and cautiously drop some into the hot cooking oil. How many you can cook at a time will depend upon the size of the fish and the size of the fryer. The fish are cooked when the bubbling subsides and they have taken on a light golden brown color (4 to 8 minutes, depending upon the type and size fish). Place the cooked fish on paper towels to drain and cool.

4. When the fish have cooled a bit, place them in layers in a dish with high sides. Salt each layer.

5. Slice the onions. Some people use thick slices, some thin, and others chop them. It is not too important. Place the onions and the olive oil in a frying pan over a medium flame. A little dry white wine may be added. Cook the onions, stirring frequently, until they are tender and about to brown. Add the vinegar and mix thoroughly. Remove the pan from the fire. Pour the onions and the juices over the fish in the dish. Press down on the surface with a fork to make sure that the fish are well immersed in the juices.

6. Allow to marinate for several hours. The fish will be even better the next day. Cover and store in a cool place but do not refrigerate. Serve with fresh Italian or French bread or cold *polenta* (page 221).

RENGHE SALAE SOTO OGIO
ARINGHE SALATE SOTT'OLIO
Salted Herring Fillets under Olive Oil

This dish serves as an antipasto *but the result is so delicious one can eat them in abundance, especially if accompanied by* polenta. *In that case the stomach must be in good form, for salted herring brings on a great thirst for wine!*

The recipe itself is very simple, but a certain amount of practice is necessary to obtain unbroken fillets. Even if broken, though, the flavor is still there.

The salted herring we use run between 4 and 5 to the pound. Each herring yields 4 fillets. They are cured by and packed in salt. As an *antipasto* allow 3 or 4 fillets per person.

FOR 16 TO 20 FILLETS:

5 cups water more or less
4 or 5 salted herring, about 1 pound
Olive oil

1. Bring about 5 cups of water to a boil in a pot.

2. While the water is coming to a boil, cut off the heads and tails of the herring. Open the belly sides of the fish. You may if you wish save the roe, washing it and setting it aside for use later in the recipe. Wash the inside of the herring, removing any bits of entrail.

3. Place the herring in a frying pan and pour the boiling water over them. The frying pan is not to be placed over the fire; it serves only as a convenient container. Allow the herring to soak until the skin can be easily scraped off with a table knife. This may take 2 or 3 minutes or slightly longer.

4. Remove a herring from the hot water and place it on a cutting board. Scrape off all the skin. You may rinse it under running water to remove the last little pieces. Rinse the cutting board also. Place the fish belly side up on the board. Open the fish and pull the meat away from the bones. Do this gently so as to avoid breaking the fillets. You will note that each side of the fish will tend to divide into two fillets, giving a total of four for each herring. Inspect the fillets to make sure that all the bones have been removed.

5. Align the fillets in a glass or ceramic dish with fairly high sides. If you have chosen to save the roe, place it in with the fillets.

6. Completely cover the fillets with olive oil. Do not refrigerate. The fillets may be eaten the next day when they have had a chance to absorb some of the oil. They will remain good for 2 weeks or even longer. Serve with fresh Italian or French bread, or with cold *polenta* (page 221).

SARDELE O ACCIUGHE SALAE
CO LE SEGOLE
SARDINE O ACCIUGHE SALATE
CON CIPOLLE
Salted Sardines or Anchovies with Onion

This dish serves as a simple antipasto, *but one so tasty that it appeals more to the palate than to reason. Pay attention not to abuse the use of this dish for it is rather heavy and of limited digestibility. Pay attention also for like the salted herring in the preceding recipe it invites one to drink in abundance.*

Salted sardines and anchovies are used interchangeably for this recipe, as they are in the recipe for *bigoli in salsa* (page 52), where we describe them in more detail.

As an *antipasto* these fillets go well with pickled vegetables and perhaps a piece of canned tuna. Because they are so rich 3 or 4 fillets per serving should be sufficient.

Served on toothpicks, they make an excellent cocktail hors d'oeuvre.

FOR 40 TO 50 FILLETS:

1 pound salted sardines or anchovies (page 52)
3 large onions
1¼ cups olive oil
¼ cup or more vinegar to taste

1. Clean and fillet the sardines or anchovies. (See page 52.)
2. Place the fillets in a glass or ceramic dish with fairly high sides. Lay them out in flat layers.
3. Slice the onions and place in layers on top of the fillets. Use more onion than seems necessary, as it will shrink considerably.
4. Mix the olive oil and vinegar together and pour over the onions and fillets. Cover and store in a cool place, but do not refrigerate. Turn the fillets 2 or 3 times a day for the first day or two. Do not worry if the layers become jumbled. The fillets will be at their best between 2 and 6 days of marinating. Serve with fresh Italian or French bread.

SGOMBRI SOTO OGIO
SGOMBRI SOTT'OLIO
Fresh Mackerel Fillets in Olive Oil

Although this dish is not as widely used in Venice as some others, it does, nevertheless, make a good antipasto *and affords a bit of variety.*

Select mackerel 7 or 8 inches in length, one per person being more than sufficient as an *antipasto*.

FOR 4 SERVINGS:

> *3 fresh mackerel, 7 or 8 inches in length*
> *Cold salted water, 1 tablespoon salt*
> * per quart of water*
> *Olive oil*
> *Lemon juice or vinegar*
> *Pepper*

1. Scale, eviscerate, and wash the fish well.
2. Place the fish in a suitable cooking vessel (a fish poacher, large frying pan, or a roasting pan) and barely cover with cold salted water. Place over a fairly high flame and bring the water almost to a boil, but not quite. The water should be just ready to simmer. Cook until the eyes bulge out of the sockets, most likely between 6 and 8 minutes of cooking. Remove the fish from the water carefully, trying to avoid breaking the fish into pieces. Place on a plate or a platter to cool a bit.
3. When cool enough to handle without burning your fingers, break off the heads and fins and discard them. Then, using a knife, scrape away the skin. Cut in along the back toward the spine and the fish should split into two fillets. Remove any bones and place the fillets in a glass or ceramic dish with fairly high sides. Take a bite of part of a fillet in order to test for salt, adding more if necessary. Cover the fillets with olive oil.
4. Serve the fillets with lemon juice or vinegar, some pepper, and fresh Italian or French bread, or cold *polenta* (page 221).

NERVETI CONSI
NERVI ALL'OLIO E ACETO
Nerve Salad

This dish is usually presented as an antipasto, *but if the stomach and appetite are both functioning well it may be served in large quantities as a main course.*

Nerveti are almost always present in Venetian wine shops as a snack. We are not sure how much, if any, of the material is actually nerve fibers, but we think probably very little. It appears to be mostly tendon. Be that as it may, the *nerveti* are located in the shin section of the legs of beef and veal, and when boiled for 2 to 4 hours they become tender. It is best to boil them with the kitchen fan going full blast, lest the neighbors think you have opened a glue factory. They are not particularly sapid in themselves, but if properly dressed they go very nicely with a glass or two of good dry wine or some beer.

FOR 4 SERVINGS AS AN ANTIPASTO:

1 pound nerveti, *see above*
Salted water, 2 teaspoons per quart of water
About 2 ounces canned tuna packed in olive oil
1 large onion, chopped
5 flat anchovy fillets packed in olive oil
  and cut into ½-inch lengths
1 cup olive oil
¼ cup vinegar

1. Place the *nerveti* in a pot, cover with water, add the salt, and bring to a boil. Reduce the flame to very low and simmer covered for 2 hours or longer for veal *nerveti* and up to 4 hours for tough beef *nerveti*. Test for tenderness by sticking with a fork. They should be easily pierced but offer some resistance. When tender, allow to cool in the cooking liquid until they may be handled.

2. Remove the *nerveti* from the pot and place on a cutting board. Cut into pieces ¾ of an inch or so in length, discarding cartilage, fat, and whatnot.

3. Put the cleaned cut-up *nerveti* in a mixing bowl. Add the tuna, onion, anchovies, olive oil, and vinegar. Mix well and correct the seasoning. Some *nerveti* absorb more oil and vinegar than others and it may be necessary to increase the quantities slightly.

4. Serve cold with fresh Italian or French bread.

FONDI DE ARTICIOCO A L'OGIO E FORMAGIO SALÀ
FONDI DI CARCIOFO ALESSI CONDITI ALL'OLIO E FORMAGGIO SALATO
Boiled Artichoke Hearts Dressed with Olive Oil, Parsley, and Salty Cheese

Here is a dish that is excellent either as an antipasto, *a vegetable course, or a light lunch. It is tasty, nourishing, and easily digested, and above all, it sets up the palate for a glass, better two or three glasses, of good dry red wine.*

Although all artichoke dishes set up the palate for a glass of wine, what undoubtedly makes this so outstanding for "drinking" is the cheese. The type we use is Sicilian, quite sharp, and very salty. Ask your cheeseman to recommend a salty cheese that is hard enough to grate.

Serve 2 artichoke hearts 2½ inches in diameter as an *antipasto* or a vegetable course and 4 hearts as a main course.

FOR EACH ARTICHOKE HEART:

Salted water
1 teaspoon finely chopped parsley
Garlic
1 tablespoon olive oil, more or less
A scant tablespoon grated salty cheese

1. See page 204 for the preparation of the artichoke hearts. Do not use canned hearts.

2. Place the hearts in a saucepan or a frying pan with cover. Add enough water to float them. Add some salt, the amount depending upon how salty the cheese is. Cover the pan and place it over a high flame. Bring to a boil and then reduce the flame to low. Cook for 10 to 15 minutes. After 10 minutes start testing the hearts for tenderness by poking them with a table fork. They should be easily penetrated but should not be mushy. While the hearts are cooking go on to the next step.

3. Pull the parsley leaves from the stems, using a piece of garlic which has been cut in half. Rub the leaves thoroughly with the garlic. Chop the parsley very fine.

4. When the hearts are tender, remove them from the boiling water, drain, and place on a serving platter side by side. Put about 1 teaspoon of parsley on each heart. Pour about 1 tablespoon olive oil over the parsley. Smoothe the parsley and olive oil evenly over the artichoke hearts and then sprinkle a scant tablespoonful of grated cheese on top. Serve at room temperature.

Recipes in other sections of the book for dishes which may be served as antipasti.

SEAFOOD:

Clam "Soup" or steamed clams (page 35). If served in large portions, omit the *minestra*.

Three stockfish recipes (pages 119, 120, and 122). These also make excellent midmorning or evening snacks.

Mantis shrimp and regular shrimp. There are four recipes starting on page 135, all of which make excellent *antipasti*.

Broiled Stuffed Squid (page 133). Delicious as it is, it may seem a lot of work for an *antipasto*. Follow with very simple courses.

Braised Scallops (page 134). Be especially careful not to overdo this one, as it is quite heavy.

Fresh anchovies cooked in olive oil and vinegar (page 128). Easy to do and it makes as good an *antipasto* as it does a main course. Serve cold.

"Scorched Finger" Anchovies (page 129). Requires last-minute charcoal broiling.

MEAT:

Meat Patties (page 187). Serve small portions.

EGGS:

Spinach Omelet (page 197). Used as an *antipasto*, but only rarely. Serve cold. It makes a good snack with a cold beer.

VEGETABLES:

Braised Artichokes (page 202) and Braised Artichoke Hearts (page 203). May be prepared well in advance and served cold.

Eggplant Venetian Jewish style (page 210). Goes very well with canned tuna.

Braised Bell Peppers (page 212). A versatile dish that goes well with many things.

Stuffed Zucchini (page 191). Heavy enough that it should be served alone.

The following antipasto items do not require a recipe, merely good judgment about how much to serve.

SEAFOOD:

Tuna, anchovies, and capers rolled in anchovy fillets, all three packed in olive oil.

MEAT:

Prosciutto crudo (Italian raw ham), *prosciutto crudo* with melon or fresh figs, salami.

VEGETABLES:

Raw carrots, spring onions, radishes, celery.

Sottoaceto (pickled vegetables): pearl onions, peppers, cauliflower, capers, etc.

Sott'olio (under olive oil): mushrooms, small artichokes, peppers, etc.

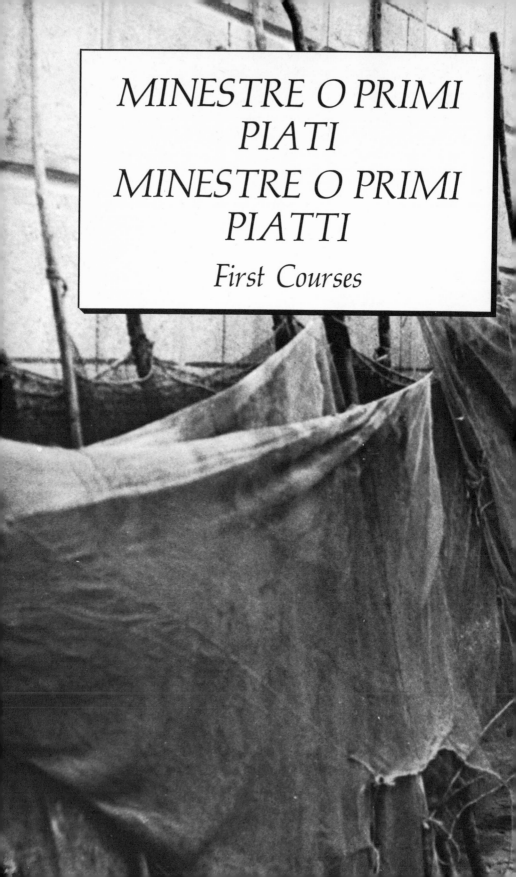

MINESTRE O PRIMI PIATI
MINESTRE O PRIMI PIATTI

First Courses

Nets at the lagoon fishing town of Chioggia.

$\mathcal{M}$INESTRE as much as anything set the Italian eating habits apart from those of other countries. The idea of consuming a plate of pasta before the main course seems strange to many Americans, but it would seem equally strange to an Italian not to do so. We have thought of a number of weak explanations for this phenomenon, but it all comes back to custom: why do Chinese use chopsticks?

Classification of the different *minestre* is difficult. Italians tend to think of two groups, *minestre in brodo*, "in broth," and *minestre asciutte*, "dry." Thus a thick rice soup is *in brodo* while a *risotto* is *asciutta* even though for four servings there is a difference of only a cup or so in the amount of broth. There are other examples of ambiguous classification, the reasoning behind which is always obvious to one of the authors and often incomprehensible to the other. The latter, however, has won out in the organization of this section and you will find an unclassical, but he hopes more readily understandable, system.

Brodeti E Sope
Brodi E Zuppe
BROTHS AND SOUPS

THE BROTHS and soups that follow offer excellent variety covering fish, meat, fowl, vegetable, and even one made with bread and little else.

Since the broths and soups are all so different from one another, we have tried to be as explicit as possible within the individual recipes.

Of all possible dishes, soups and broths in general seem more than any other to properly set up the stomach for serious wine drinking.

BRODETO DE PESCE A LA CIOSOTA
BRODO DI PESCE ALLA CHIOGGIOTTA
Fish Broth Chioggia Style

This broth is a favorite of Chioggia fishermen who wish to make a pleasing and substantial meal without a great outlay of money. The main ingredients are their catch. Hence, only a little seasoning to satisfy their strong appetites.

In order that the broth turn out well it is necessary that the fish be from the sea, and recently.

A good way to turn out a mediocre fish broth or soup is to use yesterday's fish, something that is done too often in restaurants as an economy measure. If the fish are not fresh enough to broil, fry, or poach, they are not fresh enough for broth.

This fish broth will undoubtedly seem a bit odd to most readers. It lacks saffron, a common ingredient in Mediterranean fish soups, but it has vinegar instead. A more conventional recipe follows this one, although it too is without saffron.

It is useless to lay down an exact recipe, for none exists. Further, the varieties of fish are going to be so different from those found in Venice that it is better if we merely put down the general method and let you and your fishmonger take it from there.

Here are the things to keep in mind: Everything that can be will be put through a sieve, so it does not matter if the fish is firm fleshed or not or how bony it is. For flavor, though, use a mixture of lean, firm-fleshed fish and gelatinous fish as well as some crustaceans, shrimp being the easiest to find. The only mollusks we use are mussels.

Speaking slightly more specifically about fish, some members of the scorpaenoid family, a spiny, plump group, are excellent for soup (and little else). Many types of fish heads make good broth; particularly popular in Venice is the head of the *rospo*, a member of the pediculate family. Flat fish such as sole and flounder, aside from being too expensive for soup, are rather bland and not well adapted.

Although a suitable broth can be made for two or three people, the larger the batch the better, since a wider variety of fish may be included. We give the recipe for eight to ten servings, feeling this is an optimum number, but it certainly can be made and made well for fewer people.

One last thing. Do not be afraid to try this recipe. Fish broth and fish soup should be approached in the same spirit as beef stew—as long as the ingredients are good the results will be good, although perhaps never exactly the same twice in a row.

FOR 8 TO 10 SERVINGS:

> *4 pounds mixed fish as discussed above*
> *1½ pounds fish heads*
> *12 medium shrimp, unshelled*
> *12 medium mussels, unshelled*
> *⅔ cup good olive oil*
> *2 cloves garlic, peeled and split*
> *Salt and pepper*
> *¾ cup good wine vinegar*
> *Water to cover the fish*
> *An additional 2 cups water, more or less*

1. Clean, scale, and wash the fish. Wash the shrimp but do not shell them. Scrub the mussels and remove the beards (see page 17).

2. Place a pot containing the olive oil and garlic over medium heat. When the garlic has browned, remove and discard it.

3. Carefully, to avoid splashing yourself with hot oil, add the seafood to the pot and turn it until well coated and very slightly cooked, 3 minutes or so. Add salt and quite a bit of pepper. Pour in the vinegar and enough water to barely cover the seafood. Adjust the heat to maintain a simmer and cook uncovered for about an hour, adding a little more water if too much liquid boils away.

4. In a small saucepan bring about 2 cups of water to a boil.

5. Strain the fish broth into a second pot. Place some of the seafood remains on a strainer over the second pot, and with a wooden spoon push through the juices and some of the solids. Add some boiling water to the pulp and repeat the process. Discard the pulp on the strainer and start over again with fresh seafood remains. Continue as before.

6. When all the remains have been used up, judge how much broth you have and if necessary add more water to bring it up to sufficient volume. Think in terms of a scant 2 cups broth per serving. Correct the seasoning.

7. Bring the broth back to a simmer and serve in soup bowls with either good fresh Italian or French bread or, better, with *crostini* (page 220).

SOPA DE PESCE I
ZUPPA DI PESCE I
Fish Soup I

Many people prefer fish soup to broth, presumably to have a better look at the ingredients.

Actually, there are quite a few differences between our broth and soups, but read the introductory remarks to the preceding recipe for broth, many of which apply here.

The fish in this soup are not put through a sieve, so it is important that fairly firm-fleshed fish be used. Otherwise you will have a tremendous problem with the bones.

As to the type of fish, though, again the Venetian varieties are so different that it will be necessary for you to improvise. Consult your fishmonger and use the following as a guide.

FOR 8 TO 10 SERVINGS:

4 pounds firm-fleshed fish
1½ pounds fish heads
10 medium unshelled shrimp
¾ medium onion, chopped
2 ribs celery cut into 1-inch lengths
Salt and pepper
4 tablespoons butter
6 tablespoons olive oil
2 cloves garlic, peeled and split
2 tablespoons finely chopped parsley
2 cups water
6 tablespoons tomato sauce (page 218)
16 medium mussels, unshelled

1. Clean, scale, and wash the fish. Wash the shrimp but do not shell them. Scrub the mussels and remove the beards (see page 17).

2. Put the fish, fish heads, shrimp, onion, and celery in a pot and cover with cold water. Add some salt and pepper. Bring to a simmer over a high flame and then reduce the heat to a point where a simmer is just maintained. Do not boil vigorously. Cook for 7 or 8 minutes from the time the water starts to simmer.

3. Remove the fish and the shrimp, putting them aside in a bowl. Leave the fish heads and vegetables in the pot and continue to simmer them for at least another 20 minutes.

4. When the shrimp are cool enough to handle, shell and vein them, returning the shells and scraps to the pot.

5. Place a second pot containing the butter, olive oil, and garlic over a medium flame. When the garlic has browned, remove and discard it. Add the parsley to the hot oil and remove the pot from the flame.

6. In a small saucepan bring 2 cups of water to a simmer.

7. Pour the contents of the first pot onto a strainer over the second pot. Using a wooden spoon, press out as much of the liquids as possible from the remains on the strainer. Then pour the boiling water a little at a time over the material on the strainer. Still working with the wooden spoon, squeeze out as much of the juices as possible. Estimate the amount of liquid and add more water if necessary. Try for a scant 2 cups per serving. Bring the broth back to a simmer.

8. Add the fish, shrimp, tomato sauce, and mussels to the pot. Simmer for about 10 minutes. Correct the seasoning.

9. Place the soup in a tureen or directly into soup dishes, trying to give everyone a bit of each type of seafood. Serve with fresh Italian or French bread or, better, with *crostini* (page 220).

SOPA DE PESCE II
ZUPPA DI PESCE II
Fish Soup II

Those people who fear fish bones but like fish soup will enjoy this recipe.

All the quantities and most of the procedures are the same as in the preceding recipe. The only difference is that the fish are filleted and only the bones used in making the broth.

Set the fillets aside and follow the directions for Soup I. When the broth has been made and strained and is simmering again, add the fillets. After 10 minutes, add the mussels and the shelled shrimp. Cook gently for another 5 to 10 minutes and serve.

SOPA DE CAPE E CAPE SALTAE
ZUPPA DI LAMELLIBRANCHI
Clam "Soup"

This soup is often prepared by fishermen on the open sea during pauses in their work. It is easy to do, taking only a few minutes to make. Simple as it is, it has excellent flavor, but it is a bit heavy on the stomach.

In Venetian the word *sopa* means soup and *saltae* means sauté. The difference, some say, between *sopa de cape* and *cape saltae* is that the *sopa* is cooked a couple of minutes longer and more clam juice is released. Call it what you like: they look almost the same. We have chosen soup in English since its wateriness makes it difficult to call it anything else. It is not watery enough, however, for us to be pleased calling it a soup.

Clams with shells up to about 1½ inches across may be used for this recipe. Make *risotto* or spaghetti sauce out of larger clams, or better, eat them raw.

FOR 4 SERVINGS:

About 3½ pounds of small clams in the shell
6 tablespoons olive oil
1 or 2 cloves garlic, peeled and split
3 tablespoons finely chopped parsley
(Pepper)
(Lemon juice)

1. Wash and if necessary purge the clams. See the recipe for *risotto de cape* (page 76) for details.

2. Put the olive oil and garlic in a large shallow pot or a flameproof casserole. It must have a cover. Place the cooking vessel over a medium flame. When the garlic has browned, remove and discard it.

3. Immediately add the clams and parsley. Quickly cover the pot and shake it as if you were making popcorn; or stir quickly once or twice, uncovering the pot for the shortest time possible. As soon as the clams have opened, after 3 or 4 minutes, pour everything onto a deep serving platter or into a bowl.

4. Serve into warmed soup dishes. A piece of fresh Italian or French bread is traditionally used to sop up the juice. More often than not pepper and lemon juice are added and mixed well with the liquids. Sometimes in informal company a glass of wine is added to the remaining juice after the clams have been eaten. The juice is then drunk from the soup dish. This mixture of clam juice and wine is claimed to have mild but effective purgative qualities.

SOPA DE CASTRÀ
ZUPPA DI MONTONE
Mutton or Lamb Soup

It is important to eat this soup always when the weather is either very cold or very hot, since in these times mutton has no strong odor and yet is particularly tasty.

The only difficulties in this recipe are the choice of meat and the preparation of the meat for cooking. Mutton or mature lamb will serve equally well, but all the fat and skin should be removed. Although the shank has marvelous flavor the amount of work needed to remove the fat, skin, and tendons is formidable. Therefore, unless time is no object, the upper part of the leg is recommended. Other lean cuts may also be used.

This recipe is a relative of *risoto in cavroman* (page 87), potatoes being substituted for the rice and additional meat added. Although it is quite substantial a light second course is often served after. As with most other soups and stews the dish is equally good or even better the next day, when the potatoes have had a chance to absorb some of the liquids.

FOR 4 GENEROUS SERVINGS:

> *1¾ pounds boned lean mutton or mature lamb*
> *2 quarts water*
> *1 medium carrot, diced*
> *3 ribs celery, diced*
> *1 medium onion, chopped*
> *Salt and pepper*
> *4 or 5 medium potatoes, peeled and cut into 3 pieces*
> *Grated Parmesan cheese*

1. Remove all fat and skin from the meat. Cut the meat into 1-inch cubes.

2. Place the meat and water into a pot and bring to a boil. Skim off any scum that appears. If all the fat and skin have been removed little scum will form.

3. Add the carrot, celery, onion, and some salt and pepper. Adjust the flame so that a simmer is maintained. Cover the pot. The cooking time will depend upon the cut of meat and the age of the animal, but generally between 1¼ and 2 hours will be required. If the cut is very tough it may have to be cooked even longer. Consult your butcher when buying the meat and test frequently with a fork during cooking.

4. When the meat just begins to seem a bit tender, add the potatoes. Cook for an additional 20 minutes or until the potatoes are easily pierced by a fork.

5. Serve in soup plates or bowls with a slice or two of French or Italian bread on top, or better yet, with *crostini* (page 220). Sprinkle a couple of tablespoonfuls of grated Parmesan cheese on top. Serve immediately, very hot.

CASTRADINA
ZUPPA DI CASTRATO AFFUMICATO
Smoked Lamb Soup

In the year 1630 a plague struck Venice, so the Venetians naturally promised to build a church dedicated to the Virgin if they were saved. The church, Santa Maria della Salute *took over fifty years to build and was finally consecrated in 1687.*

As tradition has it, the workmen were not given enough time off to go home for their noonday meals. Therefore, at the work site they ate a filling and nutritious soup of castradina, *smoked lamb, sold from boats on the Grand Canal. It seems improbable that such diligent workmen should require fifty years to finish the church, but such is the case.*

Today on the Festa della Salute, *November 21, the traditional dish is, of course,* castradina. *It is a tradition that is dying out, however, and many younger Venetians have never tasted* castradina *let alone know how to prepare it. None the less, it is a flavorful, robust dish, so much so that it is perhaps a bit too strong for many palates.*

This recipe presents a couple of problems, the first being to find *castradina*, smoked lamb, although it may be smoked kid, goat, or mutton.

The second problem concerns salt: use none and the soup may still be too salty (in which case add some peeled potatoes, boil until tender, and hope they absorb enough salt to make the soup palatable).

Castradina as it comes from the butcher offers a dismal picture. It has a dark brown, tough outer coating, much of which, but not all, will wash off with the aid of a stiff scrub brush. It must then be blanched and scrubbed again. Once this is done the rest is easy.

FOR 8 SERVINGS:

   4 pounds castradina, *meat and bones*
   2 pounds savoy cabbage, sliced or chopped
   (2 medium onions, coarsely chopped)

1. Have the butcher cut the *castradina* into serving-sized pieces.
2. Wash the meat under running water while scrubbing it with a stiff brush.
3. Place in a pot and cover with boiling water. Allow to soak for 2

or 3 minutes. Discard the water and again scrub the meat under running water.

4. Replace in the pot and cover with cold water. Bring to a rolling boil and skim until scum no longer forms. This may take 20 minutes or even longer.

5. Add the cabbage and, if you wish, onion. Simmer until the meat is tender when tested with a fork, 3½ hours more or less. Taste the broth toward the end of the cooking to check for salt, adding more if needed, or "removing" it with potatoes as discussed above.

6. Serve very hot with or without bread slices or *crostini*, page 220. This is such a filling dish that it is normally eaten as a one-course meal, often preceded by a light *antipasto*.

SOPA DE COA DE MANZO
ZUPPA DI CODA DI MANZO
Oxtail Soup

Here is a soup that can be served for convenience and economy, as a first course or a main course. Either way the result is flavorful and invites one to drink several glasses of red wine, full bodied and dry.

An oxtail of 3½ or 4 pounds comes from a mature animal. If the animal was too mature the meat may never become tender. If in doubt, you may wish to use two smaller oxtails.

FOR 5 OR 6 SERVINGS:

An oxtail, about 3½ pounds
Water
6 ribs celery, diced
1 large onion, chopped
1 large ripe tomato, peeled
  (seeded if you wish) and chopped
Salt and pepper
Grated Parmesan cheese

1. Divide the oxtail into pieces by cutting at each joint. Trim off and discard as much fat as possible. Wash the pieces with cold water and place them in a pot. Cover the meat with cold water, the quantity depend-

ing on whether you like your broth thick or thin and how many people you plan to serve. Place the pot over a high flame. While the water is coming to a boil, prepare the vegetables.

2. When the water boils scum will form. Turn the flame down to medium and skim off the scum. Continue skimming until no more scum forms, 15 minutes or so.

3. Add the vegetables and some salt and pepper. Reduce the flame, cover the pot, and simmer until the meat is tender, possibly as little as 3 hours, possibly as long as 4½. During cooking add water to replace that which boils off.

4. Test the meat with a fork and when it seems tender cut off a small piece and eat it. Oxtail can be stringy and deceptive, and the best test is to chew on a piece of it.

5. When the meat is tender, skim the fat off the broth. You may wish to strain out what little there may be left of the vegetables as well.

6. Place a piece or two of oxtail in a soup dish and ladle over some broth. You may serve it with or without *crostini* (page 220) or with Italian or French bread. Sprinkle some grated Parmesan cheese on top and serve immediately.

SOPA DE TRIPE
ZUPPA DI TRIPE
Tripe Soup

This appetizing soup is eaten by preference in wintertime, as it should be served very hot. Red wine is the indicated beverage with this soup.

The recipe below may be varied slightly by using ¾ of a pound of oxtail and additional water in place of the broth. If this variation is used, add extra water, about 2 cups, and for the first 15 minutes of cooking skim the soup to remove the scum. Increase the cooking time considerably, since the oxtail will probably require 3 hours and perhaps as long as 4½ to cook.

Most tripe bought in stores today has been precooked, and it is this type that is called for in the recipe. Be sure to check with your butcher about this.

FOR 4 SERVINGS:

½ pound meaty tripe
½ pound of the thin leaflike part of the tripe
¼ pound esophagus, if you can find it; otherwise,
  increase the amounts of tripe
4 tablespoons butter
2 tablespoons olive oil
1 clove garlic, peeled
2 tablespoons finely chopped parsley
Salt and pepper
¾ teaspoon thyme
6 to 8 cups chicken, meat, or vegetable broth,
  or a mixture
Crostini *(page 220)*
Grated Parmesan cheese

1. Wash the tripe and esophagus well. Cut the tripe into pieces ½ by 2 inches and cut the esophagus into washers ⅛ of an inch thick.

2. Heat the butter and oil in a saucepan. Add the garlic and cook over a medium flame until it has browned. Remove and discard the garlic.

3. Add the tripe, esophagus, parsley, some salt, and quite a bit of pepper to the saucepan. Stir periodically, keeping the pan covered between stirrings. If in the first hour of cooking the tripe does not produce enough liquids of its own and threatens to stick to the bottom of the pan, add some of the broth to be used in the next step.

4. After the tripe has cooked for about an hour, add the thyme and enough broth to make a thick soup, 6 to 8 cups. Simmer another hour.

5. Serve the soup into bowls or soup dishes. Place some *crostini* on top and sprinkle on grated Parmesan cheese. The soup should be eaten while very hot.

PASTA E OCA
PASTA CON BRODO D'OCA
Pasta in Goose Broth

The broth made from goose is both flavorful and substantial. With the addition of pasta it becomes substantial to the point of heaviness, but it makes an excellent dish nevertheless when eaten in moderation.

It is a favorite of people who work more with the muscles than the brain. Venetian gondoliers in former times ate it so often that they became nicknamed "pasta e oca."

Gondoliers today do not take kindly to being called *pasta e oca*.

The goose broth and pasta are served as the first course and the goose itself as the second. Boiled goose goes very well with horseradish and pickled vegetables, called *sottoaceto*.

The recipe is simple and the results gratifying if the goose is a good one. Try for an old gosling or a young goose, 8 to 10 pounds. Aside from being perfect for 8 people, it will be more tender and less fat than a larger bird. For fewer people, use half the goose for *pasta e oca* and roast the other half a day or two later.

The giblets are not called for in this recipe so you may wish to consult a French cookbook for a recipe for *terrine*.

FOR 8 SERVINGS:

A gosling or young goose, 8 to 10 pounds dressed
5 to 6 quarts water
2 large onions coarsely chopped
2 large carrots coarsely diced
8 ribs celery cut into ½-inch lengths
Salt and pepper
10 ounces pasta: linguine *if you can find them;*
    otherwise thick spaghetti or any other
    fairly thick pasta
Grated Parmesan cheese
Horseradish and pickled vegetables

1. Remove the neck from the goose and cut it into 3 or 4 pieces. Discard the neck skin. Cut the goose into quarters and remove all excess fat. (The fat may be rendered and used as a substitute for part of the olive oil in vegetable recipes). Wash the goose quarters and the neck pieces and place in a large pot. Cover with cold water. Bring to a boil over a high flame. Scum will form at first and must be skimmed. When scum no longer forms add the vegetables, some salt, and quite a bit of pepper. Cover the pot and reduce the flame to very low so that the water is barely simmering.

2. Cook until the goose is tender. How long this will take depends upon how the goose was raised. It will take at least 1½ hours, probably

2 to 2½ hours, and possibly as long as 3. Test by sticking with a fork. Oddly enough the hind quarters will require less cooking than the breast, and when tender should be set aside until the rest is ready.

3. During cooking degrease the broth frequently. A good way to do this is with a ladle and a baster. Dip a ladleful of broth from the surface. Return any broth in the ladle to the pot, using the baster for this purpose.

4. When all the goose is tender, remove it from the pot and set it aside temporarily. Strain 16 cups from the pot into a second pot. (An easy way to do this is to first measure 16 cups of water into the second pot. Note the level and discard the water. Fill the pot to the same level with strained broth). Return the goose to the remaining broth in the first pot and keep it warm over the lowest possible flame.

5. If necessary, degrease the broth again. Check the seasoning. The broth should be just a bit on the salty side at this point, since the pasta will require some salt. Bring the broth to a rapid boil and add the pasta. Cook the pasta until just barely tender, *al dente*. It should not be soft and mushy. (See pages 50-51 for more information about cooking pasta.)

6. Divide the cooked pasta among the soup dishes and fill them with broth. At the table sprinkle on a tablespoonful or more of grated Parmesan cheese.

7. After the broth has been eaten, serve the goose accompanied by horseradish and pickled vegetables and perhaps a green salad.

8. Use leftover broth for making a *risotto* and leftover goose for *polpete* (page 187).

SOPA D'INTINGOLO
ZUPPA CON LE REGALIE DI POLLO
Chicken Giblet Soup

Aside from being a flavorful soup, this soup also prepares the stomach for a glass of red wine; as we always hope, wine of good quality and very dry!

The *regalie* of the chicken consist of the liver, heart, gizzard, wing tips, feet (minus the toenails), neck, and the comb. Other dark red meat located inside the chicken along the backbone may also be used, but the lungs are discarded. The feet should be skinned, not an easy task.

If you cannot find all these ingredients, make up the difference in weight with those available.

FOR 4 SERVINGS:

The regalie *from two 2½-pound chickens;*
  about ¾ pound
2 tablespoons olive oil
2 ounces butter
1 celery heart, finely diced
1 small carrot, finely diced
1 medium onion, chopped
Salt and pepper
1½ tablespoons tomato sauce (page 219)
1½ cups water; or half water, half dry white wine
5 cups beef or veal broth
Crostini *(page 220)*
Grated Parmesan cheese

1. Wash the *regalie* well and cut everything except the wing tips and necks into ¼-inch cubes.

2. Place the olive oil and butter in a saucepan over a medium flame. Add the vegetables and cook until the onion is translucent, about 5 minutes. Add the *regalie* and some salt and pepper. When the *regalie* are lightly browned add the tomato sauce and the water or water and wine. Bring to a simmer and reduce the flame to a point where the simmer is maintained. Cook for about 1 hour.

3. Add the broth to the saucepan, return to a simmer and cook for another 10 minutes or so.

4. Serve very hot. The wing tips may be served with the skin still on, but remove the skin from the necks after cooking. Place some *crostini* on top of the soup and sprinkle on a tablespoonful or more of grated Parmesan cheese.

FEDEINI IN BRODO
PASTA O PASTINA IN BRODO
"Angel's Hair" in Broth

There is nothing quite like this simple broth with pasta to put one's stomach in shape either before or after serious drinking. Before, it builds a base so that the wine may be enjoyed more thoroughly. On the other

*hand, if one has already had his share and then some, it serves to restore
the equilibrium and enable him to carry on!*

Apart from the usage described above, this broth is often served
as a first course when a *bollito* (mixed boiled meat) is the main course,
since the broth is a by-product of the *bollito* recipe. (See page 146.)

Making the broth does not require as much talent as time. When the
broth is prepared it is merely a matter of adding the pasta and cooking
it until tender.

The most often used pasta is *fedeini* in Venetian dialect, *capelli
d'angelo* in Italian, or "angel's hair" in English. It is a very thin spaghetti.
The generic term for thin pasta in Italian is *pastina*. We use *pasta o pastina*
in the Italian title to this recipe instead of *capelli d'angelo* because there
are perhaps 150 other types of *pastina* or pasta that might be used, some
thin, some thick. Many of the other interesting shapes (bow ties, cart
wheels, shells, etc.) are bought by parents who hope that their children
will become more interested and eat more, much as at one time alphabet
soup was popular in America.

In Venetian homes the broth is not clarified as a rule. Perhaps this is
to show that it is really homemade and not canned or dehydrated; perhaps
it is laziness.

FOR 4 SERVINGS:

    7 cups broth (page 146)
    3½ ounces pastina, *as discussed above*
    (Salt)
    ⅓ cup grated Parmesan cheese

1. If the broth has been cooled and stored in the refrigerator, skim
off any grease or fat from the surface. If the broth is still hot, use a ladle
and a bulb baster and degrease the broth in the way described in the
recipe for *pasta e oca* (page 43).

2. Bring the broth to a rolling boil. Add the pasta and cook until
just tender but not mushy, 4 or 5 minutes for "angel's hair." Check to see
if the broth is sufficiently salted. The pasta will absorb some of the salt
flavor.

3. Add the grated cheese, stir, and serve into soup dishes. Have some
additional grated cheese on the table to sprinkle on top of the broth if so
desired.

SOPA DE VERDURA
MINESTRONE
Vegetable Soup

This is a very agreeable soup that comes out better in the spring when it is possible to buy fresh vegetables at the market. In winter one makes do with the vegetables available, but it comes out well all the same.

The recipe calls for fresh cranberry beans, which will be difficult to find. Do not confuse cranberry beans with cranberries. Dried cranberry beans, which may be found in Italian grocery stores (ask for beans to make *pasta e fagioli*), may be used, but they must be soaked overnight and parboiled for 1 to 3 hours depending upon the quality. Dried kidney beans may be substituted, but they must also be soaked and parboiled.

Some people also add pasta to this soup, but we feel that that is overdoing it, there being enough starch already.

FOR 4 SERVINGS:

2 carrots, peeled and cut into thin disks
6 to 8 ribs young celery or 3 to 4 ribs mature, diced
1 medium onion, chopped
1 large leek, chopped
2 to 3 zucchini, unpeeled, cut into ¼-inch disks
¼ pound green beans, cut into 1-inch lengths
⅓ to ½ pound shelled fresh cranberry beans or
    ¼ pound dried cranberry or kidney beans,
    soaked overnight and parboiled. See instructions
    on the package.
1½ tablespoons finely chopped parsley
3 medium-sized mature potatoes, cut into
    ½-inch cubes or smaller
⅓ cup olive oil
6 cups broth, either chicken or meat, or better, a mixture
Salt and pepper
Crostini *(page 220)*

1. Prepare all the vegetables.
2. Place the vegetables in a pot along with the olive oil and broth. Add some salt and quite a bit of pepper. If the broth does not completely

cover the vegetables, add some water. Cover the pot and bring the liquids to a boil over a high flame. When a boil is reached reduce the flame to a point where a gentle simmer is maintained.

3. Cook for at least 2½ hours. If a lot of steam escapes during cooking add more water to make up the difference. The soup should be quite thick, but still a soup and not a stew.

4. Serve into soup dishes. At the table put on 3 or 4 or more *crostini* and sprinkle on a couple of tablespoonfuls of grated Parmesan cheese.

PANADEA CO L'OGIO
ZUPPA DI PANE GRATTATO
Bread-crumb Soup

This appears to be a very light soup, but in fact it is surprisingly substantial. It is excellent for delicate stomachs, and it is claimed that it alleviates distress from intestinal disturbances. In times gone by it was popular with new mothers for its nutrient quality.

One of the authors of this book doubts that the soup has much nutrient value, but both agree that for an upset stomach it is difficult to imagine a more innocuous dish than this.

FOR 4 SERVINGS:

1½ quarts water
⅔ cup very fine (preferably sifted) bread crumbs
* made from dry Italian or French bread*
2 teaspoons or more salt
6 tablespoons olive oil
⅓ cup grated Parmesan cheese

1. Bring the water to a boil in a saucepan.
2. Gradually add the bread crumbs to the boiling water while stirring with a spoon. Add the salt and olive oil. Cover and reduce the heat to very low. Simmer for about an hour, stirring occasionally and adding a little more water if necessary. Test to see if it needs more salt.
3. At the end of cooking, add the grated cheese, stir, and serve in soup dishes.

Pasta

THERE ARE SCORES of types of pasta, ranging from spaghetti of various sizes to little bow ties, butterflies, and shells. As mentioned earlier, many of these forms are served to children to entice them to eat. This leaves perhaps a half a hundred forms that the average adult Italian would not be at all surprised to see upon his plate.

Out of all these possibilities it happens that every one of our recipes calls for the most widely known of all pasta: spaghetti. We have nothing against the other shapes; spaghetti just seems to be the most indicated for the recipes we present here. By all means, if you happen to prefer a flat noodle, or a corkscrew type, or whatever, use it instead.

Most pasta, especially the more complicated forms, is made by complex machines. However, on occasion we make at home a few of the simple things, usually *tagliatelle*, a thin flat noodle and *taglierini*, the same thing except cut into very narrow ribbons; essentially a square spaghetti. Even with a small hand pasta machine it requires so much time and effort that we rarely do it. Also, in Venice there are shops which specialize in fresh pasta. But if fresh pasta is not available, then it would seem definitely worth the trouble now and then to make it even though there are excellent dry brands on the market. An important thing to remember, however, is that there are also exceedingly poor brands in packages. For a little more money you can find good Italian pasta in America. But simply because it is Italian is no guarantee that it will be good, for there are bad Italian brands too.

The Molo *near Piazza San Marco at high tide. Gondoliers awaiting work.*

There is more than one way to make pasta. Although many recipes call for olive oil and water, the best pasta to our thinking is that made only from flour, a little salt, and eggs. To do it by hand, place 3½ cups of unsifted flour in a mound on a pastry board and make a well in the center. Add 2 teaspoons of salt. You may need 3 and possibly 4 eggs to make the flour into a dough. Start off with just 2 to be sure. They need not be beaten, merely deposited into the well. Work the flour into the eggs, adding more eggs as necessary. Knead the dough until your arms are ready to fall off. It should be uniform, quite hard, and fairly dry. Roll the dough into as thin a sheet as possible and cut into the desired form.

That is the way to do it by hand. We have a mixer that has a "pasta hook" attachment for kneading the dough. We put most of the flour and all of the salt into the bowl, turn on the machine, and start adding the eggs. If after 3 eggs the mixture is too dry we add another. If after 4 eggs the dough is too moist, we add more flour. When the dough is well kneaded, we take out our hand-operated pasta machine through which we can roll the dough to any one of 7 thicknesses. Starting with the thickest and working down to the thinnest we go through all 7 settings. After each run through the machine we fold the pasta sheet into a triple layer before going on to the next setting, thus obtaining further mixing and kneading. After the seventh setting we fold the pasta into 10 or so layers and start all over again from the thickest setting. We run the dough through the machine 3 times at each setting, 21 passes total before we are ready to cut it.

Hand pasta machines often also have cutting attachments. Ours, being a small model, cuts only *tagliatelle* and *taglierini*, but cutting by hand we are able to make *lasagna*, *ravioli*, and others.

After cutting the pasta, it may be cooked immediately or saved for later. If you do not plan to cook it the same day, though, you have missed the point, the idea of *fresh* pasta.

It is one thing to have the pasta, whether fresh or packaged, and another thing to cook it. The American coauthor of this book before coming to Venice undoubtedly ruined more than his share of pasta. By way of excuse he points out that older cookbooks often recommended long cooking and then blanching. His Venetian friends wonder how it is possible to blanch glue.

The proper way to cook pasta is to place it in fairly salty boiling water, stir so that it does not attach itself to the pot, and cook until it has just barely reached tenderness. The amount of water in the pot should be abundant and the boil should be rapid.

If pasta is overcooked it loses its starch (in more ways than one) and its flavor, and will stick together unless blanched. If you have to rinse it to remove the goo, forget it and start all over.

How do you know if it is done? Test it by fishing out a piece and biting into it. If undercooked it will stick to your teeth, be hard to chew, and be generally unpleasant. When properly cooked it will still be firm but will not stick to your teeth. You will still have to bite it, but it will not be hard to chew. This is called *al dente*, "to the tooth," and is the preferred degree of doneness.

We recommend that no matter what shape of pasta you cook, you start testing while you are sure it is still raw. This so that you have a point or reference which will make it easier for you to spot the moment when the pasta is *al dente*. This is vital when cooking fresh pasta, which cooks almost immediately; a matter of only a couple of minutes for *taglierini*, for example.

A few additional words of warning when using packaged pasta: one brand of pasta of a certain measure may require either more or less cooking than another brand of the same measure. Also, a box of pasta that has been on a shelf for a long time may need longer cooking than a fresh box. *Never mix brands of pasta and never mix the same brands unless you are sure they are of about the same age.*

When the cooking is completed, pour the cooking water into a colander depositing the pasta therein. Or, if you have cooked spaghetti or longer noodles, you can fish them out of the pot using two forks and place them directly onto the spaghetti dishes. This is sometimes done in restaurants and makes a terrific presentation, but unless you are agile, do not try it—by the time you get the last spaghetti out they may be overcooked.

Other types of pasta can be fished out with a slotted spoon or some other suitable draining device.

If you have taken the easy way, the colander, shake to drain off any trapped water and place the pasta either into warmed spaghetti dishes, a warmed mixing bowl, or a chafing dish. If into spaghetti dishes, spoon the sauce over the top and serve immediately. If into a mixing bowl, combine the pasta and sauce and serve into warmed spaghetti dishes. The chafing-dish routine is another presentation that is sometimes done in restaurants. The sauce is cooked in the chafing dish at the table and at the proper moment a waiter runs out with a plate full of hot pasta. The pasta and sauce are mixed and then served.

Another word of caution at this point: even if the pasta is cooked perfectly it will tend to stick together if it cools before it has been combined with the sauce. When cooked it should be served quickly. The sauces, which always contain some olive oil and often butter, keep the pieces from sticking to one another. This is important if, in spite of the warnings about overcooking, the pasta is too well done. Do not blanch it, but rather pour a little olive oil over it and mix quickly (before your guests see what a mess you have made of it).

Note that the recipes call for ¾ of a pound of pasta for 4 servings, a perfect amount if you are all normal eaters and are having a second course afterwards. If you are particularly fond of pasta, use a full pound for 4 servings, and if you do not plan to have a second course, double the recipe.

Along this line another thing bears mentioning. Many American visitors to Italy are surprised the first time they order pasta when they see how little sauce there is. Italians prefer pasta with sauce as opposed to sauce with pasta. Also, the Italian is more than likely thinking ahead to the second course, where Americans frequently eat the pasta as the whole meal. The sauces as given are geared to the Venetian temperament and will have to be augmented if you want to do it American style.

You may wonder how important pasta is to Venetians since we give only 7 recipes in this section. It is extremely important, but we have included only recipes that are most typically Venetian. However, at the end of the section we do list a few more that either require no recipe because they are so simple or are by-products of recipes given in other parts of the book.

BIGOLI IN SALSA
SPAGHETTI ALLA SALSA D'ACCIUGHE
O DI SARDINE
Spaghetti with Anchovy or Sardine Sauce

Bigoli in salsa *is a very simple dish, but as simple as it is, it is also tasty, stimulating, and awakening to the appetite.*

This dish is most popular when the weather is cold. In winter it is often available in the wine shops as a mid-morning snack.

The sardines or anchovies usually used are those preserved in salt. They run between 20 and 25 per pound. It is all but impossible to distinguish between salted anchovies and salted sardines since a big anchovy may be larger than a small sardine. It does not matter; they are used interchangeably for this recipe.

Preparing the fish is time-consuming if one has had no practice. The easiest method seems to be to first rinse the fish under the faucet for a few seconds. This makes it fairly simple to scrape away the skin. Do this with a table knife, but do it gently. After the skin has been removed, still using a knife, pull away the dorsal fin. This will leave a cavity. Lengthen the cavity in both directions, toward the head and toward the tail. By inserting the thumbs in the cavity and working in toward the spine, one can peel away the fillets. Scrape away the small bones along the belly side. Do not worry about this too much; no one ever succeeds in getting them all.

If all this sounds too time-consuming or if salted anchovies or sardines are not available, canned flat anchovy fillets packed in olive oil may be substituted. Actually, the use of salted fish is almost as much a matter of economy as of flavor.

Canned anchovies vary widely in quality and also quantity per can; some packers fill the cans more completely than others. The recipe calls for 2 or 3 cans, depending upon how tightly the anchovies are packed.

Properly prepared *bigoli in salsa* has little sauce because what there is has a relatively strong flavor. Since there is little sauce, it is particularly important not to overcook the spaghetti, as it is the sauce that helps prevent the spaghetti from sticking together.

The *bigoli*, or spaghetti, traditionally used for this recipe is dark, made from only partially refined flour. Fifty or sixty years ago it was considered a luxury to have white spaghetti, the cost being so much more than that for the dark. Now, though, in Italy the dark costs more and is in fact difficult to find.

FOR 4 SERVINGS:

> *10 ounces salted anchovies or sardines or*
>   *2 or 3 cans, 2 ounces each, flat anchovy*
>   *fillets packed in olive oil*
> *4 quarts water*
> *1 tablespoon salt*
> *½ cup olive oil*
> *1 large onion, fairly coarsely chopped*
> *(⅓ cup dry white wine)*
> *(1 or 2 tablespoons capers)*
> *¾ pound thick spaghetti, dark if available*
> *Pepper*
> *(1 or 2 ounces tuna packed in olive oil)*

1. Clean and fillet the fish as discussed above. Cut into ½-inch lengths.

2. Put the water on to boil and salt it. Use less than the normal amount of salt since the sauce will be quite salty due to the anchovies.

3. Place the olive oil and the chopped onion in a frying pan over a flame a little lower than medium. Cook the onion until tender and almost ready to brown, 10 to 15 minutes. After 5 minutes or so you may add some white wine and cover the pan. You may also add some capers if you wish. If you add wine, allow longer for the onion to cook.

4. See pages 50-51 for general remarks about cooking pasta. Add the spaghetti to the boiling water and stir with a fork to be sure the spaghetti does not stick to the bottom of the pot. Thick spaghetti may take 12 minutes or a little longer to cook, but start testing after 10 minutes. Go on to the next step while the spaghetti is cooking.

5. About 5 minutes before you think the spaghetti will be done, add the anchovies and a lot of pepper to the frying pan containing the onions. You may add some tuna also at this time. Increase the flame to medium or a bit more. Stir constantly. The fish should turn to paste in just a few minutes. The sauce is now ready to pour over the pasta.

6. Drain the pasta and place it in a warmed mixing bowl. Pour the sauce over it and mix well. This is a tough one to mix. If the strands stick together, add a tablespoonful or more olive oil.

7. Serve in warmed spaghetti dishes. Cheese is not used with this dish. *Bigoli in salsa* may also be eaten tepid or cold.

SPAGHETI CO LE CAPE
SPAGHETTI CON LAMELLIBRANCHI
Spaghetti with Clam Sauce

This is a choice dish, very prized by those who enjoy spaghetti prepared in interesting ways. For them it is ideal for days di magro, meatless days. Be careful, though, because it is not terribly easy to digest and should be eaten in smaller quantities if one's stomach is a little delicate.

Cape in Venetian is the generic term for clams. Almost any clam, large or small, may be used for this recipe since they are chopped into fairly small pieces. The sauce most often prepared in Venice is *co le vongole*, with cockles. Probably this is more a question of economics than flavor. A kilogram (2.2 pounds) of cockles in the shell costs about $.35 at the time of writing this book while other clams cost up to eight times as much. A kilogram of cockles, incidentally, is sufficient to make sauce for 4 servings.

A certain amount of time and effort is involved in preparing *spaghetti co le cape*, but no more than that to make a good clam chowder. The results are well worth the trouble.

FOR 4 SERVINGS:

> 2 to 2½ pounds unshucked small clams or 3 pounds unshucked large
>   clams with thick shells; between 12 and 16 ounces of shucked
>   clams and clam juice
> 6 tablespoons olive oil
> 1 clove garlic, peeled and split
> 1½ tablespoons finely chopped parsley
> 2 tablespoons tomato sauce (page 218)
> 4 quarts water
> 2½ tablespoons salt
> ¾ pound spaghetti
> (Grated Parmesan cheese)

1. Wash, purge, and open the clams. (See *risoto de cape*, page 76, for the procedure.) Separate the meat from the shells, being sure to save the juice. On a cutting board mince the clams into ¼-inch pieces or smaller. Set the chopped clams aside. Filter the juice through a fine cloth or decant it very carefully into another container to avoid any sand or dirt reaching the sauce.

2. Place the olive oil and garlic in a saucepan over a medium flame. When the garlic has browned, remove and discard it. Allow the pan to cool enough so that when the clam juice is added in the next step it will not spatter.

3. Replace the pan over a fairly high flame and add the parsley, clam juice, tomato sauce, and the chopped clams. Cook until something approaching the consistency of a thin meat sauce is reached. Or, to put it differently, cook until most of the liquids have boiled away. The sauce should be thick and the oil just beginning to separate. How long this will take depends upon how juicy the clams were and how high the flame. Think in terms of a half hour, more or less. The sauce may be prepared in advance and reheated later.

4. See pages 50-51 for general remarks about cooking pasta. Bring the salted water to a boil and then add the spaghetti, stirring it to make sure

that it does not stick to the bottom of the pot. When cooked, as little as 6 minutes for thin spaghetti up to 12 or a little more for thick, drain it.

5. Dress the spaghetti with the warmed sauce and serve in hot spaghetti dishes. If so desired, some grated Parmesan cheese may be added at the table.

SPAGHETI COI PEOCI
SPAGHETTI CON LE COZZE
Spaghetti with Mussel Sauce

This dish is best during the warmer months when the mussels are more plump and flavorful.

Prepare the mussels for cooking (see page 17). Then make the sauce exactly the same way as you would clam sauce.

About 2 pounds of mussels in the shell should be sufficient for 4 servings. If it is winter and the mussels are thin, increase the weight to compensate. As with clam sauce, 12 to 16 ounces of shucked mussels and their juice are needed.

SPAGHETI COL TON
SPAGHETTI AL TONNO
Spaghetti with Tuna Sauce

This is a dish that one appreciates particularly when he has built up a good appetite, for it is substantial and filling but without giving the impression of being terribly heavy.

This recipe is one of the simplest in this book and is very good for emergency suppers. Simple as the recipe is, it may be ruined if the spaghetti is overcooked. There is so little sauce involved that starchy, overcooked spaghetti will absorb it all and make it impossible to mix properly.

Another very good tuna sauce can be made following the recipe for *bigoli in salsa* (page 52), substituting tuna for the sardines or anchovies.

The sauce requires only a few minutes to prepare, so put the water for the spaghetti on to boil first off. If thin spaghetti is used, start the sauce cooking before the pasta. Thicker spaghetti will take a long enough time to cook that the sauce may be made while the spaghetti is cooking.

FOR 4 SERVINGS:

4 quarts water
2½ tablespoons salt
¾ pound spaghetti
3 ounces butter
5 ounces canned tuna packed in olive oil
3 tablespoons tomato sauce (page 218)
(3 tablespoons good dry white wine)
Salt and pepper
(Grated Parmesan cheese)

1. Bring the salted water to a boil. (Read the general remarks about cooking pasta, pages 50-51). Start the pasta to cook as discussed above.

2. Melt the butter in a frying pan over a low to medium flame. Break the tuna into small pieces and add it, along with the oil in which it was packed, to the butter. Add the tomato sauce, wine if you wish, and some salt and pepper. Cook for 5 or 6 minutes, mixing the ingredients thoroughly.

3. Drain the pasta and dress it with the sauce. Serve in warmed spaghetti dishes. A tablespoonful or two of grated Parmesan cheese may be added at the table.

SPAGHETI COI BISI
SPAGHETTI COI PISELLI
Spaghetti with Ham and Peas

This simple family style minestra *is delightful, but it must be prepared with a certain amount of care.*

The only trick in this recipe is to start the spaghetti cooking when the peas just show the first signs of tenderness.

Do not use canned peas.

FOR 4 SERVINGS:

2¼ pounds peas in the pod or
    1 pound frozen peas
4 ounces olive oil
2 tablespoons butter
10 ounces boiled or smoked ham, or better,
    Italian prosciutto crudo, *minced*
1 medium onion, finely chopped
1 rib celery, finely diced
1 tablespoon finely chopped parsley
1 small garlic clove, peeled and minced or
    squeezed through a garlic press
Pepper
(Salt)
4 quarts water
2 tablespoons salt
¾ pound spaghetti
Grated Parmesan cheese

1. Either shell or defrost the peas.

2. Put the olive oil and butter in a saucepan over a moderate flame. Add the peas, ham, onion, celery, parsley, and garlic. Season with salt and pepper to taste. Be careful with the salt if salty ham was used. Cover and cook until the peas are tender, stirring them every now and then. You may have to add a few tablespoonfuls of water. Cooking time for the peas will depend upon the size and whether they are fresh or frozen. Start testing frozen peas after 8 minutes. Large fresh peas may take up to 25 minutes or even longer. While the peas are cooking, go on to the next step.

3. Salt the water and bring to a boil. (Read the general remarks about cooking pasta, pages 50-51.) When the peas show signs of becoming tender, add the spaghetti to the boiling water, stirring so that the spaghetti does not stick to the bottom of the pot. When cooked, 6 minutes or slightly more for thin spaghetti, 12 or more for thick, drain and dress with the sauce. Be sure to serve in warmed dishes. Sprinkle on some grated Parmesan cheese at the table.

SPAGHETI A LA CARBONERA
SPAGHETTI ALLA CARBONAIA
O ALLA CARBONARA
Spaghetti "Carbonara"

This minestra *is a little heavy but of most pleasing flavor, inviting a good glass of dry red wine and perhaps at the end of the dinner a* digestivo.

The Venetian noun *carbonera* or Italian *carbonaia* has several meanings: charcoal kiln, charcoal pit, charcoal pile, coal cellar, and female coal vendor. How *spagheti a la carbonera* got its name is rather a mystery. The most likely guess is that the mixing bowl should be so heavily coated with pepper that it looks like the inside of a coal cellar. Another idea is that it might be named in honor of *i carbonari*, an Italian revolutionary group organized in the early nineteenth century. Whatever the origin of the name, it is an excellent spaghetti made from readily available ingredients.

Read the recipe through carefully before starting, for at one point there are three things happening at once: the sauce is cooking, the spaghetti is cooking, and the egg yolks are being beaten. It is an easy recipe, but timing is important.

FOR 4 SERVINGS:

4 quarts water
2½ tablespoons salt
Butter and pepper
4 tablespoons olive oil
4 tablespoons butter
⅓ pound lean bacon cut into ¼-inch cubes or smaller
(⅓ cup light cream)
¾ pound spaghetti
3 egg yolks
½ cup grated ewe, goat, or Parmesan cheese, the sharper the better

1. Salt the water and put it on to boil. Do this first to avoid confusion later.

2. Grease a mixing bowl with quite a bit of butter and coat it with a very generous amount of pepper. Set the bowl aside.

3. Put the olive oil and butter in the frying pan over a low flame.

Add the bacon and cook for about 10 minutes, but do not brown it: it should have lost most of its fat but should not be crisp. Go on to the next step while the bacon is cooking. Optional: add the cream when the bacon has reached the proper degree of doneness and allow it to simmer gently.

4. (Read the general remarks on cooking pasta, pages 50-51.) Add the spaghetti to the boiling water and cook until just *al dente*, 6 minutes or a little longer for thin, 12 minutes or so for thick. Try to have the spaghetti done at the same time as the bacon.

5. While the spaghetti and bacon are cooking, beat the egg yolks lightly with a fork.

6. Drain the spaghetti thoroughly. Place it in the mixing bowl and pour over it the contents of the frying pan. Mix slightly. Add the egg yolks and again mix slightly. Sprinkle on the grated cheese and mix everything thoroughly. Serve into warmed spaghetti dishes.

SPAGHETI A LA MARINARA
SPAGHETTI ALLA MARINARA
Spaghetti with Parsley and Tomato Sauce

The dish in question is delicious and loved by those with healthy appetites. It is not easy to digest, but when one has a good stomach, all goes well.

In most parts of Italy this dish is prepared with large amounts of finely chopped garlic added at the same time as the parsley and remaining in the finished sauce. In Venice very little garlic is ever used, but even so the proportions of ingredients for *marinara* will vary widely from one Venetian household to another. Here is our way of doing it.

FOR 4 SERVINGS:

> *4 quarts water*
> *2½ tablespoons salt*
> *8 tablespoons olive oil*
> *1 clove garlic, peeled and split in half*
> *¾ pound spaghetti*
> *4 tablespoons finely chopped parsley, leaves only*
> *4 tablespoons tomato sauce (page 218)*
> *Grated Parmesan cheese*

1. Salt the water and put it on to boil.

2. Put the olive oil and garlic in a frying pan over a moderate flame. When the garlic has browned, remove and discard it. Take the pan away from the flame for a couple of minutes to allow it to cool a bit.

3. (Read the general remarks on cooking pasta, pages 50-51.) Add the spaghetti to the boiling water, stirring it so that it does not stick to the bottom of the pot.

4. Place the frying pan over a medium low flame and add the parsley and tomato sauce. Mix well. Cook for 4 or 5 minutes, being careful not to burn the parsley.

5. When the spaghetti is done, 6 minutes or a little more for thin, 12 minutes or so for thick, drain it thoroughly. Dress the spaghetti with the sauce. Be sure to serve in warmed spaghetti dishes. Sprinkle on grated Parmesan cheese to taste.

OTHER PASTA DISHES, without recipe or with sauces from other parts of the book.

Pasta with butter and cheese. This is the simplest of all. Put a good-sized piece of butter on the cooked pasta and sprinkle on freshly grated Parmesan cheese. If the pasta is of good quality, properly cooked, and the cheese fresh, it makes a perfectly acceptable first course. Best with a fairly light pasta.

Pasta with tomato sauce (page 218). Good with almost any shape pasta. Use lots of freshly grated Parmesan cheese.

Spagheti camisa nera; Black Shirt or Fascist Spaghetti. A postwar invention; smile when you order it in a restaurant. It is spaghetti with Cuttlefish in Its Ink (page 131).

Pasta with sauce from Pot Roast in Wine Sauce (page 143). Best when served with a thick pasta.

Pasta with Braised Veal Tail sauce (page 156). Use thick pasta.

Pasta with Veal Stew sauce (page 155). Again, use thick pasta.

Pasta with Braised Mutton sauce (page 162). Still the same: use thick pasta.

Pasta with Braised Duckling sauce (page 170). Once again, use thick pasta.

Pasta with Braised Mushroom sauce (page 207). Excellent with tagliatelle, flat noodles, and freshly grated Parmesan cheese.

Risi E Risoti
Risi E Risotti
RICE AND RISOTTO

A FRIEND OF OURS one day made the categorical statement that there are 120 ways in which rice is prepared in Venice. We include in this collection a mere 27, the most popular and interesting. After seeing the recipes which follow, you might think it feasible to make a rice dish out of practically anything. You would be close to the truth, and if you feel like inventing one of your own there is no reason why you should not. It probably will be no more weird than numbers 100 to 120.

There are basically two ways in which rice is prepared in Venice, in broth and *risotto*. In broth the consistency is that of an extremely thick soup. When a spoonful is removed, the cavity left by the spoon will fill up slowly. A *risotto* is drier and will form a mound on the plate or in the dish. This is how it is in theory, in any case. We often see *risotti* that fill all the requirements for rice in broth.

Another explanation that is sometimes given for the difference between the two is that for rice in broth the rice is added to the broth while for *risotto* the broth is added to the rice. We have tried it both ways and found them indistinguishable if the same amount of broth is used. We conclude that it is simply a matter of adding a little more broth or a little less rice that makes the difference.

But, to complete the consistency discussion and further cloud the distinction between the two, within each category some dishes are traditionally drier or more brothy than others. A brothy risotto is almost like a dry rice in broth.

Ca d'Oro, so named for its original gold-leaf facade, said to be the finest example of Venetian Gothic architecture.

Another interesting thing is that for some reason there are certain dishes that are always served as a *risotto* and some always as rice in broth. Then there are some that are popular either way, the best example being *risoto de bisi* and *risi e bisi*, peas and rice. There is no apparent logic as to why it should be so.

The procedures for making the various *risi* and *risotti* vary somewhat from one to another, but the idea is pretty much the same throughout. Rice is added to a saucepan containing the other almost cooked ingredients. Then water or broth is added a little at a time, enough to prevent the rice from sticking. The rice is cooked to a point where it has just become tender but is still rather firm to the bite and not mushy. During the cooking the rice must be stirred frequently, especially toward the end.

The first and most obvious pitfall is the rice itself, both with regard to the type and the quality. There are several types of rice in Italy, the three best suited for our purposes being *carnaroli*, *vialone*, and *arborio*. Other types are softer and release more starch when cooked and are not well adapted. *Carnaroli*, *vialone* and *arborio* retain the starch and when cooked the grains remain reasonably discrete. Of the three we believe *carnaroli* is the best, but there are different qualities of each type. The best *arborio* would more than likely make a better *risotto* than a second quality *vialone*. Try to find the first quality Italian rice. Otherwise, use domestic short-grain rice. We have made acceptable *risotti* with American rice packaged by a Texas firm. It may be our imagination, but it seems to work better than some other domestic brands.

The next thing to consider is the broth. For a number of *risotti* the broth is made as a by-product of the preparation of the name ingredient, but for many others, particularly those involving vegetables, broth from other sources must be substituted and chosen with care. If you are making a *risotto* with an ingredient that has a delicate flavor you must be careful not to cover it up. On the other hand if you were to use only water the result might be too insipid. You have to be an equilibrist. Try for a balance of veal or light chicken broth or a mixture of the two for delicate *risotti* and beef or beef and strong chicken broth for others with more definite flavor. For seafood, fish stock may be used, but only if it will not overpower the main ingredient.

By far the best broths are, of course, those made from scratch (see *carn e polo lessi*, page 146). You may substitute veal for beef, use all chicken, or vary it in any way you may wish to come up with either a heavier or lighter broth. Goose broth (page 41), is also good. Meat and fowl left over from making broth may be used to make *polpete de carne* (page 187) or *suchete ripiene* (page 191). For fish broth see *brodeto de pesce* (page 31), but be sure to leave out the vinegar.

Even with the best quality rice and homemade broth one must pay attention to the other ingredients, be they meat, fish, fowl, or vegetable. If you put in garbage, you will wind up with garbage and rice.

This part is divided into two subsections, the *risi* first and the *risoti* after.

RISI IN BRODO
RICE IN BROTH

RISO E BISATO
RISO CON L'ANGUILLA
Rice in Eel Broth

This is a riso *for robust stomachs. In Venice it is eaten often during the cold months, particularly at Christmas when it is the traditional dish.*

It is a tradition that is dying out, not for lack of enthusiasm for eel, but because of difficulty in finding good ones. More and more often we are finding eels contaminated by petroleum and having an unpleasant flavor. When good, though, rice with eel broth is one of the best.

Only the broth is used with the rice, the eel itself being served with lemon wedges as the second course.

FOR 4 SERVINGS:

> *An eel, 1¼ to 1½ pounds*
> *Water to soak the eel*
> *3 tablespoons white wine vinegar*
> *1 large rib celery cut into 1-inch lengths*
> *1 medium onion, peeled but whole*
> *5 or 6 cups water*
> *Salt*
> *2 tablespoons olive oil*
> *2 tablespoons butter*
> *1 small celery heart, finely diced*
> *½ medium onion, finely chopped*
> *1¼ cups risotto rice*
> *3 cups water, simmering*
> *(⅓ cup grated Parmesan cheese)*

1. Have your fishmonger remove the head and clean the eel Cut it into 4- or 5-inch lengths and wash well under running water. Place the pieces in a ceramic bowl and cover with cold water. Add the vinegar and allow to soak for 45 minutes.

2. Drain the eel and place it in a pot along with the 1-inch celery lengths and the whole onion. Cover with cold salted water, 5 or 6 cups. Place over a high flame and bring to a simmer. Lower the flame so that a simmer is maintained. Avoid vigorous boiling which will cause the skin to peel off the meat. Cover the pot and simmer for about an hour.

3. Skim off the grease and strain the broth. Set the eel aside for the second course. It may be served tepid or kept warm in the oven.

4. (Read the introductory remarks about rice, page 63.) Place a saucepan containing the olive oil and butter over a medium flame. When the butter has melted, add the diced celery heart and the chopped onion. Cook until the onion is translucent, 5 minutes or a little longer. Add the rice and stir until it is well coated. Then add eel broth as necessary until it is all consumed, after which add simmering water a little at a time. This *riso* is one that should be rather brothy. Cook the rice for 18 minutes or until just barely tender but not mushy.

5. When cooked you may add grated Parmesan cheese if you wish. Stir and serve immediately in soup dishes.

RISO E LUGANEGHE
RISO CON LA SALSICCIA
Rice with Sausage

This riso *is simple but of very good flavor. The important thing is the quality of the sausage; unfortunately, it is becoming more and more difficult to find really outstanding* luganeghe.

Ask at an Italian grocery store for *salsiccie* for *minestra* for this recipe, and hope for the best. The sausages should be about 3 inches in length and an inch or so in diameter. If they appear to be excessively fat, puncture the skins in 20 or 30 places with a toothpick and boil them for 20 minutes to remove some of the grease.

The whole sausages may be cooked with the rice or they may be skinned and broken into small pieces. Better still, use one whole sausage for each serving and break the rest of the sausages into pieces.

FOR 4 SERVINGS:

3 cups beef or chicken broth, or a mixture
   of the two
1¼ cups risotto *rice*
8 salsiccie, *about 1 pound total, prepared*
   as discussed above
Salt and pepper
3 cups water, simmering
⅓ cup grated Parmesan cheese

1. Put the broth in a saucepan and bring to a boil. (Read the introductory remarks about rice, page 63.) Add the rice to the boiling broth and stir. Reduce the heat to a point where a simmer is maintained.

2. After 5 minutes add the sausages and a little salt and pepper.

3. Have 3 cups water simmering and add it to the rice as it is needed. Cook until the rice is tender but not too soft, about 18 minutes total.

4. Add the grated Parmesan cheese, mix well, and serve in soup dishes.

RISI E BISI
MINESTRA DI RISO E PISELLI
Rice and Peas in Broth

It is very well known that the farms located on the islands of the Venetian lagoon produce various vegetables and fruit of excellent and delicate flavor. Worth singling out among these are the peas, from which one can make an exquisite rice dish, provided the peas are most fresh and the skins very thin and tender.

This *riso* should present no difficulties beyond that of the choice of peas. The ideal pea, found in the late spring, is very small, sweet, and delicate. Frozen peas will work but canned peas will not since they tend to purée when stirred with rice. The cooking time will vary greatly depending upon the age of the peas. Also, Venetians seem to like their peas more cooked than Americans. The cooking time, therefore, may be anywhere from 10 minutes for frozen peas up to 25 for large fresh peas.

Risi e bisi is about as Venetian a dish as there is. Simple as it is, it is extremely delicious when prepared properly.

FOR 4 SERVINGS:

4 pounds very young peas in the pod, or
   2½ pounds older peas in the pod, or
   1 pound frozen peas
¼ pound butter
2 tablespoons olive oil
1 medium onion, finely chopped
3 tablespoons finely chopped parsley
(2 ounces ham, boiled or smoked, or better,
   Italian prosciutto crudo, *minced)*
Salt and pepper
1¼ cups risotto *rice*
6 cups chicken or veal broth, or a mixture
⅓ cup grated Parmesan cheese

1. Shell or defrost the peas.
2. Place the butter and olive oil in a saucepan over a medium flame. When the butter has melted add the peas and other vegetables, and ham if you wish. Sprinkle on some salt and pepper. Cook over medium to low heat until the peas are just turning tender.
3. (Read the introductory remarks about rice, page 63.) Add the rice to the vegetables and mix well. Add broth as needed. Cook until the rice is tender but not mushy, about 18 minutes. Stir frequently, particularly toward the end of cooking.
4. When the rice is ready, stir in the grated cheese and serve in soup dishes.

RISO E PATATE
RISO CON LE PATATE
Rice with Potatoes

Inexpensive to make, this dish was frequently served in Venice years ago during times when housewives had to appease the appetites of numerous children on very little money. Modest as it is, it is nevertheless a quite flavorful dish.

The only problem this recipe presents is having the rice and potatoes both cooked at the same time. If the potatoes are overcooked before the rice is ready the whole thing becomes pasty. Other possibilities include overcooking the rice and having raw potatoes, or worse yet, raw rice. Pay close attention to the cooking times and the size of the potato pieces. Also, know your rice. If it takes more or less than 18 minutes to cook, compensate.

FOR 4 SERVINGS:

> *½ pound new potatoes, fairly small*
> *2 ounces butter*
> *2 tablespoons olive oil*
> *2 tablespoons finely chopped parsley*
> *½ medium onion, chopped*
> *Salt and pepper*
> *3 tablespoons tomato sauce (page 218)*
> *1¼ cups* risotto *rice*
> *7 cups meat or chicken broth or a mixture of the two, simmering*
> *⅓ cup grated Parmesan cheese*

1. Peel the potatoes and wash them. Cut into 4 or 6 pieces having a maximum dimension of about 1 inch.

2. Place the butter and olive oil in a saucepan over medium heat. When the butter has melted, add the potatoes, parsley, and onion. Add quite a bit of salt and pepper and mix well. When the vegetables have warmed and the onion is bubbling along well, reduce the heat and cook slowly, stirring frequently.

3. After 5 minutes add the tomato sauce. Cook for another 5 minutes, stirring, and then proceed to the next step.

4. (Read the introductory remarks about rice, page 63.) Add the rice to the vegetables and mix well. Add simmering broth as it is needed. More liquid is required for this recipe than for most because the potatoes absorb some of it. Also, it is traditionally served a bit more brothy than most. Cook the rice for about 18 minutes and hope that the potatoes are done at the same time.

5. Add the grated Parmesan cheese, give a quick stir, and serve in soup dishes.

RISO COL RADICIO INCARDA
RICE COL L'INSALATA ROMANA
Rice with Romaine Lettuce

This minestra *is well adapted for people with somewhat delicate stomachs. Food for delicate stomachs brings to mind all sorts of insipid dishes. This one, however, is tasty and can be eaten happily at any time, but particularly in spring and summer when the lettuce is fresh and flavorful.*

As with all rice dishes the broth used is very important, but especially so with this recipe because of the relatively delicate flavor of the lettuce. The broth should be substantial, but it should not overpower the romaine.

FOR 4 SERVINGS:

1¼ pounds romaine lettuce
(½ small fennel)
2 ounces butter
2 tablespoons olive oil
1½ tablespoons finely chopped parsley
½ medium onion, thinly sliced
Salt and pepper
1¼ cups risotto *rice*
6 cups chicken, veal, or vegetable broth,
  or a mixture, simmering
⅓ cup grated Parmesan cheese

1. Discard the outer leaves of the romaine. Remove the inner leaves and wash them thoroughly. Save the stem. Dry the leaves and cut them into thin strips, cutting across grain. Wash the stem and chop it finely.

2. If you can find a small fennel, cut it in half and discard the tough stringy outer part of the ribs as well as the top. In other words, use just the heart. Chop it rather fine.

3. Place the butter and olive oil in a saucepan over medium heat. When the butter has melted, add all the vegetables. Stir for a few minutes until the lettuce wilts. Add some salt and pepper and reduce the heat to very low. Cover the saucepan and cook for about an hour, stirring occasionally, adding a little water if the mixture threatens to stick to the bottom of the pan.

4. (Read the introductory remarks about rice, page 63.) Add the rice to the saucepan and mix well. Add broth as it is needed and cook until the rice is tender but not mushy, about 18 minutes.

5. When the rice is ready, add the grated cheese, stir, and serve in soup dishes.

RISO CO LE PONTE DEI SPARASI
RISO CON LE PUNTE DEI ASPARAGO
Rice with Asparagus Tips

Here is a minestra *that is eaten often during the asparagus season, which is to say in May and June in Venice. The result is very flavorful, a favorite dish of asparagus lovers.*

Both white and green asparagus serve equally well for this *riso.*

The big trouble with this recipe is the weight of the tips (or, rather, their lack of weight) as opposed to that of the stems. More is thrown away than used. At least that is the way it is done in Venice; we recommend saving the stems, minus an inch or two from the bottoms, for making cream of asparagus soup. We do not include a recipe in this book, however, since cream soups are definitely not Venetian.

If plump white asparagus is available, use about 2 or 2½ inches of the tip. For the more slender green asparagus, save about 3 or 3½ inches. If you are lucky enough to find very slender young green asparagus having stalks about the size of a pencil, grasp the stalks at either end, one stalk at a time, and pull. If fresh and tender, they should break at a point about 4 inches from the tip. Regardless of the type of asparagus, the idea is to use only the most tender part.

FOR 4 SERVINGS:

1½ to 1¾ pounds asparagus
2 ounces butter
2 tablespoons olive oil
1 tablespoon finely chopped parsley
½ medium onion, finely chopped
1 cup chicken or vegetable broth
Salt and pepper
1¼ cups risotto *rice*
Another 5 cups chicken or vegetable broth,
  simmering
⅓ cup grated Parmesan cheese

1. Remove the tips from the asparagus as discussed above. Wash well in cold water. Cut into pieces about ½ inch in length.

2. Place the butter and olive oil in the saucepan over medium heat. Add the asparagus tips, parsley, and onion. When the onion becomes translucent, after 5 minutes or so, add 1 cup of broth and some salt and pepper. Cover the pan when the broth boils and reduce the flame to very low. Simmer for about ½ hour.

3. (Read the introductory remarks about rice, page 63.) Add the rice to the vegetables and mix well. Add more broth as needed. During cooking stir frequently, particularly toward the end of cooking. Cook the rice for about 18 minutes until it is tender but not mushy.

4. Add the grated Parmesan cheese, stir again, and serve in soup dishes.

RISO E SUCHETE
RISO CON ZUCCHINI
Rice with Zucchini

This riso *is extremely popular in early summer when young, tender zucchini just appear in the market.*

This recipe is slightly more difficult than it might seem at first glance. Two saucepans are involved and the cooking time is interdependent. The trick is to have the vegetables very lightly browned in the first saucepan when the rice is about one-third cooked in the second.

FOR 4 SERVINGS:

10 ounces zucchini
3 cups water or light broth
2 ounces butter
1 medium onion, finely chopped
1 tablespoon finely chopped parsley
Salt and pepper
1¼ cups risotto rice
Another 2½ cups water or light broth,
  simmering
⅓ cup grated Parmesan cheese

1. Wash the zucchini well and cut a little from each end and discard. Cut the zucchini into sections ¼-inch in length.

2. Bring 3 cups of water to a boil.

3. In another saucepan melt the butter over medium to low heat. Add the zucchini, onion, parsley, and some salt and pepper. Sauté until the onion becomes translucent and then go on immediately to the next step, but continue to cook the vegetables slowly.

4. Add the rice to the first saucepan and cook for 6 minutes. Then pour the rice and water into the saucepan containing the vegetables.

5. Continue cooking the rice until it is tender but not overcooked, about 12 minutes longer. Add simmering water or broth as needed. As *risi* go, this one should be rather dry.

6. When the rice is ready, add the grated cheese, stir, and serve in soup dishes.

RISO A LA VENETA
RISO CON SEDANO
Rice with Celery

This is a simple minestra, *but it is tasty, delicate, and easy to digest.*
This is one *riso* that should be quite brothy. It is also one of the easiest to prepare.

FOR 4 SERVINGS:

3 tablespoons butter
2 celery hearts, diced very fine
6½ cups veal or chicken broth, or
  a mixture, simmering
Salt and pepper
1¼ cups risotto rice
⅓ cup grated Parmesan cheese

1. Melt the butter in a saucepan over a medium flame and then add the celery. Sauté for 5 minutes, stirring every now and then.
2. (Read the introductory remarks about rice, page 63.) Add about half of the simmering broth and some salt and pepper to the saucepan containing the celery. When boiling evenly, add the rice. Adjust the heat so that a slow boil is maintained. Cook until the rice is tender but not overcooked, about 18 minutes, stirring frequently and adding more broth as required.
3. When the rice is ready, add the grated cheese, stir, and serve in soup dishes.

RISO COL SEDANO E POMIDORO
RISO CON SEDANO E POMODORO
Rice with Celery and Tomato

Very simple, easy to make, delicious, and digestible. It also prepares the stomach for a glass of good dry wine.

Follow exactly the preceding recipe, but add 3 tablespoonfuls of tomato sauce (page 218) after the celery has cooked 4 or 5 minutes. Mix well, cook for another minute or two, and proceed to the next step.

RISI E VERZE
RISO CON VERZE
Rice with Savoy Cabbage

This is another very simple minestra, *but it is also one of the very best.*

One thinks of cooked cabbage as having a strong flavor. When done with rice, though, it turns out to be surprisingly delicate.

FOR 4 SERVINGS:

   1½ pounds savoy cabbage
   3 tablespoons butter
   Salt and pepper
   6 cups chicken or meat broth, or a mixture,
      simmering
   1¼ cups risotto *rice*
   ⅓ cup grated Parmesan cheese

1. Remove and discard the outer leaves and remove the core of the cabbage. Cut the good leaves into very thin slices as if you were making coleslaw. Wash well.

2. Melt the butter in a saucepan over medium heat. Add the cabbage and some salt and pepper, and stir until the cabbage has produced some juices. If after 3 or 4 minutes the cabbage is still not giving up liquids, add a little of the broth to be used in the next step. Stir occasionally while cooking until the cabbage is fairly tender, about 20 minutes.

3. (Read the introductory remarks about rice, page 63.) Add a couple of cups of the broth to the cabbage and when boiling evenly, stir in the rice. Cook until the rice is tender, about 18 minutes, adding more broth as it is needed. Whether or not all the broth will be used will depend upon how much liquid the cabbage produced. This *riso*, however, is usually more liquid than most.

4. When the rice is tender but not overcooked, add the grated cheese, mix well, and serve in soup dishes.

RISO IN CAGNON
RISO AL BURRO CRUDO
Rice with Butter and Parmesan Cheese

Easily made, flavorful, and recommended for upset stomachs.
Use only the finest imported *risotto* rice for this recipe. Since there is neither meat, fowl, seafood, vegetables, nor broth involved, the amount of rice is greater and the quality is of the utmost importance.

FOR 4 SERVINGS:

¼ pound butter, or slightly more
2 saucepans containing:
  3 cups water, boiling
  6 cups water, simmering
Salt
1¾ cups risotto *rice*
3 ounces grated Parmesan cheese

1. Take the butter out of the refrigerator and allow it to soften.

2. Salt the 3 cups boiling water and add the rice. Cook for about 18 minutes or until just barely tender. Add water from the second saucepan as needed. During cooking the flame should be lowered to a point where a slow boil is maintained. Stir frequently, particularly toward the end of cooking. While the rice is cooking, prepare everything for the next step.

3. Warm a mixing bowl and place the butter in it. When the rice is ready, pour it over the butter and mix a bit. Add the grated cheese and mix very well. Test to see if the rice needs more salt. Serve immediately in soup dishes.

RISOTI
RISOTTI
RISOTTO

RISOTO DE CAPE
RISOTTO DI LAMELLIBRANCHI
Rice with Clams

The Venetians and, in general, the inhabitants of the islands that surround Venice are very gluttonous when it comes to crustaceans and mollusks. In particular they love clams, which are most frequently eaten uncooked because they then are more flavorful and very suitable for bringing out the best in a glass of dry wine, either white or red.

One can also make a risotto with clams which, although a bit heavy, is very delicious.

A wide variety of clams are found in the Venetian lagoon and the Adriatic Sea. Those used for *risotto* range from about the size of a nickel up to that of a silver dollar. Almost any clam will serve to make a good *risotto*, although the larger, tougher varieties should be worked through a sieve or food mill to separate the hard, less digestible parts from the flavorful, tender parts.

CLEANING THE CLAMS:

Using a brush, scrub the outsides of the clams under cold running water. If the clams are sandy or muddy inside, allow them to soak in cold salt water for 1½ hours in order that they may purge themselves. Use 3 tablespoonfuls of salt for each half-gallon of water.

OPENING THE CLAMS:

If the clams are small, place them and ¼ cup of water in a frying pan with cover over rather high heat. Cover the pan and when the water begins to boil reduce the heat. After a minute or so, uncover the pan and stir the clams around. Cover again. Repeat the process until the clams have opened. After 4 or 5 minutes discard any that have not opened. Remove the pan from the fire and allow it to cool somewhat. Separate the meat from the shells. Save the juice. The juice should either be strained through a fine piece of cloth or decanted very carefully to avoid any sand passing on to the rice.

A second method, more practical for larger clams, is to open them one by one with a knife. Do this over a bowl in order to catch the juice. Again, strain or decant the juice. Some people use this method even for small clams, claiming that the rice has better flavor when prepared with clams opened in this manner.

RISOTTO FOR 4, USING SMALL CLAMS:

> 2 to 2½ pounds small clams
> 1 clove garlic
> 3 tablespoons olive oil
> 2 cups strained clam juice reserved from
>   opening the clams: if there is not enough, make
>   up the difference with fish stock or water
> 2 tablespoons finely chopped parsley
> Pepper
> 1⅓ cups risotto rice
> Another 2½ to 3 cups clam juice, fish stock,
>   water, or a mixture, simmering
> (¼ cup grated Parmesan cheese)

1. Wash, purge, and open the clams as discussed above. Be sure to save and strain the clam juice. Set the meat aside for later use.

2. Peel a clove of garlic and place it with the olive oil in a saucepan over medium heat. When the garlic has browned, remove and discard it. Set the saucepan aside to cool a bit.

3. To the saucepan add 2 cups of clam broth, the parsley, and quite a bit of pepper. Return to the fire and bring the broth to a boil.

4. (Read the introductory remarks about rice, page 63.) Add the rice to the saucepan and adjust the flame to a point where a gentle boil is maintained. As the rice cooks add more broth from the other cooking vessel as it is needed. After the rice is about ¾ cooked, about 14 minutes, add the clams. Finish cooking the rice, about 18 minutes total, until just tender but not mushy.

5. Correct the seasoning and serve in soup dishes. Optional: Stir in ¼ cup of grated Parmesan cheese just prior to serving.

RISOTTO FOR 4, USING LARGE CLAMS:

3 pounds large clams
1 clove garlic
3 tablespoons olive oil
1 cup strained clam juice reserved from
    opening the clams
2 tablespoons finely chopped parsley
Pepper
1 cup water, simmering
1⅓ cups risotto *rice*
Another 2½ to 3 cups clam juice, fish stock,
    water, or a mixture, simmering
(¼ cup grated Parmesan cheese)

1. Wash, purge, and open the clams as discussed above. Be sure to save and strain the clam juice. Set the meat aside for later use.

2. Peel a clove of garlic and place it along with the olive oil in a saucepan over medium heat. When the garlic has browned, remove and discard it. Set the saucepan aside to cool a bit.

3. Add 1 cup clam juice, the parsley, quite a bit of pepper, and the clams. Bring the broth to a simmer, cover the saucepan, and cook for 30 minutes.

4. Remove the clams from the saucepan and place them on a strainer or food mill over another saucepan. Pour a little of the broth from the saucepan over the clams and work them with a wooden spoon until dry. Add some more broth and continue as before. When all the broth has

been consumed, use the 1 cup simmering water, repeating the above procedure. When all the water has been consumed, discard the material remaining in the strainer and bring the broth to a boil.

5. (Read the introductory remarks about rice, page 63.) Add the rice to the boiling broth, stir, and adjust the flame so that a gentle boil is maintained. Stir frequently, adding simmering broth as needed. Cook until the rice is tender, about 18 minutes. Correct the seasoning.

6. Serve in soup dishes. Optional: stir in ¼ cup grated Parmesan cheese just before serving.

RISOTO DE SCAMPI
RISOTTO DI SCAMPI
Rice with Scampi

This risotto, though not eaten all that often by Venetians, is usually associated with Venice. When properly prepared it is delicate and delightful.

There is a tremendous amount of confusion about scampi and shrimp. It is true that they are both macrural crustaceans, but they are from different branches of the family. A *scampo*, Latin *Nephrops norvegicus*, is structurally much closer to lobster, *Homarus gammarus*, than it is to shrimp. Its flavor, too, seems to us to tend more toward lobster. So if you cannot find true scampi, go ahead and make the recipe with medium size shrimp following the directions below, but please call it *risotto di gamberi*. If you can find very small shrimp, see the next recipe, that for *risotto di gamberetti*.

The scampi best suited to this recipe are small, the tail measuring 1½ to 2 inches maximum. In the markets in Venice when they are this little they come with the heads already detached since the claws when so small have no commercial value. This is too bad. We think that by using the heads and claws, the broth in which the rice is to be cooked could be made stronger without masking the scampi flavor.

More about the broth. We use the water in which the scampi have been boiled and supplement it with boiling water only. Some people prefer to use fish stock in order to give the rice a more substantial flavor. We feel that fish stock overpowers the scampi flavor and the delicateness is lost.

FOR 4 SERVINGS:

1 pound small scampi without heads
3 cups cold water
Salt
Another 2½ cups water, simmering
2 ounces butter
4 tablespoons olive oil
1 clove garlic, peeled
2 tablespoons finely chopped parsley
½ medium onion, finely chopped
Pepper
(¼ cup grated Parmesan cheese)

1. Rinse the scampi under running water and place them in a pot. Cover with 3 cups cold water and add a little salt. Use much less salt than you normally would for boiling crustaceans since the rice will be cooked in this water. Place the pot over high heat and bring the water to a boil. Cook for 7 or 8 minutes from the time the water reaches a rolling boil. If too much foam forms during cooking, skim it and reduce the flame to a point where the water boils less vigorously. After 7 or 8 minutes, remove the scampi from the broth. Strain the broth through a cloth and set aside for later use.

2. Peel the scampi and vein them if you wish.

3. Return the scampi broth to a boil. In another saucepan bring 2½ cups of water to a simmer. While the broth and water are heating, go on to the next step.

4. (Read the introductory remarks about rice, page 63.) Place a saucepan containing butter and olive oil over medium heat. When the butter has melted, add the garlic and cook it until browned. Remove and discard the garlic. Add the parsley and onion. Stir occasionally while cooking until the onion becomes translucent, 5 minutes or so. Then add about half of the scampi and some pepper. Mix well for a minute or so and then add the rice. Mix again and then start adding the broth a little at a time. When the broth is exhausted, add the simmering water as needed. After 15 minutes cooking, add the remaining scampi and continue to cook until the rice is ready, another 3 minutes or so. The rice should be tender but not mushy.

5. You may add a little Parmesan cheese, but be careful not to overdo it. Correct the seasoning and serve in soup dishes.

RISOTO DE GAMBARETI
RISOTTO DI GAMBERETTI
Rice with Small Shrimp

Patience is required of one who would make this dish, for shelling small shrimp is, if not difficult, at least time-consuming.

The proper shrimp for this recipe is the very small variety, with a tail length of about 1 inch.

The recipe for all practical purposes is the same as that for the preceding recipe, but note the following: In Venice when these small shrimp are bought they are still alive. In the cooking, rather than starting with cold water, the shrimp are thrown into boiling water. The reason for doing it this way is probably as much to keep them from jumping out of the water as anything else. At any rate, when the water returns to a boil, remove the shrimp and proceed as with the recipe for *Risoto de Scampi* (page 79).

A few hints might be given about shelling *gamberetti*. Break off the heads. Remove about half of the shell working back toward the tail. Then, pinch the tail and pull on the meat and the whole *gamberetto* should come out of the shell. *Gamberetti* are too small to vein.

If you have the time you may wish to return the heads and shells to the broth and cook them for 10 minutes or longer to strengthen it somewhat.

The same weight of *gamberetti* with heads is used as scampi without heads. The reasoning is that the flavor from the small pieces permeates the rice more evenly and thoroughly and, therefore, somewhat less useable weight is required. If the *gamberetti* are without heads, ¾ of a pound should be ample.

RISOTO DE GÒ
RISOTTO DI GHIOZZO
Rice with Fish

This risotto is considered by Venetians to be one of the best, perhaps even the best, for it is delicious and substantial, worthy of accompaniment by a white wine of exceptional quality.

The most likely translation we have been able to find for the Venetian *gò* is *goby*. In any case, the fish in question is a member of the *Gobiidae* family. Try the recipe with any bony, spiny salt-water fish having a fairly flat head. The fish should have a rather pronounced flavor and be 8 inches in length, give or take a couple. Any fish fulfilling most of these requirements ought to produce a fine *risotto*.

FOR 4 SERVINGS:

> *1½ pounds of fish as discussed above*
> *2 ounces butter*
> *½ cup olive oil*
> *1 clove garlic, peeled*
> *3 tablespoons finely chopped parsley*
> *⅓ cup finely diced celery*
> *Salt and pepper*
> *½ cup water*
> *4 cups water, simmering*
> *1⅓ cups* risotto *rice*
> *⅓ cup grated Parmesan cheese*

1. Clean and scale the fish. Do not bone them. Leave the heads and tails attached.

2. Choose a frying pan with a cover and large enough to accommodate the fish in a single layer. Put the butter, olive oil, and garlic in the pan and place the pan over medium heat. Cook until the garlic is well browned and then remove and discard it. Allow the pan to cool a bit.

3. Add the parsley, celery, and salt and pepper. Replace the pan over the flame and cook the celery and parsley for 3 or 4 minutes, stirring. Add the fish and ½ cup water. Cover the pan and when the water starts to simmer, reduce the heat to very low. Cook for about 30 minutes, turning the fish now and then.

4. Remove the fish from the pan and place on a strainer over a saucepan. Work the juices through by rubbing with a wooden spoon. Pour some of the broth from the frying pan over the fish pulp and work it again with the spoon. Continue in this manner until all the broth has been consumed. Then use about 1 cup of the simmering water, repeating the above process. When the whole cup has been consumed, discard the pulp on the strainer. (A food mill may be used in place of the strainer and wooden spoon.)

5. Check carefully to see that no bones have slipped through the strainer. It is safer to restrain the broth at this point.

6. (Read the introductory remarks about rice, page 63.) Bring the fish broth to a boil, add the rice, and stir. Reduce the heat to a point where a slow boil is maintained and cook until the rice is tender, about 18 minutes, adding simmering water as needed.

7. When the rice is ready, add the grated Parmesan cheese, mix well, and serve in soup dishes.

RISOTO COI PEOCI
RISOTTO CON LE COZZE
Rice with Mussels

This is another fine risotto, *best in summer when mussels are in season.*

This recipe is just enough different from *Risoto de Cape* (page 76) to merit its own space. (For a more detailed discussion of mussels, see page 17.)

FOR 4 SERVINGS:

2 to 2½ pounds well-filled mussels in their
  shells, more if the mussels are thin
¼ cup water
2 tablespoons olive oil
2 ounces butter
1 clove garlic, peeled
2 tablespoons finely chopped parsley
Pepper
1⅓ cups risotto *rice*
4 cups water, simmering
¼ cup grated Parmesan cheese

1. With a stiff brush scrub the mussels well under running water. Remove any sea growths that may have attached themselves to the mussels. With a knife pull away the "beard" (see page 17).

2. Place the mussels and the ¼ cup water in a frying pan, cover, and heat over a fairly high flame. When the water starts to boil, uncover the

pan and stir quickly. Cover again. After another minute repeat the process. Continue in this manner until the mussels have opened. If after 4 or 5 minutes there are still some that have not opened, discard them. Remove the pan from the flame and allow to cool a bit.

3. Separate the meat from the shells. Set the mussels aside while either straining the juice through a fine cloth or decanting it very carefully. Save the broth.

4. Go back to the mussels and remove the "interior beard," the dark, tough part of the meat which disconnected from the tender part looks rather like a rubber band. It is not absolutely necessary to remove the interior beard, but it is nicer if you do. Cut the mussels crosswise into ¼- or ½-inch lengths. Set aside for later.

5. Place the olive oil, butter, and garlic in a saucepan over a medium flame. When the garlic has browned, remove and discard it. Allow the pan to cool somewhat.

6. (Read the introductory remarks about rice, page 63.) Place the saucepan back over medium heat and add the parsley, the broth from opening the mussels, and a little pepper. When the liquid in the saucepan is boiling, add the rice and stir. Adjust the heat so that a slow boil is maintained. Stir frequently, adding simmering water as needed. Cook for about 10 minutes and then add the cut-up mussels. Continue cooking and stirring until the rice is tender but not mushy, about 18 minutes total.

7. Add the grated Parmesan cheese, mix, correct the seasoning, and serve in soup dishes.

RISOTO COL ROMBO
RISOTTO COL ROMBO
Rice with Turbot

If well made, this is one of the most pleasing risotti, appreciated by those who enjoy the fragrance of the sea. It is light, easily digestible, and rather economical because, aside from providing a rice course, the fish itself serves as the main course.

Be sure that the turbot is very, very fresh.

FOR 4 SERVINGS:

> *A 1½ to 1¾ pound turbot*
> *5 cups cold water*
> *2 teaspoons salt*
> *3 or 4 lemon slices*
> *2 ounces butter*
> *3 tablespoons olive oil*
> *A small celery heart, finely diced*
> *½ medium onion, finely chopped*
> *1⅓ cups* risotto *rice*
> *(1 cup water, simmering)*
> *(Grated Parmesan cheese)*

1. Have your fishmonger clean and scale the turbot, but scale it again at home and wash well.

2. Place the fish in a large frying pan (with cover) or other suitable cooking vessel. Add the cold water, salt, and lemon slices. If the water does not completely cover the fish, cook with the pan covered. Place over fairly high heat and bring the water close to the boiling point. Do not allow the water to boil, but reduce the heat to a point where the liquid is ready to simmer. Start timing from this point. While the fish is cooking, prepare for the fourth step. Cook the turbot for about 15 minutes. Carefully remove it from the pan and place it on a serving platter. Serve tepid as the main course. Accompany it with lemon wedges.

3. Strain the broth from the cooking of the turbot and bring it to a simmer in a saucepan.

4. Place a saucepan containing the butter, olive oil, celery heart, and onion over medium heat. Cook until the onion becomes translucent, 5 minutes or so.

5. (Read the introductory remarks about rice, page 63.) Add the rice to the onion and celery and mix well. Start adding the strained and simmering broth. Cook the rice for about 18 minutes or until tender but not mushy. Stir frequently and add broth as necessary. There should be enough broth, but if there is not, add some simmering water. This *risotto* should be fairly brothy.

6. When the rice is ready, you may add some Parmesan cheese if you wish. If so, add very little because the turbot flavor is so delicate that it can easily be covered up by the cheese. Correct the seasoning and serve in soup dishes.

RISOTO DE SEPIOLINE
RISOTTO DE SEPPIOLINE
Rice with Cuttlefish in Its Ink

This mollusk is most flavorful, especially in the hot season, July and August. During this period the younger, more tender, and more delicate cuttlefish are caught and are used to make a wonderful risotto *which some people claim is not well adapted to delicate stomachs. For meatless days, though, there are few dishes so delicious and substantial.*

The first time people see this dish served it usually comes as a surprise since the rice is black. It is made with *Sepioline in Tecia*, cuttlefish cooked in its own ink (page 131), and the rice absorbs the color very nicely. Forget its unusual appearance: it is one of the best *risotti* that can be made.

FOR 4 SERVINGS:

½ *recipe* Sepioline in Tecia *(page 131)*
5 *cups water or fish stock, or a mixture of the two*
1⅓ *cups* risotto *rice*
⅓ *cup grated Parmesan cheese*

1. In a saucepan heat the cuttlefish to boiling. At the same time in another saucepan bring the water, fish stock, or mixture of the two to a boil.

2. (Read the introductory remarks about rice, page 63.) Add the rice to the cuttlefish and mix well. Cook the rice until tender, about 18 minutes, adding liquid from the second saucepan as it is needed. Stir frequently during cooking, particularly toward the end. The rice should be tender but not mushy.

3. When the rice is ready, throw in the grated Parmesan cheese (although many Venetians say cheese should not be used in seafood *risotti*). Mix well and serve in soup dishes.

RISOTO IN CAVROMAN
RISOTTO CON CASTRATO
Rice with Mutton or Lamb

This extremely toothsome minestra *is particularly used in two periods: either when the weather is very hot or very cold. That is to say the seasons when mutton is of the best quality.*

See *Sopa de Castrà* (page 36) for general comments on the type of meat to use.

This *risotto* is substantial enough that it is often eaten as a main course. If so eaten, about half again as much meat will round it out better.

FOR 4 SERVINGS:

    1¼ pounds very lean lamb or mutton
    1½ teaspoons olive oil
    3 tablespoons butter
    1 medium carrot, finely diced
    2 ribs celery, finely diced
    1 small onion, chopped
    Salt and pepper
    1 cup meat, chicken, or vegetable broth,
      or a mixture
    ¼ cup tomato sauce (page 218)
    1⅓ cups risotto *rice*
    3½ to 4 cups broth, as above, simmering
    ½ cup grated Parmesan cheese

1. Trim off all fat and skin from the meat and cut into 1-inch cubes.

2. Place the olive oil, butter, carrot, celery, and onion in a saucepan over a moderate flame. Add some salt and pepper and, mixing well, cook until the onion becomes translucent.

3. Add the meat and turn it until lightly browned. Then add 1 cup broth and the tomato sauce. Cover and simmer until the meat is fairly tender. The time will depend upon the cut of meat and the age of the animal, possibly little more than an hour, possibly nearly 2. The recipe can be prepared in advance to this point.

4. (Read the introductory remarks about rice, page 63.) Add the rice to the meat. Adjust the heat so that a slow boil is maintained. Add

simmering broth as necessary. Stirring frequently, cook the rice until it is tender but not mushy, about 18 minutes.

5. Add the cheese, stir well, and serve in soup dishes.

RISOTO COI FIGADINI DE POLO
RISOTTO COI FEGATINI DI POLLO
Rice with Chicken Livers

This also is a popular risotto *among Venetians, particularly those who work hard at tiring jobs. This because it is very nutritious yet easily digested. As usual, it prepares the stomach for a good glass of dry red wine.*

As *risotti* go this one may be prepared rather quickly. More important, though, is the fact that it is a flavorful and interesting way to present chicken livers. It is a good way to initiate young children who often tend to regard liver of any kind with suspicion.

FOR 4 SERVINGS:

> 5 or 6 whole chicken livers, about ½ pound
> 2 ounces butter
> 1½ tablespoons olive oil
> ½ small onion, finely chopped
> 1 small carrot, finely diced
> 1 small celery heart, finely diced
> 2 tablespoons tomato sauce (page 218)
> Salt and pepper
> 1⅓ cups risotto rice
> 5 cups chicken, veal, or vegetable broth,
>   or a mixture, simmering
> ⅓ cup grated Parmesan cheese

1. Cut the chicken livers into 2 pieces in such a way that any fatty tissue or strings may be removed. Wash well under running water. Cut each half into 4 pieces. Let the livers drain while going on to the next step.

2. Place the butter, olive oil, onion, carrot, and celery heart in a saucepan over a medium flame. Cook for about 5 minutes or until the onion becomes translucent.

3. Add the chicken livers to the saucepan. Turn them for 2 or 3

minutes until they have browned slightly and then add the tomato sauce
and some salt and pepper. Continue cooking for 3 minutes more.

4. (Read the introductory remarks about rice, page 63.) Add the
rice to the vegetables and chicken livers. Cook the rice until tender, about
18 minutes, stirring frequently and adding broth as needed.

5. When the rice is tender but not mushy, add the cheese. Mix well,
correct the seasoning, and serve in soup dishes.

RISOTO DE FONGADINA
RISOTTO CON LE INTERIORE
DI AGNELLO
Rice with Lamb "Interiors"

What to do with leftover Fondagina de Agnelo in Tecia (page 163)?
Make risotto *the next day, of course.*

As mentioned there, we are not happy with the word "interiors" in
the title, but we prefer it to the euphemism "specialty cuts."

Using one complete set of *interiore* you will have enough meat and
sauce to make a generous 6-serving *risotto*. Otherwise, if two people eat
about two-thirds of the *fongadina* one day and use the other third the next
day to make *risotto*, they will have eaten substantially both days.

FOR 6 TO 8 SERVINGS:

1 4-serving recipe Fongadina *(page 163)*
2 cups risotto *rice*
7½ cups chicken, meat, or vegetable broth, or
  a mixture, simmering
½ cup grated Parmesan cheese

1. In a saucepan bring the *Fongadina* to a simmer.

2. (Read the introductory remarks about rice, page 63.) Add the
rice to the *Fongadina* and mix well. Add simmering broth as needed and
cook until the rice is tender but not mushy, about 18 minutes.

3. When the rice is ready, add the grated Parmesan cheese, mix
well, and serve in soup dishes.

RISOTO A LA SBIRAGLIA
RISOTTO CON PEZZI DI POLLO
Rice with Chicken

Risoto a la Sbiraglia *was very popular with Venetians in times past when they met for a* garanghelo, *which is to say a few hours of serious eating and drinking with a very unserious company. It was also eaten at wedding banquets when, after the* antipastò *was finished, it was considered the moment to lay a sound foundation for the succeeding food and drink, particularly the latter.*

It is a truly fine dish, substantial but not particularly difficult to digest. Above all, though, it is adapted for drinking lots of good dry red wine!

This excellent dish presents no difficulties and would be a good one to try if you have never tasted *risotto* before.

The ideal chicken for this recipe weighs from 1¾ to 2 pounds dressed, a medium-sized broiler or a small fryer. Larger, older birds may be used and actually have more flavor but, of course, must be cooked longer and may be fattier, causing the *risotto* to become more rich. If a very fat chicken is used, skim some of the grease before adding the rice.

FOR 4 SERVINGS:

A chicken, 2 pounds or a little less, dressed
3 ounces butter
2 tablespoons olive oil
1 celery heart, finely diced
1 small to medium carrot, finely diced
½ medium onion, chopped
Salt and pepper
3 tablespoons tomato sauce (page 218)
1 cup, more or less, veal or vegetable broth,
  or water, or a mixture
1⅓ cups risotto rice
4 cups water, simmering
⅓ cup grated Parmesan cheese

1. Quarter the chicken or cut it into eight pieces. Wash with cold water and allow to drain, or better, dry the pieces with a cloth.

2. Place the butter and oil in a saucepan over rather high heat.

When the butter is bubbling nicely add the chicken and vegetables and some salt and pepper. Cook for about 7 minutes or until the chicken has browned slightly. Add the tomato sauce and enough broth or water to not quite cover the chicken. Cover the saucepan and bring the broth to a simmer. Reduce the flame to very low. Stir occasionally while simmering for about an hour, depending upon the chicken. Test it with a fork from time to time. It should be fairly tender, about to fall off the bone but not quite. When done, remove from the saucepan and set aside. The broth will be used for cooking the rice and the chicken will be added when the rice is about half cooked. Note: True Venetian home style is simply to plop the pieces of chicken back in with the rice and at the table to chew at and suck on the bones. If you are not the chicken-bones-in-hand type you may wish at this point to remove the skin and bones and to cut up the chicken meat into pieces.

3. (Read the introductory remarks about rice, page 63.) Bring the broth in which the chicken was cooked to a boil and add the rice. Stir and add simmering water as needed. After about 10 minutes, add the chicken. Continue cooking until the rice is tender, about 18 minutes total.

4. Add the grated cheese, mix well, correct the seasoning and serve in soup dishes.

RISOTO CO LE SECOLE
RISOTTO CON PEZZI DI MANZO
Rice with Pieces of Beef

This risotto *is recommended for the winter season because besides being very flavorful, it is also substantial, especially adapted for those of strong constitution.*

It is a type of risotto *prepared particularly in the homes of Venetian butchers, for* le secole, *pieces of meat and muscle taken from the vertebrae of steers, are not easy to find in meat markets. To have these tender, delicious nuggets of meat one must have a friend who is a butcher or else one must be a highly esteemed client.*

The *secole* are the bits of meat from the vertebrae in the shoulder area. The further back one goes the tougher the meat becomes. Butchers in Venice look blank when asked about these pieces of meat. About the only way to have this *risotto* is by ordering it a week or so in advance at a well-connected restaurant. The recipe is so highly praised and prized by

Venetians that it would be impossible to leave it out and still call this a Venetian cookbook.

Try substituting small pieces of prime beef tenderloin for the *secole*. It will not be as flavorful, but it will give the idea and will make an excellent *risotto*.

FOR 4 SERVINGS:

>2 *tablespoons olive oil*
>3 *tablespoons butter*
>1 *small carrot, finely diced*
>1 *small celery heart, finely diced*
>1 *small onion, finely chopped*
>*Salt and pepper*
>1 *pound* secole *in pieces having about ½-inch*
>   *as the largest dimension*
>2 *cups beef or chicken broth, or a mixture*
>   *of the two*
>*(½ cup good dry red wine may be substituted*
>   *for part of the broth)*
>1⅓ *cups* risotto *rice*
>2 *cups broth, as above, simmering*
>⅓ *cup grated Parmesan cheese*

1. Place the olive oil, butter, and vegetables in a saucepan over a medium flame. Add a little salt and quite a bit of pepper. Cook until the onion becomes translucent, 5 minutes or so.

2. Add the *secole* and turn them until slightly browned, a matter of 2 or 3 minutes. Add the broth, cover the pan, and bring to a simmer. Cook until the meat is fairly tender, easily pierced with a fork but not falling apart. This may take anywhere from 30 minutes on up depending upon the quality of the meat. Go this far with the recipe well in advance in case the meat takes, say, 1½ hours, as it well might. If it takes only a short cooking time, it can be reheated with no damage to the recipe.

3. (Read the introductory remarks about rice, page 63.) Add the rice to the saucepan containing the meat and vegetables and cook the rice for about 18 minutes, stirring frequently and adding simmering broth as necessary. The rice should be tender but not mushy, while the meat with the additional cooking should be very tender but still not falling completely apart.

4. When the rice is ready, add the grated cheese, mix well, and correct the seasoning. Serve in soup dishes. A full-bodied red wine, very dry and very good, is indicated.

RISOTO DE BISI
RISOTTO DI PISELLI
Rice with Peas

Risoto de Bisi is prepared in exactly the same way as *Risi e Bisi* (page 67) except that less broth is used. Subtracting a cup and a half of broth should give the proper consistency.

RISOTO COI ARTICIOCHI
RISOTTO DI CARCIOFI
Rice with Artichokes

The little island of Murano was famous not only for its glass but also for the marvelous artichokes that its farms produced. There are few farms left, but what ones there are produce artichokes that are of fine flavor in all particulars, delicious and tender, especially if just picked and very small. These little artichokes are called spuntature *and may be used to make a wonderful risotto.*

Very fine artichokes are grown on all the lagoon islands. Venetians feel that there are no others grown anywhere to compare with them and that it is the salt air (and too often now the salt water) from the Adriatic that makes the difference.

We give below the Venetian recipe. In America it will most likely be necessary to substitute artichoke hearts in place of the small type called for, but it still makes a fine *risotto*. (If you use artichoke hearts, see page 203.) Use 2 average hearts, each cut into 8 pieces, per serving.

FOR 4 SERVINGS:

10 to 12 artichokes with bodies about
  1½ inches in length
4 tablespoons butter
2 tablespoons olive oil
1 clove garlic, peeled
1 tablespoon finely chopped parsley
Salt and pepper
(Water)
1⅓ cups risotto *rice*
4½ cups vegetable, chicken, or veal broth, or
  a mixture, simmering
⅓ cup grated Parmesan cheese

1. Remove the outer leaves from the artichokes and cut a bit off the tops, leaving bodies about 1 inch in length. Do not cut off all the stalk. Leave an inch or two. The outer fibrous part of the stalk which is quite bitter, should be removed with a potato peeler. Cut the artichokes into 4 or 6 pieces, lengthwise, not crosswise. Wash well with cold running water.

2. Put the butter, olive oil, and garlic in a saucepan over medium heat. When the garlic has browned, remove and discard it.

3. Lower the heat and cautiously add the artichoke pieces, parsley, and some salt and pepper. Cook for about 20 minutes over a very low flame, stirring frequently. It may be necessary to add a few drops of water to keep the artichokes from sticking.

4. Add the rice to the saucepan and stir. Add broth as needed while cooking the rice until it is tender but not mushy, about 18 minutes.

5. Add the grated Parmesan cheese, mix well, and correct the seasoning. Serve in soup dishes.

RISOTO COI FUNGHETI
RISOTTO DI FUNGHETTI
Rice with Mushrooms

Try this risotto *in the fall when mushrooms are more interesting, but be sure to have a light second course for it is a substantial dish.*

If you make good sautéed mushrooms (page 207), you are one short step from having a delicious *risotto*. Think carefully, though, about the type of broth. If you use mushrooms with a pronounced flavor you will not want a terribly strong broth; otherwise you will have a *risotto* that is overpowering. Neither will you want to use a strong broth if the mushrooms are very delicate, thereby masking the flavor, but it must be strong enough to prevent the *risotto* from becoming insipid. Perhaps the best solution is to use a weak beef broth for the former and moderate chicken broth for the latter. For mushrooms in between, mix the broths or use your imagination.

FOR 4 SERVINGS:

1 pound mushrooms
1⅓ cups risotto *rice*
5 cups broth as discussed above, simmering
⅓ cup grated Parmesan cheese

1. Prepare the mushrooms following the recipe on page 207, but try to catch them slightly before the tender point because they will cook some more after the rice has been added.
2. (Read the introductory remarks about rice, page 63.) Add the rice to the simmering mushrooms and mix well. Add broth as needed and regulate the flame so that a slow boil is maintained. Stir frequently while cooking the rice until tender but not mushy, about 18 minutes.
3. Add the cheese, mix well, correct the seasoning, and serve in soup dishes.

RISOTO DE SUCA
RISOTTO DI ZUCCA
Rice with Pumpkin

This risotto *is usually eaten in the fall and early winter when pumpkin is better and more sweet. It is not used too often in Venice but more so on the island near Chioggia, where there are some farms on which very choice pumpkins grow.*

The pumpkins found in Venice are quite different in appearance from those in the United States. They are much flatter and have green skins, but the meat is essentially the same.

You many substitute acorn or Hubbard squash and have equally pleasing results.

FOR 4 SERVINGS:

2 pounds pumpkin
1 tablespoon olive oil
2 ounces butter
1 medium onion, finely chopped
1 tablespoon finely chopped parsley
Salt and pepper
1⅓ cups risotto *rice*
4½ cups vegetable broth or water
⅓ cup Parmesan cheese

1. Remove the skin and seeds from the pumpkin meat. Cut the meat into very small pieces or thin slices.

2. Place the olive oil, butter, onion, and parsley in a saucepan and cook over medium heat until the onion becomes translucent, about 5 minutes. Add the pumpkin and some salt and pepper. Cover the pan. Every couple of minutes uncover the pan and stir. Do this until the pumpkin becomes very tender and begins to be pulpy. This should take 10 minutes or a little longer.

3. (Read the introductory remarks about rice, page 63.) Add the rice to the pumpkin and stir. Cook the rice until tender but not mushy, about 18 minutes, adding broth as needed. Stir frequently.

4. When the rice is ready, add the grated Parmesan cheese, mix well, and correct the seasoning. Serve in soup dishes.

MINESTRE VARIE
MISCELLANEOUS MINESTRE

THE FIVE RECIPES in this subsection are ones that are difficult to classify. *Pasta e fasioi* and *risi e fasioi* are both in a sense soups. *Pastiso de macaroni* is definitely pasta while *pastiso de melansane*, although a vegetable dish, is eaten as a *minestra* and is included here in order to keep our *pasticci* in one pie. *Gnochi de patate*, potato dumplings, are in a class all by themselves.

Forgetting the classification problems, some of the best recipes in the book are to be found in the following pages.

PASTA E FASIOI
PASTA COI FAGIOLI
Beans with Pasta

It was once stated that beans are the meat of the poor. This minestra, *aside from being very delicious, is nutritious, healthful, and relatively inexpensive. But its greatest merit is that of effectively quieting for a bit the goad of hunger.*

Pasta e fasioi is very important to the Venetian kitchen, and therefore we go into quite a bit of detail in this recipe.

The consistency of *pasta e fasioi* may vary from bean soup with pasta to pasta with bean sauce. It is eaten with a spoon if thin, with a fork if thick; with both fork and spoon if in between. It may be eaten hot, cold, or tepid.

Besides the consistency, the proportions of the ingredients may also vary widely from cook to cook. The recipe given here is a simple one—

the reader may take it from there, adding sausage, tomato, rosemary, thyme, and so on, if he so desires.

Since basically the recipe calls for beans and pasta and little else, it is particularly important to select the best quality beans possible. Cranberry beans (not to be confused with cranberries) are preferable, but dried kidney beans may be substituted. The larger the better is the general rule in selecting dried beans. The exception to the rule is large beans that do not have enough density; they may be too airy and have relatively little "meat." Either fresh or dried beans may be used. A pound of fresh beans in the pod yields about a half pound when shelled.

Almost any thick pasta is acceptable, but traditional ones include *lingue di passera*, flat noodles that before cooking are about ⅛-inch wide and 10 inches long, or *subiotini*, pasta tubes about ¼-inch in length and diameter before cooking. If a thin sauce is desired, it is wise to break noodles in 2 or 3 parts, or to use shorter, thicker pasta. Eating full-length *lingue di passera* with a spoon is a challenge, even for those practiced in the art.

The sauce may be prepared in advance and the pasta added and cooked just before serving. The sauce can be frozen, and because of the long preparation time, you may wish to make a large batch and freeze most of it for later use. Freeze only the sauce, not the sauce and pasta mixture—frozen pasta is a disaster.

FOR 4 SERVINGS:

> *1 pound fresh or ¾ pound dried*
> *cranberry or kidney beans*
> *Water for soaking the beans,*
> *if dried beans are used*
> *About 6 cups water*
> *4 ribs celery, diced*
> *1 small to medium carrot, finely diced*
> *1 medium onion, chopped*
> *1 tablespoon finely chopped parsley*
> *½ cup olive oil*
> *Salt and pepper*
> *⅜ pound pasta, as discussed above*

1. Place dried beans in a pot and cover with an abundant amount of water. Soak overnight, at least 10 hours. Fresh beans need not be soaked.

2. Pour the beans into a colander and rinse thoroughly. Return the

beans to the pot a handful at a time, still rinsing and making sure that all foreign material is removed.

3. Cover the beans with about 6 cups of water. Depending upon the beans, it may be necessary to add more water later. Place the pot over a high flame and add the vegetables, olive oil, and quite a bit of salt and pepper. When a simmer is reached, reduce the heat to the lowest point possible, cover the pot, and cook for 2½ to 3 hours for fresh beans and no less than 4 hours for dried beans. If the dried beans are of good quality, 6 hours' cooking is not too long. Stir occasionally to make sure the beans are not sticking to the bottom of the pot. If they do stick, do not scrape them off the bottom; instead pour everything into another pot. The burned beans will be lost, of course, but better that than to ruin everything. The consistency at this point should be soupy. Add more water if necessary. Optional and definitely not required: some cooks at this moment remove half of the beans, purée them, and then return the purée to the pot.

4. The sauce is now ready for the addition of the pasta, or for storage. It should be fairly salty, since the pasta will absorb some of the salt flavor.

5. Bring the sauce to a rapid boil and add the pasta. When the pasta is completely submerged in the sauce and the sauce has returned to boiling, reduce the heat. From this point until the pasta is cooked (8 to 10 minutes for *lingue di passera* and a little longer for *subiotini*) care must be taken that the pasta does not stick. Stir constantly. To be on the safe side have a saucepan of boiling water handy, so that if the mixture becomes too thick it can be quickly thinned without disturbing the boil. Do not overcook the pasta. Test it frequently toward the end of cooking.

6. Serve in soup dishes. Note: if you plan to serve it tepid or cold, the mixture should be brothy, since the pasta will continue to absorb liquid as it cools. Also, during cooling some additional cooking will take place. To minimize this, serve into the soup dishes immediately. Do not let it cool in the pot.

RISO E FASIOI
RISO E FAGIOLI
Beans and Rice

Beans in minestra *are always very good, no matter whether with pasta or rice. Perhaps it comes out a little lighter, and therefore more digestible, when made with rice.*

This typically Venetian dish, as good as it is, is not eaten all that often in Venice. The reason for this may be that the Venetians eat so much rice as *risotto* that they feel the need for a change of diet.

The recipe is identical to the one for *pasta e fasioi* except that rice is substituted for the pasta. (See the preceding recipe for the preparation of the sauce.)

FOR 4 SERVINGS:

The sauce, boiling
¾ *cup* risotto *rice*

1. Add the rice to the sauce, stir, and cook for about 18 minutes or until tender but not overcooked.
2. Serve in soup dishes. This dish may be eaten hot, tepid, or cold, and the same remarks apply here as those at the end of the preceding recipe.

PASTISO DE MACARONI
PASTICCIO DI LASAGNE
Lasagna

This is a delicious minestra; *a little heavy, to be sure, but so flavorful as to be appreciated not only by those who savor food to satisfy their stomachs, but also those who appreciate eating from a more cerebral approach.*

Some people may question *lasagna* as a Venetian dish. The answer is that *lasagna* made with peas is Venetian. Some people may question this answer, but there is no question about the results of this recipe. For the cook who is willing to take the time, the results will be well worth the effort.

We recommend the following recipe for 4 to 6 people as a *piatto unico*, a one-course meal, or for 8 to 10 people as a first course. It is probably better as a *piatto unico*, for it is difficult to come up with an act to follow.

Two other recommendations: make the *ragù* the day before; plan on at least 3 hours of hectic work even if the *ragù* is ready.

FOR A LASAGNA ABOUT 8″ BY 12″ BY 2″:

The ragù:

2 ounces dried mushrooms
1 to 1½ pounds fresh peas in the pod or
  ½ pound frozen peas. (Do not use canned peas.)
½ pound round steak or chuck
½ pound lean veal
2 ounces prosciutto crudo *or other ham*
2 chicken livers
½ pound butter
4 tablespoons olive oil
A celery heart, finely diced
A small carrot, finely diced
½ medium onion, chopped
1 tablespoon finely chopped parsley
5 tablespoons tomato sauce (page 218)
Salt and pepper
(A little water or broth)

1. Rinse the mushrooms to remove any sand or dirt and then cover them with an abundant amount of water. Allow them to soak until soft. Different types of dried mushrooms require more or less soaking, so read the directions on the package carefully. You may even have to soak them overnight.

2. Shell or defrost the peas. In the pod, you will need 1½ pounds of young peas, 1 pound of mature.

3. Take the round steak, veal, *prosciutto*, chicken livers, and mushrooms and chop them together very finely, or put them through a meat grinder.

4. Put the butter and olive oil in a saucepan over medium heat and add all the vegetables. Cook for about 5 minutes or until the onion becomes translucent. Add the meat and mushroom mixture. Cook, stirring frequently, until the meats have browned. Add the tomato sauce and some salt and pepper. When everything is simmering nicely, turn the heat down to low and cover the pan. You may have to add some water or, better, broth, from time to time to prevent the sauce from sticking. You must be very careful, for this sauce should be relatively dry and it is quite easy to burn it. Cook for 2 hours or a little longer. Correct the seasoning.

The pasta:

Salted water, 2½ tablespoons salt per gallon
1 pound lasagna

1. Fill your largest pot ¾ full with salted water. Bring the water to a boil.

2. Cooking time for *lasagna* varies tremendously from one brand to another. It also depends upon how fresh it is. Take one piece and drop it into the boiling water. If the box has cooking instructions on it, follow them for *al dente*, cooked but still resistant to the teeth. Otherwise, cook for 8 minutes. Remove this test piece and bite off a corner. If not cooked, put it back for a little longer, noting the time. Continue in this manner until you determine the cooking time. One book we have gives cooking time for *lasagna* as 10 to 25 minutes. We doubt that more than 15 minutes will ever be required.

3. Cook the *lasagna* a few at a time, depending upon the size of your pot. Be sure to stir them while cooking, for they tend to stick together. This is the reason for cooking so few at a time. If you are using a small pot and a type of pasta that takes a long time to cook you could conceivably lose 2 hours on this step alone, so plan ahead.

4. As soon as the pasta is *al dente*, pop it immediately into cold water. This stops the cooking. Then place the *lasagna* on moist cloth towels. When all the pasta has been cooked, proceed quickly to the next steps. Actually, during the cooking of the pasta, it is a good idea to prepare as much as possible for these next steps.

The béchamel sauce:

3 cups milk
1 teaspoon salt
5 tablespoons butter
5 tablespoons flour

1. Salt the milk and start warming it over a low flame.

2. Melt the butter in a second saucepan over a medium flame. Add the flour and stir with a wooden spoon. Cook for 2 or 3 minutes. It should bubble actively, but not so much that the flour is in danger of burning. Try to juggle things in such a way that when the flour has cooked for 2 or 3 minutes, the milk is just coming to a boil. Remove the butter-flour mixture from the heat and add the just-boiling milk. Beat them together with a

wire whip or your spoon. Return to heat and bring the sauce to a boil again for a half minute or so. If too thick, add a little milk and mix well. Go on to the next step immediately.

Assembling the lasagna:

> Butter
> The cooked pasta
> The ragù
> ½ pound grated Parmesan cheese
> The béchamel, setting aside ⅔ cups for the topping

1. Butter a pan 8″ by 12″ by 3″ generously. If you do not have such a pan, you can use a large ovenproof casserole or perhaps two baking dishes, or almost anything else that has sides at least 3 inches high and can be put into the oven.

2. Cover the bottom of the pan with a single layer of *lasagna*. Count the number of pieces used to form this layer and divide this number into the total number of pieces of *lasagna* with which you started. The result of this mathematical operation is the number of layers your *lasagna* will have. This tells you what part of the *ragù*, Parmesan cheese, and *béchamel* to put into each layer. For example, if 4 *lasagna* are needed to form a layer, and you started with 24 *lasagna*, you will have 6 layers, so use 1/6 of the other ingredients for each layer.

3. Place on top of the *lasagna* the proper amount of *ragù* first, cheese next, and *béchamel* last. Smooth things around and place on top another layer of *lasagna* and repeat as before. Continue until all the ingredients are exhausted, except for the remaining ⅔ cup *béchamel*. Pour this over the top to make a nice-looking surface. You may, if you wish, also sprinkle on 3 or 4 tablespoons of grated Parmesan cheese. The *lasagna* may be prepared in advance to this point.

The cooking:

1. Preheat the oven to 400 degrees.

2. Place the pan in the oven for about ½ hour or until the *béchamel* on top just begins to brown. If after ½ hour it has still not started to brown, place the pan under the broiler for a minute or two.

3. Cut the *lasagna* into squares and serve on warmed plates.

PASTISO DE MELANSANE
PASTICCIO DE MELANZANE
Eggplant Casserole

This minestra *should be prepared during the hot season when egg-plant is of better quality.*

Eggplant-eating in Italy is rather peculiar—Venetians eat the skin and thrown away the white center, and Sicilians eat the center and throw away the skin. We understand that the Romans eat everything.

At any rate, most Venetian recipes call for the long, thin eggplant, which makes sense if you are going to throw away the center. Long, thin ones will have greater surface for a given weight than will round ones.

The recipe which follows has excellent flavor and is not too difficult to prepare, but be sure to allow plenty of time. After the casserole is assembled it may be refrigerated for several hours and cooked later. Or it can be cooked immediately and served cold later.

Think of this recipe more as a guide than anything else. It is not terribly precise, since there are so many variables.

FOR 4 SERVINGS:

> *6 eggplants 8 or 9 inches in length and 2 or 3*
>   *inches in diameter, about 3 pounds total*
> *Salt*
> *Cooking oil, enough to fill a deep fryer or*
>   *saucepan ⅔ full*
> *Butter*
> *Tomato sauce (page 218)*
> *Grated Parmesan cheese*
> *Pepper*

1. Wash the eggplants and peel them into long strips. The thickness of the peelings should be about 3/16 of an inch. Discard the inside. The weight of the peelings should be about 1 pound.

2. Cut the peelings lengthwise into strips about ¼ inch wide. Place the strips on a plate, and when a layer has been formed sprinkle on a little salt. Continue laying down layers and salting them until all the peelings have been used. Allow the strips to dry for an hour or so. Some liquid will be given off and should be removed periodically.

3. Heat the cooking oil to 375 degrees or a little more. If you do not have a thermometer, throw in a small piece of eggplant skin when you

think the oil may be hot enough. If the skin bubbles immediately and rises quickly to the surface, the oil is about right. Add a medium-sized handful of strips and cook them for about 3 minutes, or until the bubbling subsides and the strips are fairly crisp and lightly browned. Remove and place on paper towels to drain. Cook the rest of the strips in the same manner.

4. Preheat the oven to 375 degrees.

5. Grease a 6- or 7-inch-square baking dish or casserole with a table-spoonful or so butter. Make a layer of the eggplant strips. Try for a layer about ½-inch thick, but do not worry if things are not very flat and the appearance is a bit ragged. Spoon about 3 tablespoons of tomato sauce over the strips. Smooth the sauce around as well as possible and try to flatten out the strips. Dot the surface with 1½ tablespoons butter divided into 8 to 10 pieces. Sprinkle on 3 tablespoons grated Parmesan cheese and a little pepper. Build up another layer as before, and so on until all the eggplant has been used.

6. Pop the baking dish into the preheated oven. Cook until the cheese just starts to brown, about 20 minutes. Serve either hot or cold.

GNOCHI DE PATATE
GNOCCHI DI PATATE
Potato "Dumplings"

The only defect this dish has is the time and patience required for its preparation.

That and the fact that though it sounds easy, it is trickier than you might think. If you do not know the secrets, you can be in for a bad time.

The secrets lie in the potatoes and their cooking. Select mature baking potatoes, those that when cooked will be the most mealy. They must be boiled until just barely tender. If the potatoes are overcooked the recipe will not work. Even if cooked perfectly the recipe still will not work if the potatoes are not mealy.

The idea is to use as little flour as possible in order that the *gnocchi* come out light. How much flour is needed will depend upon the potatoes. We have heard of (but not seen) some that require less than an ounce of flour per pound of potatoes. If you manage to stay between ¾ and 1¼ cups of flour per pound you will have good *gnocchi*. If you have to use 2 cups or more flour, they are going to be heavy.

After preparing the dough, test it by making and cooking a couple of *gnocchi*. Properly made *gnocchi* are fairly light, but not in the usual dumpling sense. There is no baking powder involved and they certainly will never become fluffy. They will be a bit doughy but should not stick to the roof of the mouth.

If the test *gnocchi* simply have not come out, do not throw away the dough. Disperse a cake of yeast in ¼ cup of water and combine this with the dough, adding enough flour to make a manageable bread dough. Allow the dough to rise for a couple of hours and briefly knead again. Place in buttered bread pans and allow to rise for another 45 minutes. Bake in a preheated 400 degree oven for 1¼ hours reducing the heat after the first 10 minutes to 375 degrees. Remove from the pans and place on cooling racks. It is not an extraordinary bread, but it beats wasting the dough.

Up till now we seem to have done little but discourage the reader from trying to make *gnocchi*, which is certainly not our intention! They make an outstanding first course and are not too difficult to prepare—if only you can find the right potatoes!

Let's be optimistic and assume your *gnocchi* come out perfectly. They may be dressed in different ways: with butter and grated Parmesan cheese, tomato sauce, meat sauce, or with most any other sauce you wish. Undoubtedly the most popular ways are with tomato sauce, lots of butter, and grated Parmesan cheese, or with the sauce from *castrà in tecia* (page 162).

FOR 4 GENEROUS SERVINGS:

> 2 *pounds mature baking potatoes, all about the*
>   *same size*
> *Water*
> *Salt*
> *1½ cups sifted flour*
> *3 ounces butter, cut into small pieces*
> *2 eggs, slightly beaten*
> *4 quarts water, salted with 2½ tablespoons salt*
> *Grated Parmesan cheese*

1. Wash the potatoes and place them in a pot. Cover with water and add salt. Bring the water to a boil over high heat and then reduce to a point where a steady but not violent boil is maintained. Cook until barely tender, 20 minutes for small potatoes, longer for large ones. As soon as a fork will penetrate to the center of the potatoes without a

battle, drain them and allow to rest 5 minutes or so, the pot covered with a towel.

2. Put about half of the sifted flour into a mixing bowl. Set the rest of the flour aside.

3. Peel the potatoes and put them through a ricer, depositing the riced potatoes on top of the flour in the bowl. Place the butter pieces on top of the potatoes and after a minute or two, when the butter has pretty well melted, sprinkle on quite a bit of salt and mix with a fork. By this time the mixture should be tepid.

4. Add the beaten eggs and combine them with the other ingredients. Using your hands, form the dough into a ball and place on a surface floured with some of the remaining sifted flour. Knead the dough, adding more sifted flour as necessary; but only as much as is really needed to prevent the dough from sticking to the surface.

5. Take a handful of the dough and roll it into a stick having a diameter of about ¾ inch. Continue doing this until all the dough has been formed into sticks. Then cut the sticks into 1-inch lengths.

6. Now comes the part that is difficult to explain. Flatten a blob of dough slightly, and using a finger, roll the dough on the concave side of a curved cheese grater (floured if the dough tends to stick). The desired form is a cocoon with a slit along one side. Why it is done this way is a mystery, but that is the way it is.

7. Lightly dust the *gnocchi* with flour and place them on a plate or on waxed paper. Do not place them one on top of another lest they stick together. The recipe may be prepared in advance to this point, but do not keep uncooked *gnocchi* more than a few hours.

8. Bring 4 quarts of salted water to a boil. If you are going to use a sauce (as opposed to only butter and cheese), start it warming now, since *gnocchi* cook quickly. When the water has reached a rolling boil, start adding the *gnocchi* a few at a time. Add them as quickly as you can without disturbing the boil. Immediately upon being added to the water they will sink to the bottom of the pot. When they rise to the surface, after about a minute, they are ready and should be skimmed off with a slotted spoon or other draining device. Note: More than likely the first *gnocchi* will be coming to the surface before the last have been added. The whole cooking process, though, will take only 3 to 5 minutes for 4 servings.

9. Place the cooked *gnocchi* directly into warmed spaghetti dishes or into a serving bowl. Dress them and serve immediately. Have plenty of grated Parmesan cheese on the table.

SECONDI PIATI
SECONDI PIATTI
Second, or Main, Courses

$\mathcal{W}$ E HAVE DIVIDED *secondi piati* into four sections: seafood, meat, fowl, and game, and miscellaneous recipes. Each section has its own introduction. At the end we list recipes from other parts of the book that are sometimes used as main courses.

Pesce E Fruti De Mar
Pesce E Frutti Di Mare
SEAFOOD

IN THIS SECTION we discuss general methods of cooking seafood, mostly fish, and then follow with some special recipes. The recipes are exceptions not covered by the general methods.

Crustaceans and mollusks appear more often as *antipasti* and *minestre* and are dealt with here only when prepared as a main course. For this reason there is a certain amount of cross-referencing between this section and the other two.

BUYING SEAFOOD

In buying seafood, as with most things, the best way to be sure of what you are getting is to pay the top price. This assuming you have done enough homework to know when and if there is a season on the seafood in question. The first and last parts of the season are the most expensive and the seafood usually not as good as it is at the peak.

Many cookbooks say to choose fish whose eyes are clear, gills red, flesh firm, and scales still attached. Most say very little about how to select shellfish. The problem is that since it is all relative, if you do not have a point of reference it is easy to fool yourself or to be fooled. After more than fifty years' experience buying seafood five or six times a week we can still be fooled.

Therefore, rather than tell you how to select fish, we suggest that you select your fishmonger instead. Choose one who is fairly old—the fish business is not learned in a year or two—but not so old that he has lost the interest and desire necessary to do the job well. He should be willing to answer questions. If you want to learn about fish you must ask questions. Last, he should not be too happy. We have never met a really first-class happy fishmonger.

COOKING SEAFOOD

People from the Venetian lagoon town of Chioggia will charcoal fish of every size and shape in their homes (but not their restaurants, for some reason). On the other hand, people from the island of Burano are noted for fried fish. There is a saying that a Chioggiotto will charcoal a minnow while a Buranese will deep-fry a whale.

The point is that often there is no best way to cook a given fish. Sole, for example, may be broiled, deep-fried, pan-fried, or poached. We have, however, listed under the different cooking methods those fish which seem particularly well adapted. We expect that some people will take exception to our classification.

The various methods of cooking fish follow.

SOUP AND BROTH

Seafood soup and seafood broth are both popular in Venice in the wintertime. We have included recipes in the *minestra* section of the book. (See pages 31-36.)

AL BURRO

This method of cooking fish is probably the least used in Venice. The fish, usually filleted, are pan-fried *al burro*, in butter, with perhaps a little cooking oil added. After washing the fillets, dry them well with a towel or allow them to drain until nearly dry. Dust them with flour seasoned with salt and pepper and fry them in a pan over medium or slightly higher heat. The cooking time will depend upon the thickness of the fillets, but think in terms of 3 or 4 minutes per side. Test with a fork, giving a little more if need be.

In Venice we use fillets of sole, flounder, sea bream, and the John Dory or San Pietro (Saint Peter's fish). In her informative book *The Blue Sea Cookbook* (Hastings House), Sarah D. Alberson lists numerous other possibilities. You may wish to consult her work, and you definitely should seek advice from your fishmonger.

POACHED

In Venice poached fish is more popular than fish *al burro*, which is not saying a lot. Aside from being simple to do, poaching preserves the natural flavor of the fish; a trait valued by Venetians, who dislike eating fish smothered in sauce. In fact, in order to keep the natural flavor the poaching is as a rule done in water, instead of wine or stock as is often done in other areas.

Venetians poach whole fish as a rule, sometimes fish steaks, and rarely fillets.

Scale and eviscerate the fish. Wash well and place in a fish poacher or a fairly deep roasting pan or a large frying pan. Cover the fish with cold water and add quite a bit of salt, 1 tablespoonful or so per quart of water. Place the cooking vessel over rather high heat and bring the water near the boiling point. Do not let it actually boil—keep it just at the point where it wants to simmer. Cook the fish until the eyes pop out of the sockets; a few minutes longer for flat fish, whose eyes tend to come out rather more easily. A fish weighing about a pound should take about 10 minutes to poach. Test with a fork. The meat should be easily pierced. Do not overcook, but be sure the fish is tender. Serve as is or with olive oil and either lemon juice or vinegar. Many people enjoy poached fish with mayonnaise. If the water was properly salted you should not need to add any more, but a little pepper might be desired.

We use the following fish for poaching: sole; turbot; some of the mullets; bar; croaker; gilt-head; eel; steaks from swordfish, small sharks, and sturgeon; slices of skate; mackerel (see page 22); hake (served with the sauce for *bigoli in salsa* [see page 52], an exception to the Venetian rule about sauces). Again consult Mrs. Alberson's book and your fish-monger for other possibilities.

With slight modification of the above procedure, the broth from poaching turbot, bar, and mullet may be used in the preparation of *risotti*. (See *risoto de rombo*, page 84.)

BOILED SEAFOOD

The only seafoods that we boil (other than in the making of broth and soup) are the crustaceans and mollusks, the recipes being given in the *antipasto* and *minestra* sections of the book.

DEEP-FRIED SEAFOOD

Possibly 90 percent of the fish consumed in Venice is either deep-fried or broiled. Which of the two is more popular is hard to say. Probably when Venetians dine out, and Venetians enjoy dining out, they tend toward broiled fish and have fried fish more often at home. Frying fish is by far the simpler to do and the results more certain.

Usually, for a given species of fish, the smaller examples will be fried and the larger ones broiled. The following are the seafoods most adapted for frying: sardines; anchovies; smelt; whitebait; goby (see *risoto de gò*, page 81); John Dory or San Pietro (Saint Peter's fish); flounder; sole; pieces of cod and whiting; eel; cuttlefish; squid; bay scallops; scampi; shrimp; soft-shell crabs; thin slices of skate.

More often than not, Venetians when frying fish will use different types and serve a mixed platter. Often this will consist of a small flounder or sole, a bit of squid or cuttlefish, 3 or 4 small scampi, and 2 or 3 sardines or anchovies. Much depends upon the season. If soft-shell crabs are available, they invariably find their way to a mixed platter, as do tiny cuttlefish and gray shrimp in season.

PREPARING SEAFOOD FOR FRYING

The fish are eviscerated, scaled, and washed well, inside and out. For some reason the heads of sardines and anchovies are removed, while they are left on other fish.

Squid and cuttlefish are best cleaned by a professional. Have your fishmonger do it for you. With cuttlefish, the ink sacs *may*, or *may not be* removed. They give a slightly bitter taste that is not at all unpleasant.

Scampi and shrimp are shelled and, if you wish, veined. Venetians usually do not bother unless the veins are ugly.

Small scallops are shucked and cleaned in the same way as large ones. (See *cape sante al forno*, page 3.)

Soft-shell crabs: if they are small, tear away the legs from the, if possible, live crab, leaving only the bodies and claws. The small legs, which contain practically no meat, tend to soak up a lot of cooking oil and make the dish less digestible.

THE FRYING

1. Heat cooking oil in a deep fryer or a saucepan to about 375 degrees. The cooking vessel should be about half filled. It is a help if you have a stainless steel basket, so that the fish may be removed and drained more easily. If you do not have a thermometer to check the oil temperature, test the oil with a piece of bread or a pinch of flour. The bread should brown quickly and the flour should cause immediate bubbling on the surface without sinking.

2. The fish should drain for ½ hour or so after washing, or dry them with paper towels. The surface should still be a bit moist but not wet. Dust with flour and drop cautiously into the hot cooking oil. Cook the fish until lightly browned and the bubbling has subsided substantially. There should still be bubbling, but much less than when the fish was just placed in the oil. With a little practice you should be able to judge this very well. The cooking time will depend upon the size and type of fish. Think in terms of 4 minutes for anchovies, shrimp, and thin fillets, up to 7 or 8 minutes for sole, flounder, eel, etc. If it takes much more than 8 minutes to fry, the fish was most likely too large and should have been broiled.

3. The best way to tell whether or not the fish is properly cooked is to taste it. Buy a little extra and cook 1 piece, noting the time. When you think it might be done, take a bite and decide if it should have been cooked more or less.

If cooked properly, the meat should come off the bone cleanly. The meat should be firm rather than slimy but moist and not dried out.

Cook the remaining fish accordingly. When done, remove from the hot oil and place on paper towels to drain.

4. Salt the fish now, not before cooking. Salt helps to break down cooking oil.

5. Serve the fish hot. Sometimes sardines, anchovies, squid, and cuttlefish are eaten tepid or cold as snacks, but it is our opinion that fried fish should be served very hot.

6. About the cooking oil. If you are not going to fry fish two or three times a week, you may as well discard the oil. Despite all the claims made by oil manufacturers as to how improved their products are, it is still not pleasant to have used oil around the kitchen. If you wish to save the oil, though, allow it to cool and settle. Then decant the light oil from the top and discard the darker oil at the bottom. You should discard about ⅓ of the oil each time. Probably the most important single thing in frying fish, other than the fish themselves, is the oil. To save a dollar's worth of oil to ruin five dollar's worth of fish makes no sense.

BATTER FRYING

Batter frying is employed quite often in Venice in cooking fillets of John Dory fish and bacalà (page 123), and very rarely for anything else.

1. Make a batter of egg and flour, 3 or 4 tablespoons of flour per egg.

2. Dip the fish in the batter and then deep-fry in the usual way as discussed above.

OR:

1. Beat an egg or two.
2. Dip the fish in the egg and then roll it in flour.
3. Fry as before.

BROILED SEAFOOD

Broiling seafood is by far the most exacting of the methods, especially charcoal broiling, the one that to our thinking yields the best results when everything goes right. There is no sure-fire set of directions on how to broil fish. It takes lots of practice. Follow the rules set down below, though, and we believe that in a short time you will have, if not a complete mastery, at least quite satisfactory results.

We shall go into considerable detail below, but here are the most important things to keep in mind. Use extremely high heat and no oil, butter, or grease. The fish is dipped into a strong salt solution prior to cooking. Have your grill rack spotlessly clean. If you follow these simple rules you should reach the desired result—meat that comes readily off the bone, neither slimy nor dried out, but instead firm and moist.

We broil the following fish: anchovies (see page 128); sardines; gray, golden, and red mullets; bar; croaker; gilt-head; mackerel; goby; John Dory or Saint Peter's fish (the only fish we can think of that Venetians broil filleted); the tail part of certain angler fish; steaks from swordfish, small shark, sturgeon, and tuna; large eels; cuttlefish; stuffed squid (see page 133); large scampi; large stuffed shrimp (see page 141). Consult Mrs. Alberson's *Blue Sea Cookbook* and your fishmonger for other ideas.

PREPARING THE FISH FOR BROILING

Clean the fish as you would for frying. They need not be drained, since they will be placed in salt water before cooking starts.

THE SALT-WATER SOLUTION

Dissolve ½ cup of coarse salt, or a little less table salt, in 2 cups water. Just before cooking, dip the fish into this solution, being sure to wet the fish thoroughly.

COOKING EQUIPMENT, TECHNIQUE, AND TIME

The cooking time obviously depends upon the size of the fish; its shape, and the heat of the broiler. The size of the fish is up to you and your fishmonger. The kind of fish presents real problems, since some are flat and take less time than those that are more tubular or simply fatter. The type of equipment determines how hot the fire is. We shall touch on this first.

Charcoal. We use a covered cooking kettle. By controlling the draft we can maintain the desired amount of heat. A layer of coals about 3 inches deep works well with the broiling rack about another 3 inches above. The rack must be perfectly clean and allowed to heat up for at least 10 minutes. The fish, after being dipped in the salt solution, is placed on the rack and the kettle covered. All dampers are left wide open. The fish is turned once when half cooked with the aid of a spatula. If your charcoal broiler does not have a cover, use a cooler flame and cook the fish for a longer time.

Overhead broilers, gas or electric. Read any clues the manufacturer may give in the instruction booklet. The chances are you will never get enough heat out of a normal home stove to do a first-rate job of broiling fish, but you should be able to come out with something that will not be bad. The main thing is to preheat the broiler and broiling rack until it hurts. Place the fish as close to the heat as possible without losing even heating; most likely 4 to 6 inches. You will have to broil fish longer with this kind of equipment than you would with charcoal.

Open-flame broiling (for lack of a better name). We have never seen a home stove in the United States equipped with this type broiler. What it is is a broiling rack on top of the stove placed over a gas flame or flames in series. It is a refinement of a still popular system, that of placing the fish between two grates, hinged on one side and having handles on the other side that can be clamped together so that the fish may be held over the open flame. A bit primitive, but yielding excellent results. Treat it in the same way as you would charcoal broiling.

Grill-top broiling (again for lack of a better name). This is a rather interesting way of cooking fish. Whether or not it can really be classified as broiling is another thing, but the results look about the same and the flavor is excellent. Two special things are required here: a stove with a large grill top and a broiling rack with larger than normal rods, ¼ to ⅜ of an inch in diameter. The rack is placed on top of the grill top with the heat on full blast. When the rack is very hot the fish is dipped in the salt-water solution, put on, and cooked as if it were being charcoaled. In order to do this properly the grill top must be terribly hot.

Broiled and baked. This falls strictly into technique, rather than equipment. Venetians do not seem to bake fish, except in the large hotels where hundreds of fish are to be served in a short period of time. Often broiled fish ordered in hotels are in fact broiled only for a minute or two on each side to give the characteristic markings. They are then placed in baking dishes and the cooking completed in hot ovens. The results are not bad but not as good as if the fish had been broiled from start to finish.

So much for equipment.

Cooking time. We are going to go out on a limb here. When charcoaling the fish listed above, only cook anchovies less than 8 minutes and only eels and tuna steaks more than 20. (This rule is probably going to get us into trouble, but we want to give you some sort of guideline.) Now, thinking between 8 and 20 minutes, look at your fish and try to decide where to put it. If it is flat and of medium size, think of about 10 minutes or so. If it is a small gray mullet, think also of 10 minutes, since it is more tubular. If the mullet is larger, 15 minutes. For a small red mullet, 8 minutes, but for a sardine of about the same length, a little longer because it is a fatty fish.

The main thing is practice. Always use about the same amount of heat, and after a time or two of cooking a certain type of fish you should have the technique down fairly well.

SERVING THE FISH

Broiled fish are served on warmed plates, often with a little olive oil, always with finely chopped parsley on top. A lemon wedge accompanies the fish, but Venetians as often as not ignore it.

Broiled fish are also excellent cold. In this case they should be generously dosed with olive oil before cooling completely. As with hot fish, sprinkle on finely chopped parsley. Do not refrigerate if you plan to eat it later the same day. Most people will not even refrigerate it if they plan to eat it the following day, but we are a bit leery of this.

BACALÀ MANTECATO
BACCALÀ BATTUTO
Stockfish Mantecato Style

This is a good dish, eaten with great pleasure in wintertime, the season when stockfish is at its best. It is particularly easy to digest; some doctors refer to it as "the stomach brush."

The word *mantecato* refers to semi-liquid ice cream. Actually, the consistency of *bacalà mantecato* should be that of lumpy paste. The color should be off-white.

Stockfish is the generic term for any fish that is air dried without salt. The most commonly used stockfish in Venice is the cod.

The most difficult part of this recipe is the tenderizing of the stockfish. The dry fish must be beaten with a large wooden mallet, club, or baseball bat until it becomes reasonably flexible. The time needed to accomplish this depends upon the quality of the fish, the size of the mallet, and the strength of the person doing the beating. Figure on an absolute minimum of 20 minutes. It is all but impossible to overbeat a *bacalà*. Place a piece of clean paper on a concrete floor or on the sidewalk and beat the fish on both sides and on the top. Continue beating until out of patience or until the stockfish reaches the point where it can be readily bent. Prebeaten stockfish is available, but even then it normally benefits from additional beating.

FOR 4 SERVINGS:

1 pound dry stockfish
Water
⅓ cup milk or light cream
Salt and pepper
Olive oil

1. Beat the fish as discussed above. Place the beaten stockfish in a pot and cover with water. It must soak at least 24 hours and can be soaked 2 or even 3 days. Change the water 3 or 4 times daily.

2. After the fish has been soaked, pour off the water and replace it with fresh water. Place the pot over high heat and bring the water to a boil. When foam forms after a minute or two of boiling, the fish is "cooked." Pour the fish and water into a colander and allow to drain and cool a bit.

3. When cool enough to handle, clean away all the bones and fins. The skin may or may not be removed. Some people maintain that the skin is the most flavorful part.

4. Return the cleaned, boned stockfish to a pot and add the milk or cream and quite a bit of both salt and pepper. Place the pot over the lowest possible flame and stir constantly with a wooden spoon or paddle. When the fish seems to have absorbed the liquid, begin to add olive oil very slowly. Stir constantly, working the oil into the fish. The amount of oil the fish will absorb depends upon how well it has been beaten and the quality of the fish. It may absorb as little as ¾ cup or as much as 2 cups. Keep stirring and adding oil until a lumpy paste consistency is attained. Correct the seasoning.

5. Serve hot or cold with *polenta* (page 221), or good fresh Italian or French bread. This dish is often eaten as a mid-morning snack.

BACALÀ A LA VISENTINA
BACCALÀ ALLA VICENTINA
Stockfish Vicenza Style

This delicious recipe is more appreciated by those whose stomachs are adapted to handling heavy foods, but anyone will enjoy it if he uses moderation.

It may seem surprising that a recipe bearing the name of another city would be so popular in Venice, but it is indeed the case. After *bacalà mantecato* this is the most widely used of the stockfish recipes.

FOR 5 OR 6 SERVINGS:

   1 pound stockfish, preferably the part
      toward the head
   ¾ cup olive oil
   A large clove of garlic, peeled and split
   Flour
   9 canned flat anchovy fillets packed in olive oil
   10 black olives, pitted and quartered
   3 tablespoons capers
   Salt and pepper
   Milk

1. Beat, soak, boil, drain, and clean the stockfish as in the preceding recipe.

2. Place a saucepan containing the olive oil and garlic over a medium flame. When the garlic has browned, remove and discard it. Turn off the heat and set the pan aside.

3. Dust the stockfish with flour. Make a layer of stockfish in the bottom of a 2-quart flameproof casserole. Use about ¼ of the stockfish. On top of this layer place 3 anchovy fillets, ⅓ of the olive quarters, and ⅓ of the capers. Sprinkle on some pepper and a very small amount of salt. The anchovies and capers are so salty that you must be careful. Make another 2 layers of stockfish, interlacing them with anchovies, olives, and capers as before. Finish with the remaining quarter of the stockfish.

4. Pour the olive oil from the saucepan over the stockfish. Push down on the surface with a fork or spoon in order to force the olive oil back to the top, thereby assuring that everything is well moistened, then add milk until everything is saturated. Set aside.

5. Preheat the oven to 350 degrees.

6. While the oven is heating the stockfish will be absorbing milk. After 15 minutes or so, add more milk—enough so that it can be seen on top but does not completely cover the stockfish.

7. Place the casserole over a medium heat on top of the stove and bring the milk to the boiling point. Immediately remove from the heat and place in the oven. When a crust forms on top and takes on a golden color, the stockfish is ready to serve. This should take 45 minutes, more or less.

8. Serve with *polenta* (page 221) or fresh Italian or French bread.

BACALÀ IN TECIA
BACCALÀ IN UMIDO
Braised Stockfish

This tasty dish is much more easily digested than the preceding stock-fish recipe. It is excellent for those with good appetites and who enjoy polenta.

Although more digestible than *bacalà a la visentina*, this is still a rich dish. Plan on having a very light first course.

FOR 4 SERVINGS:

1 pound stockfish
⅓ cup olive oil
2 ounces butter
1 large clove garlic, peeled and split in half
2 tablespoons finely chopped parsley
4 canned flat anchovy fillets packed in olive oil
Pepper
3 tablespoons tomato sauce (page 218)
(Capers)
Milk
(Salt)

1. Beat and soak the stockfish as described in the recipe for *bacalà mantecato* (page 119), but do not boil it. Remove the bones and break the fish and skin into small pieces.

2. Place a saucepan containing the olive oil, butter, and garlic over a moderate flame. When the garlic has browned, remove and discard it. Add the stockfish, parsley, anchovies, and some pepper. Do not add salt at this time. Mix well. When the anchovies have pretty well broken up, add the tomato sauce. You may also wish to add a tablespoonful or more capers. Cook for 1½ hours, adding milk as necessary to prevent the sauce from sticking. Toward the end of cooking taste to see if salt is needed.

3. Serve on warmed plates accompanied by *polenta* (page 221), or fresh Italian or French bread.

BACALÀ A CAISSONI
BACCALÀ ALL'OLIO
Stockfish in Olive Oil

This, the simplest of the bacalà *recipes, is also very good. It is most popular in the wintertime when in Venetian wineshops it is eaten as an after-work snack, accompanied by a glass of white wine and a piece of bread.*

The recipe is for 4 main-course portions. As a snack it should serve 7 or 8.

FOR 4 SERVINGS:

1 pound stockfish
4 ounces olive oil
Salt and pepper
(Finely chopped parsley)

1. Beat, soak, boil, and clean the stockfish as described in the recipe for *bacalà mantecato* (page 119).
2. Place the clean stockfish in a round bottomed pot with a cover, or any pot that can be tightly sealed. Add the oil, salt and pepper, and perhaps a little parsley. Cover the pot and shake it up and down, much as a bartender shakes a cocktail. Shake for 2 or 3 minutes or until the fish is well moistened. Correct the seasoning.
3. Serve at room temperature with fresh Italian or French bread or a piece of cold *polenta* (page 221).

BACALÀ FRITO
BACCALÀ FRITTO
Batter-fried Stockfish

Batter-fried stockfish should be served very hot, accompanied by a green salad.

In Venice it is often eaten cold or tepid in wineshops as a snack, but so served it loses a lot.

FOR 4 SERVINGS:

1 pound stockfish
Cooking oil
Batter (page 115)

1. Beat and soak the stockfish as described in the recipe for *bacalà mantecato* (page 119), but do not boil it. After the fish has been soaked, drain it thoroughly and clean away the bones, trying to keep the meat in large pieces. Discard the skin. Break the meat into pieces about 2″ by 2″ by 3″.
2. Fill a deep fryer or saucepan about one-half full with cooking

oil. (See page 113 for a more detailed discussion of deep-frying.) Bring the oil to 375 degrees.

3. Dip pieces of stockfish into the batter, coating them well. Allow the excess batter to drip off and then cautiously drop the fish into the hot oil. Cook until the bubbling subsides substantially and the crust is golden brown, about 6 minutes. Remove from the oil and place on paper towels to drain. Salt the fish and place in the oven to keep warm. Cook 3 or 4 pieces at a time.

4. Serve as soon as possible after cooking.

BISATO SULL'ARA
ANGUILLA AL FORNO
Baked Eel

The island of Murano is famous not only for its glass, but also for bisato sull'ara, *that is, eel cooked in the oven much as glass is annealed, very slowly.*

In a shallow baking dish, place the whole eel with neither sauces nor oil or butter, only a few bay leaves. The eel is cooked slowly, slowly in its own juices, and a very delicious dish results, one rather strong, but of excellent flavor.

For 3 persons an eel of about 1½ pounds will be sufficient. This is about the smallest size eel that should be used for this recipe. Eels up to 2½ pounds are acceptable, but beyond this weight they are better prepared by charcoal broiling.

Eel is an extremely rich, fatty fish and must be cooked slowly in order to allow the grease to come out. Eels are served with the skin on, but the skin should not be eaten, for it is very indigestible.

FOR 4 SERVINGS:

An eel, about 2 pounds
White wine vinegar
A few drops olive oil or a little butter
4 bay leaves
Salt and pepper

1. Have your fishmonger clean the eel. Also have him make cuts at about 6-inch intervals halfway through the eel (from side to side, not top to bottom) severing the backbone. This makes it easier to bend the eel around and fit it into the baking dish.

2. Preheat the oven to 325 degrees.

3. Wash the eel well under cold running water and place it in a ceramic bowl. Pour enough vinegar over the eel that it is well bathed. Soak it for 10 minutes, turning it to make sure all parts are exposed to the vinegar. Remove it from the vinegar and place on paper towels to drain.

4. Grease a shallow baking dish large enough to accommodate the eel. Use only enough oil or butter to prevent the eel from sticking before producing its own juices.

5. Place the eel and the bay leaves in the baking dish. Use fresh bay leaves if possible; otherwise, soak dried leaves in water for at least 15 minutes. Sprinkle some salt and pepper over the eel and place the dish in the preheated oven. Baste occasionally. After about 45 minutes, start testing the eel for tenderness by sticking it with a table fork. An hour's cooking may be necessary. It is much better to overcook an eel than to undercook it.

6. Serve on warmed plates accompanied by *polenta* (page 221), or fresh Italian or French bread.

BISATO IN TECIA
ANGUILLA IN UMIDO
Braised Eel

Of all the modes of preparing eel this is perhaps the best and most flavorful, but it results in a plate so heavy that it is not suitable for delicate stomachs.

It also is not suitable for fainthearted cooks. A freshly killed eel may continue to move for a couple of hours or more.

There is nothing difficult about this recipe except trying to describe how the eel should be prepared for cooking. Remove the entrails and wash the inside of the eel thoroughly. Make cuts along the side of the eel at about 2-inch intervals. The cuts should be deep enough to go through the spine, but they should not completely sever the eel.

The eel is cut in this manner in order to make it easier to fit it into the frying pan. It would fit even more easily if it were cut completely into pieces, but tradition dictates otherwise. Tradition also dictates that this dish be served with *polenta*, a very fine idea. (See page 221.)

FOR 4 SERVINGS:

> *An eel, about 1 pound, or 2 eels, ½ pound each*
> *White wine vinegar*
> *3 tablespoons olive oil*
> *2 tablespoons butter*
> *½ medium onion, finely chopped*
> *1 small celery heart, finely diced*
> *1 small carrot, finely diced*
> *2 tablespoons finely chopped parsley*
> *Flour*
> *3 tablespoons tomato sauce (page 218)*
> *(Dry white wine or water)*

1. Have your fishmonger prepare the eel as discussed above. Wash the eel well under running water and place it in a ceramic bowl. Pour enough vinegar over the eel to bathe it thoroughly. Soak for about 15 minutes, turning the eel occasionally to make sure it is well moistened. Remove the eel and place it on paper towels to drain.

2. Use a frying pan or other suitable cooking vessel large enough to accommodate the eel. Put the olive oil, butter, and the vegetables in the pan and place it over medium heat. Stir while cooking until the onion becomes translucent, about 5 minutes.

3. Dust the eel with flour and place it in the pan with the vegetables. Keep moving the eel until it has warmed enough to produce some grease of its own and will not stick to the pan.

4. After 5 minutes of cooking, add the tomato sauce and mix well. Reduce the flame to very low and cook the eel uncovered for about an hour. Turn the eel occasionally, adding a little dry white wine or water if necessary to keep the sauce from sticking.

5. Serve this dish very hot on warmed plates and accompany it with *polenta* (page 221) or fresh Italian or French bread. Do not eat the skin of the eel—it is too difficult to digest. If the eel has been cooked long enough, the skin will peel away easily.

BODOETI IN TECIA
PICCOLI CEFALI IN UMIDO
Braised Small Gray Mullets

Simple to make and flavorful. Be sure, though, to buy mullet that are neither too small nor too large. Also, they should be the variety that has the very small mouth. As with all dishes having sauce, polenta is the indicated contorno.

As good as this recipe is, it is a bit dangerous. Small mullet are exceedingly difficult to bone and one must pay attention when eating this dish.

Mullet cooked in this way become very tender, and care should be taken not to break them into pieces during cooking and serving. Also, when the fish have just been put in the frying pan you must be careful that they do not stick and lose their skin. Shake the pan until the fish have had a chance to become well coated with oil.

Try to find mullet about 7 inches long.

FOR 4 SERVINGS:

8 mullets 7 inches long, weighing
 about 1¼ pounds
⅓ cup olive oil
1 clove garlic, peeled
2 tablespoons finely chopped parsley
Salt and pepper
3 tablespoons tomato sauce (page 218)
½ cup good dry white wine

1. Clean and scale the fish.
2. Place the frying pan containing the olive oil and garlic over medium heat. When the garlic has browned, remove and discard it. Allow the pan to cool a bit. Replace the pan over low heat and add the parsley and fish, aligning the latter neatly so that they do not overlap. Shake the pan while doing this. After a minute or two, carefully turn the fish, still shaking the pan. Add some salt and pepper and the tomato sauce. Mix the tomato sauce with the other ingredients by spooning the juices over the fish. Cook for about 15 minutes over very low heat with the pan uncovered.

3. Add the wine. Mix well as before and continue cooking until the sauce becomes quite dense. This should take about 10 minutes more.

4. Serve on warmed plates accompanied by *polenta* (page 221) or fresh Italian or French bread.

SARDONI A LA MARINARA
ACCIUGHE ALLA MARINAIA
Anchovies in Oil and Vinegar

This plate is flavorful, easy to prepare, and costs little. It is a fishermen's dish, prepared either during the tiring hours of labor or upon their return home.

Even people who hate canned anchovies like this recipe. The fresh anchovy bears little resemblance to its tinned brother.

FOR 4 SERVINGS:

1¼ pounds fresh anchovies
⅔ cup olive oil
1 clove garlic, peeled and split
Salt and pepper
½ cup vinegar

1. Scale the fish, a very easy job. Break off the head with a twisting motion and pull it away from the body. With a little practice and some luck it is possible to pull out all the entrails in one piece. If they do not come out with the head, gently open the belly of the anchovy with a finger. Wash well under running water and place on a slanted surface to drain.

2. Place a large frying pan containing the olive oil and garlic over medium heat. When the garlic has browned, remove and discard it. Allow the pan to cool enough so that when the anchovies are added in the next step the oil will not spatter.

3. Add the anchovies to the frying pan, placing them side by side. Do this while shaking the pan so that the anchovies do not stick. Sprinkle on some salt and quite a lot of pepper. Cook for 5 minutes, continuing to shake the pan. You may turn them during this time, but it is not necessary.

4. Add the vinegar, mix the juices a bit, and cover the pan. Cook until the vinegar is absorbed, stirring occasionally. This should take between 10 and 15 minutes. If after that time not all the vinegar has been absorbed, cook uncovered for a couple of minutes more until the sauce seems to be mostly oil.

5. Place the anchovies on a warmed serving platter and pour the liquids over them. They may be served either hot or cold, but we prefer them hot. They go very well with *polenta* (page 221) either hot or cold.

SARDONI A SCOTA DEO
ACCIUGHE ALLA GRIGLIA
"Scorched Finger" Anchovies

The cooking of anchovies in the manner described below is widely employed by fishermen after they have made a good and abundant catch of these fish. The season is May to September for anchovies, hence also for this dish.

As soon as the anchovies have been taken from the sea the heads and entrails are removed. Then, after the fish are scaled and washed with the water at hand, they are sprinkled with some pepper and a little olive oil. Finally, using the fingers, they are put one at a time, nicely aligned, on a grill over a hot charcoal fire. They are cooked for a short time, 3 minutes or so on one side, and then they are turned, still with the fingers, onto the other side and cooked a like amount of time. The cooked anchovies are picked off the grill, always with the fingers, and served with either hot or cold polenta.

Good as this dish is, it is included largely for the Venetian phrase *a scota deo*, roughly "scorched finger," the result of the recipe if the cook is not careful.

The fish should be broiled over a very hot fire. The cooking time is, of course, short. The "water at hand" referred to is sea water, so the anchovies need not be salted. If the grill is perfectly clean, the anchovies do not need to be oiled either.

TON IN TECIA
TONNO IN UMIDO
Braised Fresh Tuna

This fish is best if caught in the hot months in the Mediterranean waters. Its meat, because of its oiliness, brings to mind that of pork, and reminds us that tuna is also not easily digested. But it is very flavorful and Venetian gourmets go mad for it. It is quite true that "the throat kills more than the sword," but one continues to eat tuna, and usually too much of it!

The tuna best suited for this recipe are not terribly large. A slice of tuna 1 to 1½ inches thick and 6 inches in diameter will weigh about a pound; 2 such slices are more than enough for 4 people of normal appetite, and they are easier to handle than 1 slice of large diameter. Some people claim that tuna of this size have better flavor than the large ones.

FOR 4 SERVINGS:

2 pounds fresh tuna
Milk
3 ounces olive oil
4 tablespoons butter
1 medium onion, finely chopped
1 medium carrot, very finely diced
¼ cup tomato sauce (page 218)
⅓ cup milk (not the same milk
   used to soak the fish)
⅓ cup good dry white wine
Salt and pepper

1. Remove the skin from the tuna. Wash the meat and place it in a suitable container, a bowl or a dish, and cover with milk. Allow to soak for at least ½ hour.

2. Place the olive oil, butter, and vegetables in a flameproof casserole or a frying pan over medium heat. Stir while cooking until the onion becomes translucent, 5 minutes or so.

3. Remove the tuna from the milk and after drying it add it to the cooking vessel containing the vegetables. Brown lightly on both sides and

add the tomato sauce, milk, wine, and salt and pepper. Mix well and cover. Cook over very low heat for an hour or a little longer, stirring occasionally. During cooking the liquids should be just barely simmering. Toward the end of cooking, correct the seasoning.

4. Serve the tuna on warmed plates and pour the sauce on top. *Polenta* (page 221), fresh Italian or French bread, or potatoes all go well with this dish. If you use potatoes you may cook them at the same time and in the same cooking vessel as the tuna, 20 to 25 minutes for small potatoes, longer for large ones.

SEPIOLINE IN TECIA
SEPPIOLINE IN UMIDO
Cuttlefish in Its Ink

Here is a dish well suited to those who like polenta *since both the cuttlefish and the sauce go nicely with it.*

The cuttlefish is a squid-like mollusk having ten sucker-bearing arms and an internal shell, the cuttlebone. The latter, incidentally, is the thing canaries always seem to have in their cages. All of which sounds like a highly unlikely place to start preparing a delicious dish.

The cuttlefish eaten in Venice range in body length from about two inches (*sepioline*) up to ten inches or so (*sepie*). They run from about eighty to a pound down to only two or three to a pound. The smaller they are, the better, since they are more tender. But, the smaller they are, the longer it takes to clean them and they are more expensive.

The type of cuttlefish used in this recipe contains ink for its defense against predators. Diluted enough this ink is supposed to give a dark brown color, sepia, the same word as the name of the cuttlefish in Venetian. Actually, the color we get tends more toward a violet.

There are numerous variations on the cuttlefish theme. If you leave out all the ingredients listed below in parenthesis, you will come out with an excellent dish truly tasting of the sea. The more optional ingredients added, the less the sea taste, but it is still a wonderful dish and more likely to appeal to the uninitiated.

FOR 4 SERVINGS:

3 pounds cuttlefish (this is the weight
  before cleaning)
4 tablespoons olive oil
2 ounces butter
1 clove garlic, peeled
(¾ medium onion, finely chopped)
2 tablespoons finely chopped parsley
½ cup good dry white wine (or ½ cup good dry
  red wine if tomatoes, listed below, are used)
Salt and pepper
(A 10 ounce can peeled Italian plum tomatoes)
(2 dashes Worcestershire sauce)
2 tablespoons cognac

1. Have your fishmonger remove and discard the mouth, eyes, and digestive tract, but have him save the ink sacs and the *latte*, the milk. (The *latte* are white globs about the size of a quail's egg in a 5-inch female cuttlefish. Those of the male are much smaller and of a somewhat different shape.) Also, have him skin the cuttlefish and cut it into bite-sized pieces.

2. Place the olive oil, butter, and garlic in a saucepan over medium heat. Cook until the garlic has browned and then remove and discard it.

3. Optional: add the onion and cook until translucent, 5 minutes or so. Allow the saucepan to cool enough that the oil will not spatter when the cuttlefish are added in the next step.

4. Add the cuttlefish and the parsley to the saucepan. Replace the pan over medium heat and stir. Add the wine and the ink sacs, breaking the latter or cutting them with a pair of scissors. Lightly salt and pepper the mixture.

5. Optional: add the peeled tomatoes and bring to a simmer. You may also at this time put in a little Worcestershire sauce.

6. When everything is bubbling nicely, reduce the flame to very low, cover the saucepan, and simmer for about ½ hour for small cuttlefish, 45 minutes for larger ones. Stir often while cooking. Particularly toward the end you must be careful that the cuttlefish do not stick to the bottom of the pan. If necessary, add some water. On the other hand, if the cuttlefish were very wet when added to the saucepan, you may have to cook with the cover off for the last 10 or 15 minutes. The sauce should be moderately thick.

7. When the cuttlefish are tender, correct the seasoning and add the

cognac. Mix well and serve on warmed plates accompanied by *polenta* (page 221.)

CARAMAI RIPIENI A LA GREA
CALAMARI RIPIENI ALLA GRIGLIA
Broiled Stuffed Squid

These mollusks when small have delicate and sapid meat. For those who enjoy fish, this dish is one that should not be missed. Serve 1 or 2 small ones as an antipasto *or 4 of larger size as a main course.*

This is one of the finest recipes in the book. The only problem in carrying it out is to find the proper size squid. If they are large they become too chewy, but they must be big enough to prevent the cook's going mad trying to stuff them. The right size squid has a body length of 3 to 4 inches. Note that this length is for the body only, not the total length which would include the head also.

Cleaning squid is almost exactly the same proposition as cleaning cuttlefish, with only a couple of differences. One, in place of the cuttlebone there is a clear, seemingly plastic cartilage. It looks different, but it is removed in the same way. The second difference is that the body of the squid is not cut. Merely pull the body and head pieces apart. This will leave the body a cylinder having one end closed, very convenient for stuffing.

Squid, large or small, are often deep-fried. Small ones are fried whole after cleaning, while large ones are cleaned, skinned, and cut into pieces. Small squid, and even those for this recipe, need not be skinned.

FOR 4 MAIN COURSE SERVINGS:

16 squid having bodies 3 or 4 inches in length,
  about 1½ pounds
A clove of garlic, peeled and cut in half
⅓ cup very fine bread crumbs
2 tablespoons finely chopped parsley
Salt and pepper
Olive oil

1. Clean the squid, discarding the eyes, mouth, digestive tract, and ink sac. It is not necessary to skin them, but it is essential to wash them

very thoroughly, since sometimes they contain a lot of sand which is not easy to remove. When perfectly clean, place them on a slanted surface to drain.

2. Rub the inside of a small mixing bowl with the garlic. Place the bread crumbs and parsley in the bowl and add some salt and pepper.

3. When the squid have drained for about half an hour, cut the heads and tentacles into pieces, discarding any tough parts. The pieces need not be terribly small—½ to ¾ of an inch is about right. Add these squid pieces to the contents of the mixing bowl.

4. Moisten thoroughly the bread crumb mixture with olive oil. The amount of oil is not critical. Mix well.

5. Divide the stuffing equally among the squid bodies and place it as far inside as possible. Use your fingers and don't worry about neatness. Close the squid using skewers or toothpicks. The squid are now ready to be cooked.

6. (See page 116 for directions for broiling fish.) For this recipe make the following changes: do not dip the squid in salted water, and if you are cooking with charcoal use a fire a little less hot than you would normally use. Since broilers in home stoves generally run cooler anyhow, use full heat with this type apparatus. Cook the squid 12 minutes or a little longer, 6 minutes on each side. Squid is one of the easier things to broil. Do not overcook them, though, or they will become rubbery.

7. Place the cooked squid on a warmed platter and pour a few drops of olive oil over each one. Serve immediately.

CAPE SANTE IN TECIA
CONCHIGLIE DEI PELLEGRINI
IN UMIDO
Braised Scallops

Serve this delicious dish with either polenta *or bread, according to your preference.*

(See *cape sante al forno*, page 3, for the discussion about scallops.)

FOR 4 SERVINGS:
  2 pounds cleaned scallops, with or
    without the coral
  1 large clove garlic, peeled and split

4 tablespoons olive oil
3 ounces butter
1 tablespoon finely chopped parsley
1½ tablespoons tomato sauce (page 218)
Salt and pepper
½ cup good dry white wine
(More wine or water)

1. Wash the scallops well and place them on a slanted surface to drain.

2. Brown the garlic in the olive oil and butter over medium heat, then remove and discard it. Allow the pan to cool a bit.

3. Add the parsley, tomato sauce, and scallops to the pan and place over low to medium heat. Sprinkle on a little salt and quite a bit of pepper. Regulate the heat so that the sauce simmers gently. Cook uncovered for 10 minutes, turning the scallops 3 or 4 times.

4. After 10 minutes, add the wine. Continue cooking uncovered. Turn the scallops occasionally while cooking for another 10 to 15 minutes. At the end of cooking most of the wine should have boiled away, leaving a rather thick sauce. There should be enough liquid, though, to prevent the tomato sauce from burning. Add more wine or water if necessary.

5. Correct the seasoning and serve on warmed plates, accompanied by *polenta* (page 221), or fresh Italian or French bread.

CANOCIE DE MAR
CANNOCCHIE O PANNOCHIE
Mantis Shrimp
and
GAMBARONI
GAMBERONI
Large Shrimp

Canocie *are Adriatic Sea crustaceans, very tasty, but rather better from mid-February to mid-April, when they are more meaty than usual and contain a reddish caramel-like material along the back called "wax" or "coral," which is the repository of the eggs.*

Although a variety of mantis shrimp is abundant in the waters of the American East Coast, it seems never to find its way to market. If you are an enterprising fisherman, read Euell Gibbons's *Stalking the Blue-Eyed Scallop* for the method of catching them.

The mantis shrimp is an extremely popular crustacean in Venice, and since we want to give an accurate picture of the Venetian kitchen, we include the following four recipes. Large shrimp, readily available in the United States, may be substituted for the *canocie* with excellent results. The shrimp recipes follow the corresponding *canocie* recipes.

CANOCIE LESSE
CANNOCCHIE O PANNOCHIE ALESSE
Boiled Mantis Shrimp

This is the simplest manner in which *canocie* are served. Boiled in salted water and allowed to cool, they are eaten with the fingers and, if you wish, a pair of scissors. Tear off the two meaty front legs, which resemble those of a praying mantis. The leg shell is tender and the meat may be easily extracted. Next pull the thorax away from the abdomen, then peel away the top part of the shell to expose the body meat. The scissors will help at this point. Snip along the sides of the *canocia* and the top shell may be easily removed. The meat may be eaten directly from the shell or removed and placed on a plate to be served later as *canocie condite*, with dressing. (See the following *canocie* recipe.)

Boiled, *canocie* are normally eaten as an *antipasto*.

FOR 4 SERVINGS:

2 *pounds* canocie; *12 to 20 pieces, depending*
upon the size and the season
Salted water; 3 tablespoons salt per quart water

1. *If the* canocie *are alive*, place them in a pot and cover with cold water. Add the salt. Place the pot over high heat. When the water begins to boil, reduce the heat to maintain a slow boil. Cook the *canocie* for 7 or 8 minutes from the moment the water comes to a boil.

2. *If the* canocie *are dead*, bring the salted water to a boil first and then add them. When the water returns to a boil, start timing and cook as before, 7 or 8 minutes.

3. In either case, when the *canocie* are cooked drain them and place them flat on a plate to cool. When cool, they are shelled and eaten as discussed above.

GAMBARONI LESSI
GAMBERONI ALESSI
Boiled Large Shrimp

Boiled shrimp, though normally eaten as an *antipasto*, make a fair main course when served with mayonnaise and lemon.

FOR 4 GENEROUS ANTIPASTI—5 LARGE SHRIMP EACH SERVING:

1⅓ pounds shrimp without heads, *15 per
  pound in the shell
or 2¼ pounds shrimp* with heads, *9 per
  pound in the shell
Salted water, 3 tablespoons salt per quart water*

1. Prepare and cook in the same manner as for *canocie* in preceding recipe, boiling the shrimp for 7 or 8 minutes. If the shrimp are smaller than the specified size, they will require proportionately less cooking.
2. Drain the shrimp and allow them to cool. Pull away the thorax and peel away the shells. Venetians tend not to vein shrimp unless the veins are ugly. If you do vein them, try to remove only the black part, leaving any coral that might be present beside the vein.
3. Serve the shrimp with mayonnaise and lemon or see the following recipe.

CANOCIE O GAMBARONI CONSI
CANNOCCHIE O GAMBERONI CONDITI
Mantis Shrimp or Large Shrimp
with Dressing

Prepare and shell *canocie* or large shrimp following the directions in the preceding recipes.

FOR 4 SERVINGS:

The canocie *or shrimp*
Olive oil
(Salt)
Pepper
Vinegar or lemon juice
(Finely chopped parsley)

1. Place the *canocie* or shrimp on a serving platter. Pour some olive oil over them and turn until well coated. Sample one to check on the salt situation.

2. Sprinkle on some pepper and a bit of vinegar or lemon juice. Spoon this dressing back over the crustaceans until it is reasonably homogeneous. You may add a bit of very finely chopped parsley if you wish.

3. This recipe is unique among the *canocie* series, in that it is the only one that can be eaten easily with a knife and fork instead of the fingers.

CANOCIE IN TECIA
CANNOCCHIE O PANNOCCHIE
IN UMIDO
Braised Mantis Shrimp

Prepared this way *canocie* make a good main course. They may also be served as an *antipasto*, but because the sauce is so rich the portions must be reduced.

There is nothing complicated about this recipe other than realizing when the *canocie* are done but not overcooked. The recipe calls for an hour's cooking, but much depends upon the heat, the eye, and the *canocie*. Keep the heat very low and the pan covered except when turning the *canocie*. When almost all the liquid has escaped or been absorbed, test the *canocie* by eating one. It should be still moist, but not soggy! It should not be dry and tough.

FOR 4 SERVINGS AS A MAIN COURSE:

2 pounds canocie
2 cloves garlic, peeled

¾ cup olive oil
⅓ cup finely chopped parsley
Salt and pepper
Water, preferably that preserved from the
  preparation of the canocie. *(See below.)*

1. Wash the *canocie* well with running water, being careful if they are alive not to be bitten or spiked. Hold them by the thorax. With a pair of scissors, cut off about ½ of the head. Snip off the small front legs, but leave the two large meaty ones. Cut off the fins that run along the belly side of the *canocie*. Clip along the sides of the *canocie* so that when cooked the shell may be easily opened, but not so much that the top and bottom shells are completely detached from one another. Place the prepared *canocie* in a dish or bowl in order to collect the water and juices that will drain from them.

2. Use a frying pan large enough to accommodate all the *canocie* in a single layer. Brown the garlic in the olive oil over medium heat, then remove and discard it.

3. Align the *canocie* in the frying pan and add the parsley, some salt, and quite a bit of pepper. Cover the pan and reduce the heat to low. After 3 or 4 minutes, turn the *canocie*. The juices should be just barely simmering.

4. Continue cooking the *canocie*, turning them every 5 or 10 minutes. If it appears that the liquids are escaping too rapidly, replenish them with the water reserved from the first step in the recipe. But do not add too much: all that is necessary is enough liquid to form some steam. This can be seen easily by tilting the frying pan and observing whether or not a puddle of liquid forms under the oil.

5. Cooking should take about an hour, all things done properly. When ready, place the *canocie* on a platter and spoon the juices over them. Serve immediately or allow to cool. Either way, *polenta* (page 221) goes very well with this dish.

GAMBARONI IN TECIA
GAMBERONI IN UMIDO
Braised Large Shrimp

Follow the preceding recipe, but because shrimp absorb less oil than *canocie* and are therefore not as rich, the portions should be somewhat larger. Note too that if the shrimp are without heads it is better to cut back on the oil a bit.

FOR 4 MAIN COURSE SERVINGS—7 OR 8 SHRIMP EACH:

2 pounds shrimp without heads, *15 per*
    pound in the shell
or 3¼ pounds shrimp with heads, *9 per*
    pound in the shell

1. Do everything the same way as for *canocie in tecia*, the preceding recipe, with the following exception: if the shrimp are without heads, cut the oil back to ⅔ instead of ¾ cup.

2. Serve hot or cold, preferably with *polenta* (page 221).

CANOCIE ROSTE
CANNOCCHIE O PANNOCCHIE
ARROSTE
Broiled Stuffed Mantis Shrimp

This particularly fine recipe is not used as extensively as the preceding ones, possibly because it requires somewhat more work to prepare. Whatever the reason, it is regrettable that they are served so seldom, for *canocie* so prepared make a delicious dish, either as an *antipasto* or a main course.

FOR 4 SERVINGS AS A MAIN COURSE:

2 pounds canocie
1 clove garlic, peeled and cut in half
⅔ cup bread crumbs
¼ cup finely chopped parsley
Salt and pepper
Olive oil

1. Wash the *canocie* under running water. Hold them by the thorax so as not to be bitten or spiked. Cut off half of the heads, the small front legs (leave the large ones), and the fins along the belly. Do not cut along the sides. Using a sharp knife, make a slit up the middle of the back running the length of the *canocia*, starting at the tail and ending at the

thorax. Avoid cutting all the way through or the stuffing will fall out during cooking. Do not remove any coral that may be inside.

2. Rub a small mixing bowl with garlic. Put the bread crumbs and parsley into the bowl. Add quite a bit of salt and pepper. Mix well.

3. Preheat the broiler.

4. Stuff each *canocia* with 2 or 3 teaspoonsful of the bread-crumb mixture, more if possible. Spoon olive oil over the stuffing. The bread crumbs do not readily accept the oil, but by spooning slowly and carefully they will eventually absorb enough. The crumbs should be thoroughly moistened.

5. Put the *canocie* in a broiling pan or shallow baking dish, stuffed side up, and place under the broiler. The distance between the *canocie* and the flame should be about 6 inches. Turn the heat down to medium or slightly higher and cook for 10 minutes or until the bread crumbs have browned. Remove from the broiler and spoon the pan juices over the *canocie* or pour a little olive oil over them. Serve immediately. This dish is best when very hot. As usual, eat the *canocie* with the fingers.

GAMBARONI ROSTI
GAMBERONI ARROSTI
Broiled Stuffed Shrimp

The preceding recipe, *canocie roste*, adapts particularly well to large shrimp.

FOR 4 SERVINGS AS A MAIN COURSE—7 OR 8 SHRIMP EACH:

2 pounds shrimp without heads, *15 per*
pound in the shell
or 3¼ pounds shrimp with heads, *9 per*
pound in the shell

1. Follow the preceding recipe exactly, paying special attention to the section dealing with splitting the shell along the back. With shrimp it is more practical to cut off the heads and to work back toward the tail. Also, be especially careful not to cut all the way through the shrimp, which is very easy to do.

2. Serve the shrimp very hot.

Carne
MEAT

THE RECIPES in this section are for the most part easy and straight-forward, and should present few problems. Naturally, Venetians do not confine themselves to the small number of recipes given in the following pages. They also eat steaks, chops, and roasts much as Americans do. We have selected popular Venetian recipes which we hope you will find interesting and unusual as well as flavorful.

CARNE PASTISSADA
CARNE DI BUE PASTICCIATA
Pot Roast in Wine Sauce

This is a method of preparing pot roast with a particular taste, pleasing to the palate of those who appreciate interestingly prepared cuisine.

Any very lean piece of beef may be used for this recipe, but preferably eye of the round or a good rump roast.

This dish may be served in different ways. Often part of the sauce is used on thick pasta such as *rigattoni*, as a first course, or pasta and meat are served on the same plate as a *piatto unico*. You may add potatoes for the last part of cooking, or serve it with *polenta* (page 221).

No matter how it is served, this is an extremely appealing and delicious dish; but somewhat rich.

High tide at the Molo. *Gino Macropodio, the gondolier, with two men who help passengers in and out of gondolas.*

FOR 4 SERVINGS:

1½ pounds eye of the round or lean rump roast
A good, rather heavy red wine, very dry
1 clove garlic, peeled and split in half lengthwise
1 strip bacon, cut in half crosswise
2 ounces butter
½ cup olive oil
4 ribs celery, finely diced
1 medium onion, chopped
1 medium carrot, finely diced
¾ cup tomato sauce (page 218)
2 cloves
Salt and pepper
(Water)

1. Place the meat in a suitable container, cover with wine, and place it in the refrigerator for 8 hours or more.

2. Remove the meat from the wine, reserving the wine, and make a slit at either end of the roast, an inch and a half or so deep. Wrap the half-cloves of garlic in the bacon and insert in the holes in the meat.

3. Place the butter, olive oil, celery, onion, and carrot in a heavy-bottomed pot or large saucepan. Cook over moderate heat until the onion becomes translucent, 5 minutes or so.

4. Add the tomato sauce, cloves, meat, ¾ cup of the wine in which the meat was soaked, and some salt and pepper. Bring to a very slow simmer and cook for 3 hours, turning the meat occasionally. Add some water if the sauce becomes too thick and threatens to stick to the bottom of the pan.

5. After 3 hours, remove the meat and carve it into 4 or 8 slices. Return the meat to the pot and cook until it is very tender, perhaps ½ hour. Do not overcook the meat, lest it become too dry; if it is very tender when carved, merely return it to the sauce but do not cook further. Reheat it when ready to serve.

6. Correct the seasoning and serve very hot on warmed plates.

CARNE IN UMIDO PICANTE
MANZO ALL'UNGHERESE
Goulash

This typically Hungarian dish is very popular with Venetians, particularly when it is cooked in the Venetian way. It comes out appetizing, but certainly not adapted to faint stomachs.

Although in general Venetians have few good words to say for the Austro-Hungarian Empire, occupier of Venice for many years, they nevertheless continue to enjoy this import. As with many dishes cooked in Venice, everyone has his idea of the only way it should be done. This is one version.

Use any lean, relatively inexpensive cut of beef. The amount of paprika depends upon its quality and how spicy a goulash is desired. Start with two teaspoonfuls and work up.

For a one-course meal, increase the amounts by about ⅓. The portions are already on the generous side.

FOR 4 SERVINGS:

1¾ *pounds onions, thinly sliced*
4 *tablespoons olive oil*
(Water)
1¾ *pounds lean meat, pot roast or*
eye of the round
Flour
4 *tablespoons butter*
2 *cups water, or* 1½ *cups water and*
½ *cup good dry red wine*
Salt
2 *teaspoons or more paprika, to taste*
8 *small to medium-size potatoes*

1. Put the onions and olive oil in a heavy bottomed pot over medium heat. Stir every few minutes at first. When the onions have warmed and are beginning to produce juice, cut the heat back to very low. Cook covered for an hour until the onions have become quite pulpy. Stir often. If the onions show any signs of sticking, add the smallest amount of water to eliminate the problem. The onions should not brown, but

neither should they be swimming in liquid. While the onions are cooking, go on to the next step.

2. Trim off any fat and skin and cut the meat into 2-inch cubes. Roll the meat in flour.

3. Add the butter to the onions and turn the heat up to somewhat below medium. Add the flour-coated chunks of meat and brown them lightly, stirring constantly and being careful not to burn the onions. When the meat is slightly browned, add the water or water and wine, and some salt. Bring to a boil, cover, and reduce the flame to very low.

4. When the meat has simmered for 1½ hours, add the paprika and mix well. Continue cooking with the pot covered. Stir occasionally and if necessary add some water to prevent the sauce from becoming too thick and possibly burning. Do not use a lot of water, though, since the sauce should be very thick. Total cooking time for the meat should be between 3 and 4 hours, depending upon the quality and cut. Toward the end of cooking test the meat with a fork and check the seasoning carefully.

5. Peel and boil the potatoes. Serve the goulash on warmed plates accompanied by the potatoes.

NOTE: The recipe as given above is the easy way to do it. A better way is to brown the floured meat in a frying pan and then transfer it to the pot containing the onions. Use the water or water and wine to clean the skillet, adding the liquids to the pot.

CARNE E POLO LESSI
BOLLITO MISTO
Mixed Boil

Where is the gourmet who would disdain a well prepared bollito? Bollito *means a slice of beef, a piece of chicken, a bit of veal head, and some* cotechino *sausage, perhaps with a tomato sauce, or best of all* sottoaceti, *small hot green peppers, pickled onions, pickled carrots, etc. All accompanied by a fresh green salad, and, of course, a dry red wine of the first quality.*

This is not a typically Venetian dish, but it is so popular in Venice in the winter that we feel compelled to include it.

A more elaborate *bollito* than the one described above also will have *zampone* (another sausage), turkey, veal tongue, a veal trotter, and possibly other things. To do a complete *bollito* like this you should plan on having about a dozen people to eat everything. Our recipe below, more modest, may seem meager to those who have seen the real thing.

Here is what it is all about: In one pot you cook chicken, beef, and perhaps some turkey. The resulting broth from this pot may be used for *pastina in brodo* (page 44), for a first course. In a second pot you cook the *cotechino*, and if you wish, *zampone* and veal tongue. In a third pot you cook the veal head and perhaps a veal trotter. When everything is ready and the soup has been eaten, give each person a little bit of each thing, beef, chicken, veal head, etc., served on a warm plate and accompanied by any of the condiments mentioned above. Other condiments such as horseradish or *salsa verde*, green sauce, also go very well with this dish.

Although the actual cooking is very simple, you will need practice and skill in testing the various components in order to tell when they are properly done. For example, if you have a tender piece of meat and a tough chicken, they may both be ready at the same time. On the other hand, if the chicken is tender and the meat tough, there may be a 2-hour difference in the cooking times. How do we resolve this problem? We don't. Put everything on to cook at the same time, 4 or 4½ hours before you plan to serve it. As the various parts of the *bollito* become tender, remove them from the pots and either place them on the serving platter to be served tepid later, or keep them warm by putting them in a roasting pan containing a half inch of water or broth. Cover the pan and place it in an oven warm enough to keep the water hot but not boiling.

Any leftover beef and chicken may be used for *polpete*, meat patties (page 187) or stuffing for zucchini (page 191). You may also use some of the leftover sausage for these dishes, but the veal head is too fatty.

FOR 6 TO 8 SERVINGS:

The first pot:

    1½ pounds beef, eye of the round, rump,
      or other lean stewing meat
    A stewing chicken, 3 to 3½ pounds dressed
    Approximately 1 gallon cold water
    8 ribs celery, cut in 1-inch lengths
    2 medium carrots, coarsely diced
    2 medium onions, peeled but whole
    Salt and pepper

1. Trim any excess fat from the meat. Place the meat in a large heavy-bottomed pot.

2. Wash the chicken and place it in the pot along with the meat. You may add the giblets if you wish. They too can be used for *polpete* or stuffed zucchini.

3. Cover the meat and chicken with cold water and place the pot over high heat. When a boil is reached, reduce the heat. Skim off any scum that forms. When scumming has ceased, add the vegetables and some salt and pepper. Cover the pot, reduce the heat, and simmer until the chicken and meat are tender. If the chicken is tender before the meat, as will probably happen, keep it warm as discussed above.

4. The broth may be used for *pastina in brodo* (page 44) for a first course, or may be saved for making *risotti* or other dishes another day. In either case, strain the broth and skim off the grease. Re-strain it through a piece of cloth, if you wish.

The second pot:

> A young veal head, in 2 pieces and boned
> Cold water
> Salt and pepper

1. Wash the veal head and place it in a pot. Cover with cold water and add some salt and pepper. Cook following the procedure for the first pot. The veal head should take something in the neighborhood of 3 hours to cook, but start testing after 2 hours because if overcooked it will fall apart too easily. It should be tender but still firm, and it goes from tender to mush very quickly.

2. When cooked remove from the water and place with the other meats to be kept warm. Discard the cooking water.

The third pot:

> A 1-pound cotechino or 2 ½-pound ones,
>   or a 1-pound zampone, or both
> Water

1. *Cotechino* is a sausage made from the ears, skin, jowls, and just about any other parts of the pig that no one has figured out how to use otherwise. The amazing thing is that when properly made it is delicious. *Zampone* is about the same story except that the meat is stuffed into the skin of a pig trotter instead of a normal sausage skin.

2. Using a toothpick, poke a lot of holes into the skin of the sausage—the more the better, but at least 100. This will prevent the skin from breaking and will allow grease to escape.

3. Place the sausage in a pot, cover with water, and place over high heat. When a boil is reached, reduce the heat and cook until the sausage may be easily pierced with a fork. This may take as little as 2 hours or as long as 3½ or even 4 hours.

4. When ready, remove from the water and place with the other meats to be kept warm. Discard the cooking water.

5. The *bollito* is now ready to be served. Place the various components on a platter and accompany them with the condiments mentioned earlier.

Salsa verde:

> *1 hard-boiled egg*
> *Soft part of 3 slices of bread*
> *Vinegar to taste*
> *¼ pound finely chopped parsley*
> *2 chopped gherkins*
> *3 tablespoons chopped capers*
> *Olive oil*
> *Salt*

Blend above ingredients thoroughly.

TRIPA AL FORMAGIO PARMESAN
TRIPPA ALLA PARMIGIANA
Tripe with Parmesan Cheese

This dish saves time and money. One can prepare it in just a few minutes and tripe costs very little. It is delicious and easy to digest, and suggests a glass of wine, or better, some good cold beer.

Ask the butcher for the meatier, thicker part of the tripe. Also, check with him to be sure that the tripe has been precooked.

FOR 4 SERVINGS:

1¼ pounds meaty tripe
¼ pound butter
Salt and pepper
⅓ cup or more grated Parmesan cheese

1. Wash the tripe and cut it into strips about ¼ inch by 3 inches.
2. Melt the butter in a saucepan over medium heat. Add the tripe and some salt and pepper. Keep stirring the tripe, because it will quickly absorb the butter. After 5 or 6 minutes, pour the tripe and butter, which will by now be milky, onto a very hot serving platter and sprinkle generously with grated Parmesan cheese.
3. Serve immediately, accompanied by fresh Italian or French bread.

TRIPA IN TECIA
TRIPPA IN UMIDO
Braised Tripe

For those not practiced in eating tripe this is a good way to begin, for the tripe becomes very tender and the sauce delicious.

Although any part of the tripe may be used, the meatier pieces are better adapted to this recipe. Depending upon the tripe, the amount of broth or water needed may vary from almost none to a cup or even more. The sauce should be very thick, so add only enough to prevent the tripe from sticking to the bottom of the pan.

When you buy the tripe, be sure that it has been precooked.

FOR 4 SERVINGS:

1¼ pounds tripe
1 clove garlic, peeled
⅓ cup olive oil
6 tablespoons butter
1 tablespoon finely chopped parsley
6 tablespoons tomato sauce (page 218)
Salt and pepper
About 1 cup veal or chicken broth, or water
(Grated Parmesan cheese)

1. Wash the tripe and cut it into pieces about ¼ inch by 3 inches.

2. Brown the garlic in the olive oil over medium heat, then remove and discard it. Allow the saucepan to cool a bit before going on.

3. Add the butter and place the saucepan over medium heat. Add the tripe, parsley, tomato sauce, quite a bit of salt and enough pepper to make the sauce fairly spicy. Mix everything well and bring to a simmer. Reduce the heat to very low and cover the saucepan. Simmer gently for 2 hours, stirring frequently, and adding broth or water as necessary, but only enough to prevent the sauce from sticking.

4. Serve very hot on warmed plates, accompanied by *polenta* (page 221), or fresh Italian or French bread. Some grated Parmesan cheese may be added at the table.

RODOLETI DE VEDEO COL PARSUTO
ROTOLINI DI VITELLO
AL PROSCIUTTO
Veal and Prosciutto Rolls

Rodoleti *are made in various parts of Italy. As the name may change from region to region, so the recipe may change also. But the idea is always the same: roll something up in a thin slice of veal and cook it! The following recipe is how we do it. It is important to pay attention not to eat too much, for it is quite rich. Also be careful about the wine, for* rodoleti *tempt one to drink that extra glass.*

Unless you are very careful you may have trouble with the rolled veal sticking to the bottom of the pan. Try to keep all the cheese inside the rolls, for it will almost immediately mess up the pan, sticking and browning.

An un-Venetian idea which might have application in the United States would be to cut the veal rolls into slices and serve them as cocktail hors d'oeuvres.

FOR 4 SERVINGS:

1¼ pounds good lean veal: cutlet, round,
  eye of the round
10 ounces prosciutto crudo, Italian ham,
  cut paper thin
⅓ to ½ cup grated Parmesan cheese
3 ounces butter
2 ounces olive oil
⅓ cup veal or chicken broth
1 tablespoon flour
¼ cup water

1. Use a cut of veal that is absolutely fat free and the more tender the better. Have the butcher cut 10 very thin slices having a total weight of about 1¼ pounds. Then have him flatten these with the side of a cleaver or some other instrument to a thickness of ⅛ inch or less; which is to say about as thin as he can.

2. Cut each slice in half. You should wind up with 20 slices 2 to 3 inches wide and 4 to 5 inches long. They will not be perfect rectangles, of course, and it really does not matter much.

3. The *prosciutto* must be cut paper thin. If cut properly you should have roughly one slice of *prosciutto* for each slice of veal. Divide the slices evenly laying them flat on top of the veal. Put 1 or 2 teaspoons of grated cheese on each piece of *prosciutto*, trying to keep it away from the edges. You now have the thin veal slices on the bottom, then the *prosciutto*, and the grated cheese on top.

4. Starting from the widest side of the veal slice, roll it as tightly as possible, forming a cylinder with the *prosciutto* and cheese trapped inside. You now have 20 veal rolls ready for cooking.

5. Place a large frying pan containing the butter and oil over fairly high heat. When the butter has melted and is quite hot, add the veal rolls. Do not move them for 3 or 4 minutes; if you try to move them immediately they will unroll. When the veal rolls have browned a bit and don't seem terribly anxious to stick any more, turn them over with a spatula. Brown the other side and continue to turn them until evenly browned.

6. Add the broth and cover the pan. Reduce the heat and simmer for 7 or 8 minutes, turning the rolls a couple of times. While the rolls are cooking, mix 1 tablespoon flour in ¼ cup water. After the 7 or 8 minutes of cooking, pour the flour and water mixture through a strainer depositing

a little on each roll. Spoon the sauce over the rolls. At this point you may have to reduce the heat even further. Cover again and cook for another 8 to 10 minutes, turning the rolls another couple of times and spooning sauce over them.

7. Serve the *rodoleti* immediately on warmed plates, or later either tepid or cold.

VEDEO TONÀ
VITELLO TONNATO
Veal with Tuna Sauce

This dish is most delicious; even though a little heavy, it is always pleasing. It makes a delightful change from the ordinary.

The unusual idea of serving meat with a tuna sauce may put some people off. Try to put this prejudice aside—it would be a shame to miss such an excellent dish because of preconceived ideas of what things do and do not go together.

Vitello tonnato is widely used in Italy and varies from region to region. Our recipe, though rich, is less so than the majority. Certainly it is simpler to make than most and we believe it is easily as pleasing as the more complicated recipes.

It is a wonderful dish for summer. Serve a light first course, and the recipe should be ample for 7 or 8 people.

FOR 7 OR 8 SERVINGS:

> *2½ pounds very lean veal,*
> *eye of the round or rump*
> *8 canned flat anchovy fillets packed in olive oil*
> *1½ quarts water, more or less*
> *2 ribs celery, cut into 1-inch lengths*
> *½ medium onion, coarsely chopped*
> *1 medium carrot, coarsely diced*
> *Salt*

1. An eye of the round of veal of this weight may be too long to fit any pot you may have, in which case it should be cut into 2 pieces of equal length. Make long slits in the meat and insert the anchovy fillets.

With an eye of the round this is very easy. With thinner cuts the slits should be made in such a way that when the meat is rolled the anchovies will be on the inside. Tie the meat with string so that the anchovies will remain trapped inside. The technique is not terribly important. The idea is that the anchovy flavor has a chance to permeate the meat during cooking.

2. Place the meat in a pot just large enough to hold it comfortably. In a second pot bring the water to a boil. Pour the boiling water over the meat and place the pot over a high flame. There should be enough water to cover the meat and then some. When the water returns to a boil some scum will form. Keep skimming until the scumming stops. Add all the vegetables and a little salt and then adjust the heat so that a simmer is maintained. Turn the meat occasionally.

3. Cook the meat for 1½ hours, or a little longer if the meat was rolled into a particularly large form. Remove from the broth and allow to cool to room temperature, or refrigerate it if you prefer cold meat really cold.

4. (Strain and save the broth. It may be used in the preparation of a *risotto* for a first course or refrigerated and used another day.)

The sauce:

> A 3¼-ounce can of tuna packed in olive oil
> 6 flat canned anchovy fillets packed in olive oil
> ⅓ cup or slightly more olive oil
> ¼ cup lemon juice
> 1½ or 2 ounces capers

1. If you don't have an electric blender, you are in for a bit of work here. Place the tuna and anchovies on a strainer over a saucepan and work the mixture with a wooden spoon. When the mixture becomes dry and no more will pass through the strainer, add several drops of olive oil and lemon juice. Continue rubbing the mixture into the strainer or sieve until it is dry again. Add more olive oil and lemon juice and proceed as before. Do this until all the tuna-anchovy mixture has been pushed through. The problem here, of course, is to come out even with the solids and the fluids. You can recycle some of the contents of the saucepan if necessary and add a little more oil.

2. An electric blender is much easier and yields better results. Put the tuna and anchovies into the blender jar along with the olive oil and

lemon juice. Blend until smooth. At first it may be necessary to stop the blender once or twice to push the ingredients to the bottom, but the whole operation should take no more than a couple minutes, as opposed to half an hour or longer by hand. When the sauce is well blended, place it in a soup dish.

Assembling the dish:

1. Cut the meat into very thin slices, ⅛-inch thick or even thinner. If you have a meat slicer, all the easier.

2. Coat both sides of the meat slices with the tuna-anchovy sauce in the soup dish and place them on a serving platter. Overlap the slices to form an agreeable pattern. When all the meat slices have been placed on the platter, pour the remaining sauce over and smooth it around.

3. Distribute the capers evenly on top of the sauce. This dish goes exceptionally well with a green salad.

SPEZATINO DE VEDEO IN TECIA
COI BISI
SPEZZATINO DI VITELLO COI PISELLI
Veal Stew with Peas

This is a dish that loves polenta. *It is quite substantial but with excellent flavor that invites one to drink a good glass of red wine. After eating, however, it is advisable to take a long walk.*

People with very healthy appetites may wish to increase the amount of sauce and serve some of it over pasta as a first course.

Ask your butcher's advice as to which piece of meat to buy. Many different cuts may be used. Tell him you want something fairly lean but something which will not dry out too much when stewed.

FOR 4 SERVINGS:

1⅓ pounds lean veal suitable for stewing
1½ pounds fresh peas in the pod or
   ½ pound frozen peas
⅓ cup olive oil
4 tablespoons butter
2 ribs celery, finely diced
1 small onion, chopped
1 medium carrot, finely diced
1 tablespoon finely chopped parsley
6 tablespoons tomato sauce (page 218)
1 cup veal or chicken broth or good dry
   white wine, or a mixture
Salt and pepper

1. Cut the meat into 1½-inch cubes. Trim off any fat.
2. Shell or defrost the peas. Do not use canned peas.
3. Place a pot containing the olive oil, butter, celery, onion, carrot, and parsley over medium heat. Cook, stirring frequently, until the onion becomes translucent, about 5 minutes.
4. Add the veal and turn it until lightly browned.
5. Add the peas, tomato sauce, broth or wine, and some salt and pepper. Reduce the heat to very low and simmer gently. At the end of cooking the sauce should be very thick, so cook uncovered, being careful that the sauce does not stick. If it becomes too thick add a little water, broth, or wine. Simmer the meat until tender, 1 to 1¼ hours for the better cuts of veal, as long as 1¾ hours or perhaps slightly longer for more economical cuts. The meat should be very tender when tested with a fork, but it should not be completely falling apart.
6. Serve on warmed plates, accompanied by lots of *polenta* (page 221).

COE DE VEDEO IN TECIA
CODE DI VITELLO IN UMIDO
Braised Veal Tails

This is a main course that is preferably eaten with polenta, *but if one does not care too much for* polenta, *he may substitute bread.*

Potatoes may be substituted also. Peel and quarter medium-sized potatoes and cook them with the veal tails for the last 20 or 25 minutes.

FOR 4 SERVINGS:

2 or 3 young veal tails, total weight
   about 2½ pounds
3 ounces olive oil
4 tablespoons butter
2 small onions, chopped
2 medium carrots, finely diced
3 ribs celery, finely diced
¾ cup good dry white wine
2 medium-sized tomatoes, peeled and seeded
   or ⅓ cup tomato sauce (page 218)
½ cup water

1. Cut the veal tails into pieces, one piece for each joint toward the large end, 2 or more joints at the tail end. Wash under running water.

2. Place the olive oil, butter, and vegetables in a large casserole or frying pan with high sides over medium heat. Stir for a minute or two to mix the vegetables well with the olive oil and butter. Add the tails and brown them slightly, turning them regularly. This should take 7 or 8 minutes.

3. Pour the wine into the cooking vessel and raise the heat to fairly high. Cook uncovered for 3 or 4 minutes, then add the tomato and water. Mix well, cover, and reduce the heat to very low. Simmer until the meat is tender, an hour or a little longer for small veal tails up to 1¾ hours for larger ones. Turn the meat occasionally. Toward the end of the cooking, test often for tenderness with a fork. Try to have the sauce come out thick, but not too thick. You may have to cook with the pan uncovered or add some water in order to get the proper consistency.

4. Serve on warmed plates, accompanied by *polenta* (page 221) or fresh Italian or French bread.

FIGÀ A LA VENEZIANA
FEGATO ALLA VENEZIANA
Calf's Liver Venetian Style

He who wishes to have a good and flavorful luncheon without too much loss of time may make fegato alla veneziana.

But, if one does want to have a quick luncheon of *fegato alla veneziana,* we hope that he has made *polenta* the day before, for *polenta,* traditionally served with this dish, requires nearly an hour to prepare.

This is one Venetian dish that can be found almost anywhere in Italy. The widespread popularity of this recipe that carries the Venetian label is surprising, since the Venetians themselves do not eat it terribly often.

FOR 4 SERVINGS:

1 pound calf's liver
6 ounces butter
¾ cup olive oil
2 medium onions, chopped
Salt and pepper
(Flour)

1. Cut the liver into thin bite-size slices, ⅛-inch thick maximum.

2. Place the butter, olive oil, and onions in a frying pan over medium heat. Add some salt and pepper. Stir frequently while cooking until the smallest pieces of onion just begin to take on a golden color.

3. Some cooks dust the liver lightly with flour before adding it to the onions. Add the liver to the onions and brown it, turning constantly. This should take no more than 4 minutes, probably less, depending upon the thickness of the slices. Test a piece after 2 minutes. It should have just barely lost its red color and should be firm but not tough. Do not overcook the liver, for it will quickly become too chewy and lose its flavor.

4. Serve the liver and onions and a goodly amount of the sauce onto warmed plates, with lots of *polenta* (page 221).

FIGÀ GARBO DOLSE
FEGATO AGRO DOLCE
Sweet and Sour Calf's Liver

This dish may be served not only as a second course but also as a hearty breakfast. Fairly easily digested and very delicious, it goes well with a couple of glasses of good beer and creates a delight to exacting palates.

The origin of this dish may well date back to the period when Venice controlled the trade routes to the East. Do not expect, though, that this will come out like sweet and sour dishes at your favorite Chinese restaurant. The sauce is simpler, and much thinner.

FOR 4 SERVINGS:

1 pound calf's liver
4 tablespoons fresh lemon juice
4 teaspoons sugar
5 ounces butter
4 tablespoons olive oil
Flour
Salt and pepper

1. Cut a slice of liver ⅛ inch thick or less and going almost, but not completely, through the liver. Then make a second cut, the same thickness and parallel to the first, but this time going all the way through. Open the liver along the first cut so that you have a flat, very thin slice twice the size of a single cut. Continue until you have sliced the whole pound into 16 pieces.

2. Squeeze the lemon juice and put it in a glass along with the sugar. Mix well.

3. Place a large frying pan containing the butter and olive oil over medium heat. While the butter is melting, dust the liver with flour. When the oil and butter are hot, add the floured liver slices. Sprinkle on a little salt and pepper. Cook for 3 to 5 minutes, turning the liver as necessary (the liver will have a tendency to curl). After 3 to 5 minutes the liver should be slightly browned if the temperature was right. Make a cut in one slice to check that it has almost lost its red color.

4. Add the lemon-juice-sugar mixture. Cook the liver for another

minute or two and then place it on warmed plates or a platter and pour the hot juices on top. Serve immediately with fresh Italian or French bread, or with *polenta* (page 221).

ROGNON TRIFOLÀ
RENE TRIFOLATO
Braised Veal Kidneys

A dish of few pretensions, easy to prepare, and pleasing to gourmets; wonderful for those who have little time at their disposal but who also enjoy an interesting meal.

Be sure that the kidney is from young, tender veal. Have the butcher remove the exterior fat, but it is better to do the rest at home—in our experience, butchers tend to leave too much of the interior fat.

FOR 4 SERVINGS:

1 pound veal kidney, cleaned of all exterior fat
5 ounces butter
4 tablespoons olive oil
(¼ cup dry red wine)
3 tablespoons finely chopped parsley
Salt and pepper

1. Cut the kidney away from all the interior fat. The meat should show no traces of fat. Slice the kidney into very thin pieces, no more than ⅛ inch in thickness; the thinner the better.
2. Put the butter and olive oil in a frying pan over fairly high heat. When the butter has melted and is bubbling rather vigorously, add the kidneys and perhaps a little red wine. While cooking the kidneys will give up quite a bit of liquid. Stir constantly and after 7 or 8 minutes most of this liquid will have boiled away. Add the chopped parsley, some salt, and quite a lot of pepper. Continue to stir until the last of the liquid has boiled away and the sauce becomes fairly clear.
3. Serve immediately on warmed plates, accompanied by *polenta* (page 221) or fresh Italian or French bread.

ROGNON AI FERI
RENE ALLA GRIGLIA
Broiled Veal Kidney

Accompanied by a good salad or some other vegetable, this is appropriately served as a light lunch. It may also be served as a second course for a larger lunch or dinner if the first course is of abundant proportions.

If you understand how to broil a steak, this recipe presents no problems.

FOR 2 SERVINGS:

An entire young veal kidney, about 1 pound
Olive oil
Salt and pepper
(Lemon wedges)

1. Have the butcher remove all the exterior fat from a fresh young veal kidney. At home split the kidney slightly more than halfway through lengthwise and remove all the interior fat.

2. Place the kidney in a soup dish and coat it well with olive oil. Sprinkle on quite a bit of salt and pepper. Allow to marinate for ½ hour or longer, turning it several times.

3. Broil the kidney exactly as if you were broiling a steak. It should be fairly well done, however. Start with the inside of the kidney toward the flame. As it cooks the kidney will tend to curl up into its original shape, so it should be placed fairly far away from an overhead broiling unit. The resulting dish is much more pleasing if the kidney is charcoal broiled.

4. Serve immediately on warmed plates. Many people squeeze a few drops of lemon juice on top.

CASTRÀ IN TECIA
CASTRATO IN UMIDO
Braised Lamb or Mutton

A very appetizing dish, good with bread or potatoes, but better with polenta.

As with *risoto in cavroman* (page 87) or *sopa de castrà* (page 36), use any very lean cut of meat, the thigh part of the leg being preferred because the fat and skin may be trimmed off easily. (See page 143 for additional comments about the type of meat.)

FOR 4 SERVINGS:

1⅓ pounds very lean lamb or mutton
⅓ cup olive oil
4 tablespoons butter
½ medium onion, chopped
1 medium celery heart, finely diced
1 small carrot, finely diced
Salt and pepper
3 tablespoons tomato sauce (page 218)
⅓ cup broth, dry red wine, or water

1. Remove all the fat and skin from the meat and cut it into cubes of about 1½ inches.
2. Put the olive oil, butter, vegetables, salt, and pepper in a saucepan over medium heat and cook, stirring frequently, until the onion becomes translucent, about 5 minutes.
3. Add the meat to the vegetables and turn until lightly browned.
4. Add the tomato sauce and broth, wine, or water, or a mixture. Mix well and bring to a simmer. Cover and cook until the meat is tender, at least 1¼ hours. If the cut of meat is tough or the animal old, 1¾ hours or even longer may be necessary. Stir often during cooking. You may have to add a little more liquid if the sauce threatens to stick. Do not add much, because the sauce should be quite thick.
5. Serve on warmed plates with fresh Italian or French bread or *polenta* (page 221). Or small new potatoes may be cooked in the same saucepan as the meat. Peel them and add to the saucepan when the meat first shows signs of becoming tender, and cook for 20 minutes or longer.

FONGADINA DE AGNELO IN TECIA
INTERIORE DI AGNELLO IN UMIDO
Lamb "Interiors" with Sauce

Here is a dish that the aroma alone fa lecar i dei, *makes you lick your fingers, as the Venetian saying goes. It should be accompanied by polenta or bread and one or two or more glasses of good dry red wine.*

We prefer the word "interiors" to the euphemism "specialty cuts," a term which tells very little. The interiors used are the liver, heart, lungs, and sometimes the kidney and spleen. We are not sure about the availability of lungs and spleen in the United States, but there should be little problem finding the other parts. The Americans with whom we have spoken are less than convinced that the whole thing is a good idea, but for those brave ones around there remains a true treat. The recipe presents no particular difficulties, but allow plenty of time for chopping the interiors and the vegetables.

FOR 4 SERVINGS:

Heart, liver, lungs, kidney, and spleen of a
young lamb, 1¼ to 1½ pounds total
4 ounces butter
3 tablespoons olive oil
4 ribs celery or a medium celery heart, finely diced
1 medium carrot, finely diced
1 medium onion, chopped
(Broth or water)
½ cup dry red wine

1. Remove all fat and extraneous material (skin, windpipe, etc.) from the meat. Chop everything into small pieces, ¼-inch to ½-inch cubes being about the right size.

2. Place the butter and olive oil in a large frying pan over medium heat. When the butter has melted, add the meat and turn until browned. Add the vegetables, stir, and cover. Stir every few minutes at first to be sure that the meat does not stick to the pan. If necessary, add a little broth or water. Reduce the heat to very low and simmer for 30 minutes.

3. Add the red wine to the pan, stir, and cover again. Cook for another 15 minutes.

4. Remove the cover and continue cooking, stirring frequently until most of the liquids have boiled off, 10 to 15 minutes. The sauce should be very thick.

5. Serve immediately, very hot, accompanied by Italian or French bread or *polenta* (page 221). Leftovers may be used to make an excellent *risotto* (page 89).

SANGUETO A LA VENEZIANA
SANGUE DI MAIALE IN TEGAME
Coagulated Pork Blood Venetian Style

This is a very economical dish and one that can be made quickly, but it should not be eaten terribly often for it is hard to digest.

In Venice there are two types of shop for meat products: the *macelleria* and the *salumeria*. The former is a normal butcher shop, but usually does not carry pork. The latter is more of a delicatessen than a butcher shop, but it is where pork and pork products are sold.

One of these products is *sangueto*. We do not know the process by which pork blood is made to congeal, but there it is, nevertheless. It comes in blocks perhaps 10 inches by 16 by 6 or 7. The *sangueto* is cut off the block in slices and is used in place of calf's liver in the recipe for *fegato alla veneziana* (page 158). The *sangueto* is cut into small pieces just as if it were liver. A scant ¼ pound is sufficient for a serving.

We have never tried it, but Venetian friends living in America tell us that blood sausage, *blutwurst*, makes a passable substitute for *sangueto*.

As with *fegato alla veneziana, polenta* (page 221) is traditionally used to sop up the sauce.

PARSUTO COI BISI
PROSCIUTTO CON PISELLI
Italian Ham with Peas

This good second course is best in spring, the season when it is easy to find fresh peas, small and tender, with excellent flavor.

Substitute ham steaks if you are not able to find *prosciutto crudo*, and frozen peas for fresh if necessary. It will not be exactly the same, but it will be good.

A first course can be made by doubling the amount of peas and then using half of them to make *risi e bisi* or *risoto de bisi* (pages 67 and 93). In these recipes mix some of the ham broth with other meat or chicken broth for the liquid. Reheat the ham and peas for the second course.

FOR 4 SERVINGS:

1½ pounds prosciutto crudo *in 1 or 2 slices*
Water
4 pounds very young peas in the pod,
  or 2½ pounds mature peas in the pod, or
  1 pound frozen peas
3 tablespoons olive oil
2 ounces butter
½ medium onion, finely chopped
2 tablespoons finely chopped parsley
⅓ cup or a little more broth from the first
  step below
(Salt and pepper)

1. Trim the excess fat from the meat. Place the meat in a saucepan or frying pan and barely cover with water. Bring to a simmer, reduce the heat, cover, and cook for 1½ hours, adding a little water as needed.

2. Shell or defrost the peas. Do not use canned peas.

3. Place a large saucepan or frying pan containing the olive oil, butter, onion, and parsley over medium heat. Cook until the onion becomes translucent, about 5 minutes, and then add the peas. Mix well.

4. Place the *prosciutto* in with the vegetables and add about ⅓ cup of the broth from cooking the meat. Cover and reduce the heat to simmer. Cook until the peas are very tender, how long depending upon the peas and your personal preference. Venetians like them very well done and for this recipe will cook large fresh peas for 45 minutes, frozen peas for about 30 minutes. During cooking stir occasionally and add more broth as needed. When finished there should be practically no broth left in with the meat and peas. Correct the seasoning. You probably will not need to add salt since the ham may be salty enough, but you may add some pepper if you wish.

5. Serve on warmed plates, accompanied by fresh Italian or French bread.

Polastri E Selvagina
Pollame E Cacciagione
POULTRY AND GAME

IN THE Venetian diet poultry comes in a bad third after seafood and meat. Venetians are probably eating as much chicken as ever, but certainly they are enjoying it less now that scientific feeding methods have been so widely employed. One happily pays a premium for a *sgraffatera*, a "ground scratcher," a skinny bird that has had to shift for itself augmenting its meager ration of food by eating seeds, berries, and all those unscientific things that give him the delicious flavor he was meant to have. Even so, unless one is lucky enough to have friends on a small country farm, it is almost impossible to find the real article. Many people are skeptical about the difference, but it is only necessary to make a broth from a *sgraffatera* and to confront it with that made from a "scientifically" raised chicken. The latter comes out like dish water by comparison.

Ducks and geese, on the other hand, being somewhat more backward than their scientific friends, are still quite good, while guinea hens fall somewhere in between.

Venetians enjoy game, but there is, of course, a season and it can be had only at certain times of the year. Also, it is becoming harder and harder to find it in the market. There is almost no chance for a householder to buy wild boar, for example, which is almost always snapped up by the restaurants before going on display at the butcher shops.

After painting such a bleak picture, we still think you will find the recipes in this section most pleasing.

Venice in winter fog. Docking area for gondolas, near Piazza San Marco.

ANARA ROSTA COL PIEN
ANATRA ARROSTA RIPIENA
Roast Stuffed Duckling

Duckling is very delicious but a rich dish. To derive most satisfaction from duckling it is advisable to omit the first course, or at least to limit it to something very light, a cup of broth for example.

Per la festa del Redentor,
Anara rosta e pesce in saor.

Traditionally this dish is eaten on the Feast of the Redeemer, Redentore, *either in a boat decorated with lights or in one of the many* osterie *or* trattorie, *wine shops or modest restaurants. Unfortunately, on* Redentore *it is also traditional to eat* pesce in saor, *marinated fried fish, another substantial dish. If one were to eat a pasta course between these two dishes he certainly would have need of help, if not from the Redeemer Himself, at least from bicarbonate of soda.*

Our method of roasting duckling may seem strange to many people, since most cookbooks recommend a cooking time of about 20 minutes per pound. For small ducklings we recommend at least twice that, and one and one-half times as much for larger ducklings. Our ducklings remain moist because of the stuffing and the frequent basting. It will, of course, be less fatty than duckling cooked only 20 minutes per pound.

We roast a 3-pound duckling (the weight of the dressed bird, not including the weight of the giblets) about 2½ hours and we increase the cooking time to about 3 hours or slightly more for a 5-pound bird.

FOR 4 SERVINGS:

A duckling, about 4½ pounds, 3 pounds
  dressed (not counting the giblets)
½ small carrot, coarsely diced
1 rib celery, cut into 1-inch lengths
¼ medium onion, chopped
Water
1 clove garlic, peeled and cut in half crosswise
Salt

3 ounces Italian prosciutto crudo, *or substitute*
  any other type ham
1½ ounces salt pork (for the stuffing)
1 large egg, slightly beaten
4 tablespoons grated Parmesan cheese
Pepper
(Salt)
Bread crumbs, a scant ¼ cup up to a
  generous ⅓ cup
6 slices salt pork, about 6 by 1½ by ⅛ inches

1. Have your butcher dress the duckling, saving the heart, liver, and gizzard. Snip off the neck at its origin inside the body, but leave enough skin from around the neck to use in trussing later. Also snip off the wing tips.

2. Do these 2 steps the night before, if possible. Place the neck, wing tips, and vegetables in a small saucepan of water over a high flame. Cover the pan, and when the water comes to a simmer, reduce the heat to very low. Cook for 1½ hours, adding more water as necessary. The neck and wing-tip meat will be used in the stuffing, and the broth may be used for making a *risotto*.

3. Cut or pull away all fat from the body openings. Wash the duckling well, or wipe it with a damp cloth. Allow the duckling to dry or dry it with a towel. Rub it inside and out with the garlic. Sprinkle the outside of the duckling with a generous amount of salt. While the duckling is absorbing the garlic and salt, prepare the stuffing.

4. Clean away any fat or strings from the heart and liver. Cut away the tough skin from around the gizzard, leaving only the dark red meat. Take the giblets, *prosciutto*, salt pork, and the meat from the neck and wing tips and put everything through a meat grinder or mince as finely as possible. Put the ground meats in a mixing bowl and add a slightly beaten egg. Mix well. At this point the mixture will be quite runny. Stir in the grated Parmesan cheese and rather a lot of pepper. Do not add salt if you have used *prosciutto crudo*; even if you have used boiled ham, go slowly with the salt. Add enough bread crumbs so that the mixture loses its runniness and may be shaped. It still should be very moist and soft, however. How much bread crumbs will depend upon a variety of things (the size of the liver, the size of the egg, etc.), but start with a scant ¼ cup and work up cautiously. Be sure to mix everything thoroughly. The stuffing is now ready to go inside the bird.

5. Preheat the oven to 350 degrees.

6. Place the stuffing inside the body cavity and truss the duckling. Do this by whatever method you can devise, but be sure that both the lower-body and the neck openings are securely closed.

7. Grease a roasting pan very lightly with olive oil and place the duckling inside, breast side up. We do not use a roasting rack. Place about ½ the salt-pork strips on parts that seem likely to brown first, the legs and the breastbone. Do not worry about the wings too much, since they are going to be very crisp whatever you do. Place the roasting pan in the oven. After 20 minutes, start basting the duckling, and baste religiously every 12 to 15 minutes. Place the rest of the salt pork over any area that seems to be browning too quickly. Cook for 2½ hours as discussed in the introduction to this recipe. We do not prick the skin of the duckling; although by so doing you lose fat more quickly, you lose the juices even faster.

8. Roasted bell pappers go very nicely with the duckling, as do green beans or a green salad.

ANARA NOSTRANA IN TECIA
ANATRA NOSTRANA IN UMIDO
Braised Duckling

This flavorful dish is best in late summer or in early autumn when ducklings are at their best.

This recipe will turn out even if the duckling is not *nostrana*. In English we do not have a really good word to express the Italian *nostrano*. Literally it means "local," but when used with reference to food and wine there is also the connotation of excellence. One of the most often heard expressions in Venetian markets is, "È *nostrano?*"

A great way to serve this dish is to use ⅔ to ¾ of the sauce to dress pasta for a first course, having the rest of the sauce and duckling for the second. Otherwise, serve a light first course and have lots of *polenta* with the duckling in order to soak up the sauce.

The sauce may or may not be made with chopped giblets. If it is, add the finely chopped heart and gizzard (free from the tough skin, the dark red meat only) at the same time as the vegetables. The chopped liver should be added later, after an hour and a half of cooking.

Be sure to cook the giblets even if you choose not to chop them for the sauce. Duckling giblets are extremely flavorful and may be cooked whole along with the rest of the duckling. Again, remove any tough skin from the gizzard. Add it and the heart at the same time as the other pieces of meat, but add the liver after about an hour and a half of cooking.

FOR 5 OR 6 SERVINGS:

A 4½-pound duckling, about 3 pounds
  dressed, not counting the giblets
3 ounces butter
3 tablespoons olive oil
A large onion, chopped
5 ribs celery or a fair-sized celery heart,
  finely diced
1 medium carrot, finely diced
4 tablespoons tomato sauce (page 218)
½ cup water
Salt and pepper

1. Cut the duckling into 8 pieces plus the neck, divided as evenly as possible. Remove all fat. Wash well and set the pieces aside on a slanted surface to drain, or dry them with a cloth. (See the introduction to the recipe for how to treat the giblets.)

2. Place the butter and olive oil in a large frying pan or in a flame-proof casserole over fairly high heat. When the butter is sizzling, add the pieces of duckling. Cook them for 3 or 4 minutes on a side or until lightly browned. Remove from the pan and set aside.

3. Reduce the heat to below medium and add the vegetables to the pan. When the onion becomes translucent add the tomato sauce and water, along with some salt and pepper.

4. Return the pieces of duckling to the pan and bring the liquids to a simmer. Cover the pan and reduce the flame to very low. Cook the duckling 2 hours or somewhat longer, turning it occasionally and adding more water if necessary to prevent the sauce from sticking. Start testing the duckling for tenderness after 1¾ hours by poking it with a fork.

5. When tender, serve the duckling and sauce both very hot on warmed plates, accompanied by *polenta* (page 221). Or serve in 2 courses, as discussed in the introduction.

FARAONA ROSTA CO LA SALSA
FARAONA AL FORNO CON LA SALSA
Roast Guinea Hen with Caper
and Giblet Sauce

This exquisite dish serves as an excellent change of pace, thanks to the interesting sauce.

There is nothing terribly difficult here, but allow quite a bit of time and be sure to baste the bird frequently, since it dries out easily.

FOR 4 SERVINGS:

A guinea hen, 3 to 3½ pounds dressed
1 rib celery, cut into ½-inch lengths
½ small onion, chopped
½ carrot, diced
Water
4 ounces salt pork cut into 5 or 6 strips
* 6 inches long by 1½ inches wide by ⅛ inch thick*
2 tablespoons butter
2 tablespoons olive oil
2 ounces prosciutto crudo *or other ham*
Another 1½ tablespoons olive oil
Another 2 tablespoons butter
2 tablespoons or more capers, to taste
Pepper

1. Do this step well in advance, the day before if you wish. Remove the neck from the guinea hen, cutting it off as far back in the body cavity as possible, and clip off the wing tips. Place the neck and wing tips in a small saucepan along with the celery, onion, and carrot and enough water to cover. Bring to a simmer over a high heat. Cover the pan and reduce the heat to very low, and cook for 1½ hours. During cooking add water to replace that which boils off. Do not add any salt at this time. The neck meat and the broth will be used later in the recipe in making the sauce.

2. Preheat the oven to 375 degrees.

3. Set the giblets aside. Wash the hen and dry it with a cloth. Sprinkle with some salt, inside and out. Place the strips of salt pork on the legs and breast. You may tie the pieces on if you want to be sure they do not

fall off. Save a strip or two so that parts of the hen that are browning too quickly may be protected later.

4. Grease a roasting pan with the butter and olive oil and place the hen inside. You may or may not use a rack, as you wish. Place the pan in the preheated oven and cook the hen for 1¾ hours or until tender and well browned. After the first 20 minutes of cooking, baste the hen every 12 to 15 minutes. Do this without fail or the hen will dry out. While the hen is cooking, prepare the sauce in the next step.

5. Remove the neck from the saucepan and separate the meat from the bones. Do not bother with the wing tips, since there is so little useable meat there. Strain the broth and save it. Remove any fat, strings, or tough skin from the heart, liver, and gizzard. Take the cleaned giblets, neck meat, and the *prosciutto* and put everything through a meat grinder or mince very finely by hand. Put the additional olive oil and butter into a small saucepan over fairly high heat. When the butter is sizzling, add the minced meats. Stir until browned and then add the broth. When simmering, cover the pan, reduce the flame and cook gently for about an hour. At this point add the capers and some pepper. Do not add salt because chances are the capers will be salty enough. Cook for another ½ hour or until the guinea hen is ready. It may be necessary to add some water if the sauce becomes too thick and threatens to stick. If the sauce is too thin, remove the cover, increase the heat, and boil away some of the liquid. The sauce will never be thick and creamy, but neither should it be watery.

6. When the hen is ready (test by wiggling the legs and poking the breast with a fork), remove it from the oven and cut it into quarters. Place the quarters on warmed plates or on a warmed serving platter.

7. Add 4 tablespoons of the pan drippings to the sauce in the saucepan. Bring to a rapid boil for a moment, correct the seasoning, and then pour over the quartered guinea hen.

8. Serve immediately. This dish goes very well with a green salad and, of course, *polenta* (page 221).

OCA ROSTA COL PIEN
OCA ARROSTA RIPIENA
Roast Stuffed Goose

Because this main course is so rich, it is better not to serve pasta first. But be sure to have plenty of good dry red wine on hand, for both the goose and the stuffing invite one to imbibe freely.

This is a straightforward recipe, relatively simple to do, and ideal for serving 8 people if an old gosling or a young goose is used. Try to limit the size of the bird to 10 pounds dressed, since larger ones are too fatty and somewhat tougher.

The neck, feet, and wing tips make an excellent broth when simmered slowly for 3 hours with some celery, onion, and carrot. A small vegetable *risotto* made with the broth could be served as a light first course if your guests are hearty eaters.

The excess fat may be rendered and substituted for part of the olive oil or other fat in the cooking of vegetables.

FOR 8 SERVINGS:

A young goose or gosling, 8 to 10 pounds dressed
4 ounces prosciutto crudo *or other ham*
3 ounces spicy salami
½ clove garlic, peeled and very finely minced, or
    ¾ clove garlic, peeled and squeezed through
    a garlic press
3 eggs, slightly beaten
3 tablespoons finely chopped parsley
½ cup grated Parmesan cheese
Salt and pepper
1 to 1½ cups bread crumbs
Another clove garlic, peeled and cut
    in half crosswise
Salt pork, 8 slices about 6 by 1½ by ⅛ inches,
    5 or 6 ounces total
Olive oil

1. Remove the neck, feet, and wing tips from the goose (and make broth with them as suggested above). Pull or cut away the fat from

around the body openings and wash the goose thoroughly inside and out. Place the bird so that it can drain.

2. Clean the giblets, cutting away any fat or strings. It is particularly important to remove the tough skin on the gizzard, leaving only the dark red meat.

3. Run the giblets, *prosciutto crudo*, and salami through a meat grinder, or chop everything extremely fine. Place in a mixing bowl.

4. Add the garlic to the mixing bowl and mix well. Then add the eggs, parsley, and the cheese. Add some salt,.but little if you used *prosciutto* or other salty ham. Use some pepper, but not too much if the salami was very spicy. Mix well with a fork.

5. Start adding the bread crumbs. How much should be added will depend upon the size of the giblets and eggs and how absorbent the crumbs are. Add crumbs until you have a mixture that is no longer runny, thick enough to be shaped, but still very moist. This should take between 1 and 1½ cups.

6. Preheat the oven to 350 degrees.

7. If the goose is still wet, dry it with a towel. Put the stuffing inside and close the body openings with skewers or large needle and thread. Tie the legs together so that they remain close to the body. Do the same with the wings.

8. Rub the skin with a piece of garlic and sprinkle on some salt. Place the strips of salt pork over the breast and legs. Protect the latter particularly well.

9. Add a few drops of olive oil to a roasting pan and smear it around. Put the goose in the pan and the pan into the preheated oven. Cook a 9-pound bird 4 hours; cook an 8-pounder 15 minutes less and a 10-pounder 15 minutes more. During cooking baste the bird every 15 minutes after the first 45. After each basting prick the skin with a fork to allow grease to escape. Do this over as much of the bird's surface as possible. Do not go in deep with the fork, just enough to break the skin.

10. Serve on a platter and carve at the table. Goose goes well with a green vegetable or salad.

POLASTREI A LA DIAVOLA
POLLASTRELLI ALLA GRIGLIA
Broiled Chicken

This dish makes the mouth water; one can almost taste the chicken just by seeing it! Readily digestible, very flavorful, and most pleasing to those looking for an excuse to enjoy a light dry red wine of the first quality.

Here is another simple, straightforward recipe. It is best when the chickens are small broilers, a pound and a half being ideal, but slightly larger birds may also be used with excellent results.

FOR 2 SERVINGS:

A small broiling chicken, about 1½ pounds
   dressed
Olive oil
Salt and pepper
(Lemon wedges)

1. Using poultry shears or a sharp knife, cut along one side of the backbone of the chicken, then the other, and remove it. Use it, the neck, and the wing tips to make broth for another day.

2. Place the chicken skin side down, and chop the breastbone with a large sharp knife just enough to make the chicken lie flat. Turn the bird over and hit it with the flat side of a meat cleaver to flatten it further. Do not overdo it, though, or you will break every bone in its body. The idea is to flatten the bird but not completely crush it.

3. Rub the chicken with some olive oil, coating it thoroughly inside and out. Sprinkle with quite a bit of salt and pepper and place on a platter. Allow to marinate for an hour or more; 2 hours is not too long. Turn the chicken occasionally while it is marinating.

4. Preheat the broiler.

5. Place the chicken on a broiling rack, skin side toward the flame. Place in the broiler about 6 inches from the heat. (The heat should be from medium to high, depending upon the type of equipment you have.) If you are using charcoal, cook the chicken 6 inches from a medium or slightly less than medium fire.

6. Baste frequently during cooking with the olive oil in which the chicken was marinated. Cook for 10 minutes, turn, and cook the other

side the same amount of time. Turn again and cook until tender and well browned, another 10 minutes or so. Use these instructions as a rule of thumb. You may have to flip the chicken again and give it still another 10 minutes. Test with a fork for tenderness.

7. Cut the chicken into 2 pieces and serve very hot on warmed plates. Venetians often squirt a little lemon juice onto the chicken. A green salad or a green vegetable will go nicely with this dish. If only a light first course was served, you may wish to have potatoes also.

POLASTRO IN SQUARQUACIÒ
POLLO IN UMIDO
Chicken in Umido

Here is a delicious dish which one may eat happily at any time, but especially when the appetite makes one listen and the stomach asks for something substantial.

We have retained the expression *in umido* in the title because neither stewed nor braised seems to describe it exactly. It certainly is less liquid than a stew, but still more liquid than braised.

The recipe below is sufficient for 4 people if a first course has been served. As a *piatto unico*, a one-course meal, the size of the chicken and the other ingredients should be increased, as well as the cooking time.

A small or medium-sized chicken may be quartered to make 4 serving pieces. If the chicken is larger, save the wing tips, backbone, neck, and gizzard to make broth.

FOR 4 SERVINGS:

A 1¾ pound chicken, dressed
4 tablespoons butter
5 tablespoons olive oil
3 ribs celery, finely diced
1 medium carrot, finely diced
1 small onion, chopped
½ cup good dry white wine
5 tablespoons tomato sauce (page 218)
Salt and pepper
(8 small new potatoes, peeled)
(Water)

1. Cut the chicken into pieces as discussed above. Wash well and dry.

2. Put the butter, olive oil, and vegetables in a flameproof casserole or other pan large enough to hold all the pieces of chicken in one layer. Cook over medium heat, stirring occasionally, until the onion becomes translucent, about 5 minutes.

3. Add the chicken and brown on both sides, then add the wine, tomato sauce, and salt and pepper. Mix well and cover the cooking vessel. When a simmer is reached, reduce the heat to very low and cook until the chicken is tender, an hour or a little longer depending upon the chicken.

4. A little more than halfway through the cooking, small peeled new potatoes may be added.

5. Stir the chicken every now and then while cooking to be sure that the sauce is not becoming too thick and threatening to stick to the bottom of the pan. It may be necessary to add a little water. After an hour, start testing the chicken for tenderness by poking it with a fork.

6. When the chicken is tender, serve it on warmed plates or a warmed platter. Pour the sauce on top. If you choose not to use potatoes, serve with *polenta* (page 221), or with fresh Italian or French bread.

POLO ROSTO
POLLO ARROSTO CON PEPERONE
Roast Chicken with Bell Pepper

An ordinary dish without pretensions, this is pleasingly flavorful and makes one relish a good glass of red wine. Neither should one scorn a glass of beer with chicken so prepared.

Use a broiling chicken for this recipe instead of a roaster. It should weigh not more than 2 pounds; 1½ is ideal. It will serve 4 people adequately if a pasta course has been eaten before, or 2 people as a one-course meal.

FOR 4 SERVINGS AS PART OF A 2 COURSE MEAL:

A broiling chicken 1½ pounds dressed
1 fairly large green bell pepper
Butter
Salt and pepper
Olive oil

1. Wash the chicken and drain, or dry it with a cloth.

2. Preheat the oven to 400 degrees.

3. Cut the bell pepper in half and remove the seeds and the stem part. Wash thoroughly. Generously butter the inside of the pepper halves.

4. Sprinkle some salt and pepper inside the chicken. Put the pepper halves back together and place inside the chicken. It may be necessary to close the chicken with skewers in order to keep the pepper from popping out.

5. Rub the outside of the chicken with olive oil and sprinkle with a generous amount of salt and pepper.

6. Butter a shallow casserole or a baking dish. Use a goodly amount of butter and add a tablespoonful or so of olive oil. Place the chicken in the casserole and the casserole in the preheated oven. Turn the chicken about every 10 minutes so that a different part is facing up, basting at the same time. Cook for an hour or until the skin has taken on a golden color and the meat is tender. Test for tenderness by wiggling the legs of the chicken and by piercing the breasts with a fork. A 1½ pound bird should need an hour and a quarter maximum, a heavier bird slightly longer.

7. Serve the chicken and pepper either hot or cold with a green salad or a cooked green vegetable.

POLENTA E OSEI
UCCELLI CON POLENTA
Birds and Polenta

This is a dish for hunting season. The birds preferred are the types becco gentile, *which is to say birds with rather long and very thin beaks,* beccofichi, *those that eat figs, and* allodale, *larks.*

Actually, almost anything that has wings seems to be fair game in Italy, sparrows and pigeons included.

The recipe given below is for cooking on top of the stove. Broiled birds are also good, but then there is no sauce for the *polenta*.

FOR EACH SERVING:

> *5 or 6 birds, about 2 inches long and*
> *1 inch wide, after skinning*
> *4 or 5 slices of salt pork, each 1" by 1" by ¼"*
> *Fresh sage leaves, or dried sage leaves*
>   *soaked in water for 15 minutes*
> *Olive oil*
> *Salt and pepper*
> *Butter*
> *(Water)*

1. Skin and clean the birds. Do not bother to save the giblets. Often the heads are left attached so that the diner may suck out the brains.

2. Alternate the birds, the pieces of salt pork, and the sage leaves on a skewer, starting and finishing with a bird. Coat everything with a generous amount of olive oil and sprinkle with salt and pepper.

3. Melt enough butter in a frying pan to coat the bottom lightly. Add a like amount of olive oil. Set the heat at medium or slightly lower and add the skewered birds. Cook covered, but check every few minutes at the beginning to see that the birds are not sticking. Turn the birds several times during cooking and baste them. If the birds and salt pork do not provide enough juices for basting, add a little water. The idea is to have just enough liquid for basting, but not so much that the birds are swimming. Cooking can take surprisingly long; as long as 40 minutes. This is a tricky recipe for timing, so start testing early and often by wiggling the legs and poking the breast with a fork.

4. Serve the skewered birds on warmed plates and pour the sauce over them. Serve with *polenta* (page 221).

LEPRE A LA CACIATORA
LEPRE ALLA CACCIATORA
Hare Hunter's Style

Game is not often eaten in Venice, but during hunting season there are few gourmets who do not endeavor to make a feast of it. One of the preferred types of game is hare, which when prepared a la caciatora results in a truly exquisite dish, delicious but rather heavy.

This recipe is not especially difficult, but it requires plenty of time to prepare. The hare must be soaked in vinegar for at least 3 hours before cooking, and the cooking time may be as long as 4 hours. The latter depends upon the age of the hare, what kind of a life it led, and how long it has been hung.

Some people who have had dishes *alla cacciatora* in restaurants may be surprised by the color of this sauce, which is not red, but rather a very dark brown.

FOR 5 OR 6 SERVINGS:

> *A hare, about 5 pounds, 3½ pounds dressed*
> *White wine vinegar*
> *5 ounces butter*
> *3½ ounces salt pork cut into ½-inch cubes*
> *1 cup olive oil*
> *1 large onion, chopped*
> *⅔ cup good dry red wine*
> *1 stick cinnamon*
> *3 cloves*
> *Salt and pepper*
> *(Water)*

1. Have the butcher clean the hare and cut it into serving pieces. Save the liver for later in the recipe. Wash the pieces of hare thoroughly and place them in a ceramic bowl. Completely cover the hare with vinegar and allow to soak for 3 hours, turning it occasionally. We have soaked hare overnight, but the resulting dish comes out more like pickled hare than hare *a la caciatora*.

2. Remove the hare from the vinegar and rinse with running water, and allow to drain well.

3. Place the butter, salt pork, and olive oil in a frying pan or flameproof casserole, preferably large enough to accommodate the hare in a single layer. The cooking vessel must have a lid, as later in the recipe the hare will be cooked covered. Add the onion and place the pan over medium heat. Cook the onion until translucent, 5 minutes or so.

4. Add the hare and turn the pieces once or twice while cooking, for about 15 minutes. The hare should provide enough liquid to prevent the onions from browning, but it may be necessary to lower the flame somewhat.

5. Add the wine, cinnamon, cloves, a little salt, and quite a bit of pepper. Mix well, cover, and reduce the heat to a point where a very gentle simmer is maintained. If much liquid escapes during simmering, add a little water to replace it.

6. Cook the hare until it just begins to become tender, 1½ to 3 hours. While the hare is cooking, prepare all the ingredients for the following sauce.

The sauce:

3 salted anchovies (page 128), or 8 canned
    flat anchovy fillets packed in olive oil
4 ounces hare liver, or hare and calf's liver mixed
3 thick slices lean bacon
1½ tablespoons butter
1 ounce finely diced citron
¼ teaspoon grated nutmeg
Salt and pepper

1. Prepare the salted anchovies in the manner described on page 128, or if canned anchovies are used, merely cut them up into small pieces.

2. Chop the liver and bacon extremely fine, or better, put them through a meat grinder.

3. When the hare has just started to show signs of tenderness, melt the butter in a small frying pan over medium heat. Add the anchovies, liver, bacon, spices, and salt and pepper. Stir until the meats are well browned. This will take about 5 minutes.

4. Add the sauce to the frying pan containing the hare, mix well, and continue cooking until the hare is very tender; perhaps as long as an hour longer, but probably much less. Add water if necessary to keep the sauce from sticking.

5. The hare may be served immediately or reheated later. If reheated, add some water if there seems to be too little liquid to provide steam readily.

6. Serve on warmed plates, accompanied by *polenta* (page 221).

ANARA SELVADEGA
ANATRA SELVATICA O GERMANO
Wild Duck

Although Venetians as a group do not eat much in the way of game, there are, naturally, exceptions. Among these are the marsh hunters who wait in ambush for the migratory birds that in late autumn seek the more temperate climates of South Europe and North Africa. One of these birds is the mallard, which when properly prepared results in a delicious dish.

Before the postwar development of the mainland near Venice there were many marshes where ducks going to winter could stop. These marshes are mostly gone now and there is very little hunting left. This recipe is rapidly becoming a curiosity.

A mallard is called for, but other types may be substituted. The recipe should be of great value to hunters who have come home with "fish" ducks, since the marinade and the sauce should cover up or clear up the offensive flavor.

FOR 2 VERY GENEROUS SERVINGS:

Marinating the duck:

A mallard, 2 to 2¼ pounds before dressing
Water and vinegar, 2 parts water to
  1 part vinegar
2 ribs celery, cut into 1-inch lengths
1 medium carrot, coarsely diced
½ medium onion, coarsely chopped
8 rosemary leaves, fresh if possible,
  slightly crushed

1. Remove all the feathers and dress the duck. Do not skin it. Save the giblets. Discard the neck or leave it on, as you please. Cut the duck into quarters and wash it well.

2. Place the duck quarters in a ceramic bowl and cover with the water-vinegar mixture.

3. Add the vegetables and the rosemary. Cover and place in the refrigerator. Allow to marinate for 24 hours.

Cooking the duck:

The duck giblets
1 salted anchovy (page 128), or 3 flat canned
    anchovy fillets packed in olive oil
1 ounce prosciutto crudo or other ham
1 ounce spicy salami
Salt and pepper
3 tablespoons olive oil
2 tablespoons butter
3 ribs celery, finely diced
½ medium carrot, finely diced
½ medium onion, finely chopped
1 tablespoon finely chopped parsley
1 tablespoon capers
1 cup dry white wine

1. Wash the giblets well, removing any strings and fat. Pay particular attention to remove the tough outer skin from the gizzard, leaving only the dark red meat.

2. Prepare the salted anchovy (page 218), or use canned fillets. Run the giblets through a meat grinder along with the *prosciutto*, salami, and the salted anchovy (or the canned anchovy fillets). If you do not have a meat grinder, mince everything thoroughly.

3. Remove the duck pieces from the bowl and wash under running water. Dry the pieces well and sprinkle them with salt and pepper. Discard the marinade.

4. Put the olive oil and butter in a flameproof casserole or a fairly deep frying pan large enough to hold the duck in a single layer over medium heat. The cooking vessel must have a lid. When the butter has melted and is sizzling, add the vegetables and the duck. Cook, stirring regularly, until the onion becomes translucent and the duck is lightly browned, 5 to 8 minutes. Add the giblet-ham-salami-anchovy mixture and the capers. Mix well and cook 3 minutes or so until the giblets have browned a bit. Pour in the wine and mix well. Cover the pan and reduce the heat to a point where a simmer is maintained. Turn the pieces of duck occasionally. If during cooking the sauce thickens too much and threatens to stick, add more wine. At the end of cooking the sauce should be thick. If it is too thin, remove the cover and boil away the excess liquid.

5. It is difficult to say how long the duck will take to cook, since that will depend upon its age and where it has been. It may take as long as 2½ hours; start testing, however, after 1½. It is a dish that may be reheated without fear.

6. When the duck is tender, correct the seasoning and serve on warmed plates. Pour the sauce over and accompany with *polenta* (page 221).

Secondi Piati Vari
Secondi Piatti Vari
MISCELLANEOUS MAIN COURSES

THERE ARE A couple of good recipes in this section for finishing up leftover meat and fowl: a simple and quick one with sausage, a number dealing with eggs, two for asparagus, and finally a joke on the hunter who returns home empty-handed: escaped birds.

Besides being fun, these recipes are some of the most practical in the book from the standpoint of economy and convenience.

POLPETE DE CARNE
POLPETTINE DI CARNE
Meat Patties

This is a very economical dish because the main ingredient is leftover meat. Beef, veal, and chicken are all acceptable, alone or in combination, no matter whether boiled or roasted. It is not a pretentious dish but one that can be served without excuses, for when properly prepared it turns out very nicely, tasty and easy to digest.

High tide in Piazza San Marco.

FOR 4 SCANT OR 3 GENEROUS SERVINGS AS A MAIN COURSE:

½ pound cooked beef, veal, or chicken,
   or a mixture
⅛ pound prosciutto crudo *or other ham,*
   or salami
2 tablespoons finely chopped parsley
½ cup grated Parmesan cheese
½ cup moist bread without crusts,
   broken into very small pieces
Milk
1 large or 2 small eggs, lightly beaten
(Bread crumbs)
Salt and pepper
3 tablespoons butter
Flour
(¾ cup tomato sauce [page 218])

1. Mince the meat and the ham or salami, or better, put them through a meat grinder. Place in a mixing bowl.

2. Add the parsley and cheese.

3. Put the bread into a measuring cup. Add some milk and stir with a fork to break up the bread pieces until the mixture becomes a paste. The total volume of the bread and milk should be about ½ cup. Add the paste to the bowl. Mix well.

4. Add enough of the beaten egg to the ingredients in the mixing bowl to attain a consistency somewhat like that of ham or tuna salad. The measure is not terribly critical, but the mixture should be moist rather than runny. If too runny, add some bread crumbs.

5. Add the salt and pepper and mix everything very well. Divide the mixture into 12 equal parts. Each part should be about the size and shape of a golf ball or a little larger.

6. Place a frying pan containing the butter over medium or slightly higher heat.

7. While the butter is heating, roll the meatballs in flour, flatten them to a thickness of about ¾ of an inch, and place them in the pan. Cook for about 4 minutes or until nicely browned and then turn them with a spatula. Cook for a like amount of time on the second side. Remove and place on warmed plates.

8. To improve this dish pour some hot tomato sauce (page 218) on top of the patties. *Polpete* may also be served cold.

LUGANEGHE AL BUTIRO E POLENTA
SALSICCIE AL BURRO CON POLENTA
Sausages in Butter and Vinegar
with Polenta

This dish makes a good breakfast, but be careful because salsiccie, *like all types of salami and sausage, are not easily digested, particularly when cooked in butter. Nevertheless, they make a nice meal, accompanied by a couple of glasses of white wine or beer and lots of* polenta.

If you have access to a good Italian grocer, ask him for the leanest *salsiccie* he has. The ideal ones are about 3 inches in length and an inch or more in diameter, and not overly fatty (all *salsiccie* are quite fatty, but some are really ridiculous).

If you cannot find *salsiccie*, substitute pork sausage or pork sausage patties. It will not be exactly the same but will give a pretty fair idea.

An excellent variation of the recipe as given below is to charcoal-broil the sausages before putting them in the pan with the butter and vinegar.

FOR EACH SERVING:

2 salsiccie *as discussed above, about ⅓ pound*
3 tablespoons butter
2 tablespoons vinegar, or more, to taste

1. Split the sausages lengthwise, cutting about ⅔ of the way through. Open the sausages and flatten them.

2. Cook the sausages slowly in a frying pan over low heat until most of the grease has come out, 15 minutes or more. Turn them every now and then.

3. When cooked, pour off most of the grease and add the butter. When the butter is sizzling, add the vinegar. Some people cover the pan upon adding the vinegar and simmer the sausages for 3 or 4 minutes so that they will absorb more.

4. When the butter and vinegar are well mixed and very hot, place the sausages on a warmed plate and pour the pan juices over them. *Polenta* (page 221) is almost a necessity with this dish, but fresh Italian or French bread will do in a pinch.

POLENTA E OSEI SCAMPAI
POLENTA E UCCELLI SCAPPATI
Polenta and Escaped Birds

In Venice there is an old saying: In mancanza dei gamberi, xe bone anche le sole zampe; *lacking shrimp, shrimp legs are also good. So if the hunter comes home empty-handed, use pieces of lean pork or veal in place of the birds. The result is a flavorful dish which should be eaten with* polenta.

Choose any lean cut of pork or veal as long as it is tender. It is particularly good with pork tenderloin. Allow about a pound and a quarter up to a pound and a half maximum for 4 servings. Follow the recipe for *polenta e osei* (page 179), substituting cubes of meat for the birds. The cooking time will be about half that for true birds.

SPARASI DE BASSAN COI VOVI DURI
SPARAGI DI BASSANO CON
UOVA SODE
Asparagus with Hard-boiled Eggs

(Follow the recipe on page 215 for the amount of and the method of cooking.)

Place sliced hard-boiled eggs on top of the asparagus on a hot serving platter. Dress the eggs as well as the asparagus with olive oil, salt, pepper, and vinegar or lemon juice.

Allow 1 or 2 eggs per person.

SPARASI COI VOVI L'OCIO DE BÒ
SPARAGI CON LE UOVA ALL'OCCHIO
DI BUE
Asparagus "Bull's Eye"

(Follow the recipe on page 215, but do not put dressing on the asparagus.) Put the asparagus on a hot platter and place eggs fried in butter on top, one egg per serving.

SUCHETE RIPIENE
ZUCCHINI RIPIENI
Stuffed Zucchini

This dish can be served either as a main course or as a vegetable course. Stuffed zucchini are very tasty and, depending upon the appetite, one can eat 4 or even 5 of them.

As a vegetable dish 2 zucchini per person should be sufficient, 3 a bit of an exaggeration, and 4 about right for a main course for people of normal appetite.

A mixed veal and ham stuffing is called for in this recipe. However, most any cooked meat or combination of meats may be used. It is a great way to clean out the refrigerator and still present an interesting meal.

FOR 10 STUFFED ZUCCHINI:

10 medium-sized zucchini, about 6 inches long
3 ounces cooked veal
3 ounces prosciutto crudo or other ham
2 large eggs, lightly beaten
Salt and pepper
3 ounces, more or less grated Parmesan cheese
2 ounces butter
3 tablespoons olive oil
(Water or broth)

1. Wash the zucchini thoroughly. Cut a little off of each end. Without breaking the skin of the zucchini, remove the center, using a slender knife, a vegetable peeler, or any other implement that will accomplish the job. The desired result is a zucchini tube with walls roughly ¼ inch thick. If the walls are too thick, the hole will be too small to allow the zucchini to be easily stuffed. If the walls are too thin, the zucchini may break during cooking or the stuffing run out the ends.

2. Mince the veal and ham or put them through a meat grinder. Combine the meat, eggs, and some salt and pepper in a mixing bowl and add enough cheese to bind the ingredients. The mixture should be solid enough not to leak out of the zucchini, but it should not be terribly dry. About 3 ounces of cheese should give the proper consistency, but much depends upon the size of the eggs and the quality of the cheese.

3. Fill the zucchini with the stuffing, not quite to the ends because the stuffing will expand during cooking.

4. Put the butter and oil in a frying pan over medium to medium-low heat. When the butter has melted, add the zucchini. Cover the pan. Turn them every 5 minutes or so, but turn them carefully, particularly toward the end of cooking, to avoid breaking them. Should they begin to stick, add a little water or broth to the pan.

5. Cook for about 30 minutes. The zucchini should be very tender when tested with a fork. They may be served immediately or allowed to cool.

VOVI
UOVA
Eggs

After meat eggs are probably the most nutritious protein food. Some people claim they are even superior to fish. Venetians, however, do not make great use of eggs. Eggs are given to babies so that they can obtain nutrition without having to chew too much, and they are given to elderly people for the same reason. They are also given to sick people, those in convalescence, and especially to women after childbirth.

In the following pages we shall try to systematically describe how Venetians eat eggs, starting with the most simple and working up.

VOVI CRUI
UOVA CRUDE
Raw Eggs

There are three ways in which Venetians eat raw eggs.

The first has no particular name but might simply be called *a bere*, to drink. The egg, both white and yolk, is drunk, usually out of the shell, with the addition of only a pinch of salt and pepper and a drop or two of lemon juice.

The second way is *a l'ostrega* in Venetian, *all'ostrica* in Italian;

"oyster style." Use only the yolk, holding it in a soup spoon. As before, add salt, pepper, and lemon juice.

The last way is more elaborate, and probably more acceptable to those not accustomed to eating raw eggs. Venetian *vovi batui*, Italian *uova battute*, "beaten eggs," are made by placing egg yolks, 1 or 2 per serving, in a glass or a bowl along with 2 teaspoonfuls of powdered sugar for each yolk. Beat thoroughly with a fork, wire whip, or egg beater. Whip until the mixture becomes very thick. Then add some marsala wine, 1½ table-spoonfuls for each yolk. In place of marsala you may use white wine, better red, even better good cognac. Mix well and serve with a biscuit. It makes an unusual but substantial breakfast.

VOVI COTI NE L'ACQUA
UOVA COTTE NELL'ACQUA
Eggs Cooked in Water

First, consider poached eggs, *vovi in camisa*, in Italian *uova in camicia*. (*In camisa*, incidentally, means "in its shirt," whatever that has to do with it.) Break the eggs gently into almost simmering water in a frying pan over low heat. Do this very carefully to avoid breaking the yolk. As soon as the white seems well set but the yolk still soft, remove the egg from the water with a slotted spoon so that the water drains off. Eggs so cooked are dressed with a little olive oil, vinegar, and salt and pepper, or with melted salted butter poured over and a dash of pepper on top. In either case some grated Parmesan cheese is sprinkled on and the eggs served on warmed plates.

The other way of cooking eggs in water is to boil them. Boiled eggs are prepared in three ways: *bazoti*, very soft, little more than warmed, to be drunk or eaten with a spoon; *molecai*, soft, but neither too soft nor too hard, eaten with a teaspoon; and *duri*, hard, but just barely. *Hard* hard-boiled eggs are not prepared in Venice except by mistake; or for use in another dish.

The eggs are placed in a saucepan and covered with cold water. Bring the water to a boil over medium to medium-high heat. When a rolling boil is reached, reduce to a slow boil and start timing, 2 minutes for *bazoti*, 4 for *molecai*, and 8 for *duri*. Remove the saucepan from the fire and place the eggs under very cold water to arrest the cooking. Serve the eggs *bazoti* or *molecai* immediately, but allow the eggs *duri* to cool completely before serving. Keep them in cold water, better ice water, for 15 minutes or so. This will prevent the yolks from discoloring. Eggs *duri* are shelled and sliced in half lengthwise, salted and peppered, and if so desired, dressed with a little oil and vinegar.

VOVI IN FORTAGIA
UOVA AL BURRO
Eggs Cooked in Butter

Eggs cooked in butter are divided into three categories: fried, scrambled, and omelets. The 2 recipes below are extensions of simple scrambled eggs. We also give 1 recipe for an omelet. First, though, let us look at fried eggs.

VOVI A L'OCIO DE BÒ
UOVA ALL'OCCHIO DI BUE
Eggs "Bull's Eye"; Fried Eggs

These eggs are merely fried in butter, something every American understands. Melt butter in a frying pan over fairly low heat and crack the eggs into the pan, being careful not to break the yolks. When the whites are firm but the yolks still soft, remove the eggs and serve them on warmed plates.

Scrambled eggs may be livened up by the addition of any one of a number of ingredients, the most common being tomato sauce (page 218), chicken livers, onion, bacon, or salami. The following 2 recipes give the idea.

VOVI STRAPASSAI CO LE SEGOLE
UOVA STRAPAZZATE CON CIPOLLA
Scrambled Eggs with Onions

FOR 4 SERVINGS:

1 large onion
3 ounces butter
3 tablespoons olive oil
Salt and pepper
8 eggs

1. Cut the onion into very thin slices.
2. Place a frying pan containing the butter, olive oil, and onions over a moderate flame. Add some salt and pepper. After the onions are well coated with butter and oil and have warmed, cover the pan and lower the heat. Cook for about a half hour stirring every now and then at first, and frequently toward the end. If after a half hour there is still a lot of liquid from the onions, remove the cover and cook a little longer over slightly higher heat. The onions should be light golden but not brown.
3. Break the eggs into a mixing bowl and beat lightly. Add some salt and pepper and beat again.
4. Pour the eggs into the pan containing the onions and cook them until firm but not dry. While cooking, move the eggs often using a spatula or fork. Serve immediately on warmed plates.

FORTAGIA ROGNOSA
UOVA STRAPAZZATE CON SALAME
Scrambled Eggs with Bacon and Salami

FOR 4 SERVINGS:

4 ounces sliced bacon
3 ounces salami, sliced
8 eggs
Salt and pepper
3 ounces butter

1. Cut the bacon slices crosswise into ½-inch lengths.

2. Cut the sliced salami into 1-inch pieces.

3. Cook the bacon until lightly browned in a frying pan over low heat. If the salami is very fat, it should be cooked with the bacon. If lean, add it just before the eggs in step 5.

4. Break the eggs into a mixing bowl and beat slightly. Add some salt and pepper and beat again.

5. Discard most of the grease from the pan containing the bacon and salami. Add the butter, and when it has melted pour the beaten eggs into the pan. Cook as usual, stirring frequently with a spatula or fork until the eggs are firm but still moist.

6. Serve immediately on warmed plates.

The last way eggs are cooked in butter is *fritada*, the omelet.

FRITADE
FRITTATE
Omelets

For lack of a more descriptive term we use the word omelet in the English title to describe a *fritada*. It is in fact a cousin of the French omelet, but a distant cousin. In the Venetian omelet the eggs and the filling are incorporated prior to being placed in the frying pan. Sometimes the eggs are added to the already cooking filling. The Venetian omelet is not shaken in the pan to give the characteristic oblong shape of French omelets. It is round and hard, cooked completely through.

The following recipe, probably the most popular *fritada*, will serve as a model. Other possibilities for *fritade* include ones made with salami, chicken livers, ham, soft cheese, grated hard cheese, tomato sauce (page 218), parsley, onion (cooked or raw), boiled zucchini slices, boiled asparagus tips, peas sautéed in butter, or mushrooms sautéed in butter and olive oil.

FRITADA COI SPINASI
FRITTATA CON SPINACI
Spinach Omelet

FOR 4 SERVINGS:

1 pound spinach
2 tablespoons butter
1½ tablespoons olive oil
1 tablespoon finely chopped parsley
½ medium onion, finely chopped
(Water)
6 large eggs
Another 2 ounces butter

1. Break off and discard the spinach stems. Tear large leaves into 2 or 3 pieces. Wash thoroughly, using several changes of water. When the spinach is sand free, put it in a pot and place the pot over a low flame. The water remaining on the spinach from the washing is sufficient—it may even be too much. The idea is to slightly cook and dry the spinach at the same time. Stir frequently and press down with a wooden spoon in order to squeeze out the moisture. Continue in this way until the spinach just begins to stick to the bottom of the pan. This should take about 10 minutes.

2. Place a frying pan containing the butter and olive oil over a low heat. When the butter has melted, add the parsley, onion, and spinach. Mix well and cook for about 20 minutes. If you have done your job too well in the first step above, the precooking of the spinach, you may need to add a few drops of water at this point. You should have the mixture quite dry, but not so dry that it might burn. After 20 minutes, set the pan aside and let the contents cool.

3. Break the eggs into a mixing bowl and lightly beat them. Combine the cooled contents of the frying pan with the eggs and mix well.

4. Take a second frying pan and place it over a medium flame. Add the butter and when it is bubbling nicely, pour the contents of the mixing bowl into the pan. Cook as if you were scrambling eggs, using a fork or spatula to scrape the eggs from the bottom of the pan. When the eggs begin to firm up but are still rather runny, stop stirring and allow a crust

to form on the bottom. Work a spatula under and peek to see when the crust is light golden brown.

5. Now comes the tricky part, turning the omelet. The easy way is to have another frying pan buttered, warmed, and waiting. Place it over the first pan like a lid and then in one quick movement reverse the pans. Be sure before doing this that the omelet is completely detached from the bottom of the first pan. If you do not have a second frying pan, try to flip the omelet with two spatulas, or cut the omelet into halves or quarters and flip each piece separately.

6. Brown the second side and transfer the omelet to a warmed serving platter. Serve immediately. It may also be eaten cold later.

RECIPES IN OTHER SECTIONS OF THE BOOK for dishes which may be served as main courses:

Boiled Eel (page 65). The only time we serve boiled eel is when a *risotto* has been made with the broth for a first course.

Baked Scallops (page 3). Double or slightly more than double the recipe as a main course. Six large scallops in three shells make a generous serving and present an appealing picture.

Crab (page 13). For some reason only rarely eaten as a main course.

Poached Turbot (page 84). The by-product of an excellent *risotto*.

Beef Nerve Salad (page 23). Quite rich. Better to serve a light first course.

Braised Savoy Cabbage (page 217). An excellent vegetable dish that becomes even better as a main course with the addition of spareribs. Quite heavy.

Beans in Sauce (page 206). As close as you can come in Venice to baked beans, though they are not baked but cooked on top of the stove.

Braised Artichoke Hearts (page 203). A good substitute second course when the first has been particularly heavy.

Boiled Artichoke Hearts with Salty Cheese (page 24). The salty cheese helps build a pretty fair thirst.

Braised Eggplant (page 211). Gives the impression of being heavier than it is, but still substantial.

Baked Tomatoes and Onions (page 213). For those who are fond of onions, this goes well after a heavy first course.

Braised Green Beans (page 216). You may wish to add a few bits of diced bacon to this one.

Contorni
VEGETABLES, SAUCES, ETC.

THE ITALIAN WORD *contorno* has several meanings, one of which is "vegetable." For our purposes here we prefer the meanings "outline" and "border," since we also include in this part tomato sauce, *polenta*, and *crostini*, Italian croutons. These things as well as vegetables in a sense surround the *minestra* or *secondo piatto*.

We have given only the most interesting and useful dishes and it should not be concluded that Venetians limit themselves to the few *contorni* included here. They eat potatoes, cauliflower, Brussels sprouts, spinach, etc., but there is nothing special about their preparation, so they have been omitted.

Salads have also been omitted, but we should say something about them. A much greater variety of salad greens is available in Italy than in America. They may be eaten singly but are more often mixed and combined with green tomatoes (which are less juicy than ripe ones and therefore they do not dilute the dressing), fennel, carrots, and celery. The result is called *insalata capricciosa*, capricious or whimsical salad. Salads are always dressed with olive oil, vinegar, and salt and pepper, the relative amounts to taste.

A last word about vegetables. Venetian vegetable dishes are so flavorful because the vegetables themselves are so good. Hothouse, frozen, and canned vegetables are used only as a last resort. For greater enjoyment try to plan your vegetable dishes around those things that are grown locally or those which arrive in the market really fresh.

Venice's main market area, from the Rialto Bridge.

ARTICIOCHI IN TECIA
CARCIOFI IN TEGAME
Braised Artichokes

This dish is usually served as a vegetable course, but because artichokes prepared in this manner are so tasty, one can eat 3 or 4 in place of a second course, accompanied by bread.

The artichokes adapted to this recipe are those about 2½ inches long from the base to the top of the leaves. They have little or no choke (the furry material attached inside the artichoke to the heart) and, therefore, require a minimum of preparation for cooking.

The same recipe may be applied to globe artichokes, the variety most often found in the United States, but the results will not be quite so successful. Cut globe artichokes in halves or quarters and remove as much of the choke as possible, removing the rest after cooking but before serving. Follow the recipe below, but cook globe artichokes longer, 45 minutes or more.

FOR 4 SERVINGS AS A VEGETABLE COURSE OR 2 AS A MAIN COURSE:

8 artichokes, 2½ inches from base to top
Olive oil
4, 5, or more sprigs of parsley, enough to give
  3 tablespoons of chopped leaves
1 clove garlic, peeled and cut in half crosswise
Salt and pepper
More olive oil, 1½ tablespoons for
  each artichoke
(Water)

1. Cut off and save the artichoke stems; cut off and discard about ½ inch from the tops. Remove the outer leaves and discard. Wash thoroughly with running water. Open the tops of the artichokes to a diameter about equal to that of the bases.

2. Lightly coat the bottom of a flameproof casserole or a saucepan with olive oil. Put the artichokes upright in the cooking vessel. (If globe artichokes are used, they will, of course, be lying on their sides, the tough outer leaves in contact with the bottom of the pan.)

3. Wash the parsley and shake dry. Rub the parsley leaves with the

cut side of the garlic, pulling the leaves away from the stems. Do this on a wooden cutting board if possible. When the leaves have been separated from the stems, rub the leaves with the other piece of garlic. Chop the leaves very fine.

4. Divide the parsley evenly among the artichokes, sprinkling it on top of them. Shake some salt and pepper onto the artichokes and pour about 1½ tablespoons of olive oil over each one. Cover the cooking vessel and place over medium heat. After 2 or 3 minutes move the artichokes to be sure that they do not stick to the bottom. Reduce the heat to very low. The residual water from the washing of the artichokes should provide enough liquid for the first 10 to 15 minutes of cooking. When and if necessary, add additional water. There should be only enough to produce some steam. While the artichokes are cooking, go on to the next step.

5. Peel the artichoke stems. The center of the stem has excellent flavor, but the outside is extremely bitter. It is easy to distinguish the good part from the bitter, the good appearing as a tube surrounded by a fibrous casing. Using a potato peeler or a knife, cut away the outside casing and scrape away any stringy pieces adhering to the center. Slice the stems into 2-inch lengths and add to the artichokes after the latter have cooked for about 20 minutes.

6. The artichokes should be tender after 30 minutes. Test by sticking the artichoke bottoms, not the leaves, with a fork. Place the artichokes on a serving platter and spoon the juices over them. Serve either hot or cold.

FONDI DE ARTICIOCO IN TECIA
FONDI DI CARCIOFO IN TEGAME
Braised Artichoke Hearts

This vegetable dish goes very well with both meat and chicken, either boiled or roasted. But, not to burden the stomach, 3 or 4 artichoke hearts may be served in place of a main course.

As a vegetable course, 2 artichoke hearts 2½ inches in diameter should make an ample serving.

We do not recommend canned artichoke hearts for this recipe, nor any other for that matter.

FOR EACH ARTICHOKE HEART:

> *An artichoke with a base about 2½ inches across*
> *Olive oil*
> *Finely chopped parsley, 1½ teaspoons,*
>   *more or less*
> *Garlic*
> *Salt and pepper*
> *More olive oil*
> *Water*

1. Separate the artichoke heart from the stem, leaves, and choke (the furry material inside the artichoke attached to the top of the heart) by the following method: Slice off the stem right at the base. Then, starting at the bottom, work around the circumference, cutting off the leaves just at the point where they are attached to the heart. Continue working around the circumference and upward until the top of the heart has been reached. Then cut across the artichoke parallel to the base, removing the top leaves and all the choke. The result should be a disc about 2½ inches in diameter and about ½ inch high.

2. Wash the artichoke heart. Artichoke hearts may be stored for several hours in cold water. If stored longer they tend to become woody.

3. Coat the bottom and sides of a frying pan with a generous amount of olive oil. The pan should be large enough to hold all the hearts in a single layer without overlapping. Place in the pan base side down.

4. Chop the parsley. If just a little bit of garlic is desired, cut a peeled clove of garlic in half crosswise and rub the parsley with it. For more garlic either use a garlic press or mince the garlic very finely with a knife. Combine the garlic and parsley and mix well. Spread about 1½ teaspoons of the parsley evenly on top of the artichoke heart. Sprinkle on some salt and pepper and pour about 1 teaspoon of olive oil over the heart.

5. Add a little water to the frying pan, cover, and place over a moderate flame. Reduce to very low when the water starts to boil. At the end of cooking most of the water should have boiled off, but check also to be sure that there is always some water, as it is the steam that does most of the cooking. Using a spatula, move the hearts occasionally during cooking to make sure they do not stick to the bottom of the pan.

6. Cook for 25 minutes, more or less, depending upon whether you like artichoke hearts very soft (as the Venetians do) or more firm. Test them with a fork for tenderness. If at the end of cooking there is still a

lot of water in the pan, cook uncovered over a higher flame for a minute or two to drive it off.

7. Serve immediately on a warmed plate, or later, cold. Either way, spoon on top the oil remaining in the pan.

FASIOI LESSI
FAGIOLI ALLESSI
Boiled Beans

All one needs to prepare beans properly are a pot, water, and salt; and most important, patience!

Cranberry beans, the Italian *fagioli*, can be found in Italian grocery stores in America. Kidney, navy, pinto, and most any other type of bean may be cooked in the same way.

There is the problem that some varieties of beans will purée on prolonged cooking. We have had some supposedly good cranberry beans turn to mush after only an hour and a half. Consult your grocer, but even he may not know. There seems to be no answer to this problem other than to try the beans and hope for the best. If you find yourself holding a bag of beans that purée, use them for *pasta e fagioli* (page 97) rather than throw them out.

FOR 4 SERVINGS:

1 pound fresh beans or ¾ pound dried beans
Water
Salt
Olive oil
Vinegar
Pepper
(More salt)
(Chopped or sliced onion)

1. If the beans are fresh they need not be soaked. Otherwise, soak dried beans overnight, at least 10 hours. Place in a pot and cover with an abundant amount of water.

2. Pour the soaked beans onto a colander and rinse under running water. Return the beans to the pot a handful at a time while continuing to wash them in order to remove any foreign matter.

3. Cover the beans with water as before and add a little less salt than you might think necessary. Bring to a simmer and cook fresh beans 2½ hours, dried beans 4 hours or more. This may sound like a long time, but your gastric tract will thank you for your patience.

4. When the beans are cooked, add cold water to the pot. This will help prevent the skins from breaking. Allow the beans to cool in their water and then drain them.

5. Dress with olive oil, vinegar, pepper, and more salt if needed. You may also add some onion. Serve at room temperature.

FASIOI IN TECIA
FAGIOLI IN UMIDO
Beans in Sauce

This is a good side dish for boiled meats, but it also goes well with roasts. People who like beans and do not suffer many visceral disturbances can eat them as a main course, accompanied by polenta or bread.

(See the remarks about beans in the preceding recipe.)

FOR 4 SERVINGS AS A SIDE DISH:

1 pound fresh beans or ¾ pound dried beans
Water
Salt
3 ounces salt pork
3 tablespoons olive oil
1 medium onion, chopped
2 tablespoons finely chopped parsley
3 tablespoons tomato sauce (page 218)
(½ cup dry red wine)
Pepper

1. Follow the first 2 steps in the preceding recipe.

2. Barely cover the beans with cold water, add a very little salt, and place the pot over high heat. When a simmer has been reached, reduce the heat to very low and cover the pot. Simmer until half cooked, 1¼ hours for fresh beans, 2 hours for dried beans. It is very easy to burn the beans, so stir them frequently adding water as needed.

3. While the beans are still cooking, put the salt pork through a meat grinder or mince it extremely fine. Put the salt pork and olive oil in a second pot over medium heat. When the salt pork just begins to take on a golden color, add the onion and cook until it becomes translucent, 5 minutes or so. Add the parsley and tomato sauce, stir, and reduce the heat to very low.

4. Drain the beans in the first pot, but save the cooking water. Put the drained beans with the other ingredients in the second pot and mix well. Add enough of the reserved liquid to prevent the beans from sticking. A half cup of red wine may be substituted for part of the other liquid. Stir often.

5. After ½ hour or so add some pepper and check to see if more salt is needed. Finish the cooking, stirring regularly and adding more liquid as necessary. The sauce should have about the same consistency as that for baked beans or perhaps slightly thinner.

6. The beans may be served hot, tepid, or cold. They may also be reheated.

FUNGHETI IN TECIA
FUNGHETTI IN UMIDO
Braised Mushrooms

The mushrooms preferred are those of middle size, which is to say those of proper maturity. Larger, they become too soft and pulpy, while the small are too hard.

This excellent vegetable is reputed by some to be one of the most nutritious, but it is probably prized for its aroma and flavor more than for its healthful properties.

There are many varieties of edible mushrooms, but the one least popular in Venice is the one found most often in the United States, the *champignon*. If you are fortunate enough to have access to other varieties, try them, particularly the tougher ones that have more pronounced flavor.

The cooking time from one type of mushroom to another varies tremendously. For *champignons* ½ hour at the most should be sufficient, while for some other varieties you may need up to 2 hours. The only thing to do is to test them regularly during cooking.

Another factor to consider is the quantity of mushrooms to buy. A pound of one variety may seem in taste like 2 pounds of another. Think in terms of 1 pound for 4 servings (understanding that quite a bit will be lost in cleaning) and hope for the best.

You may wish to try this recipe with dried mushrooms. They will definitely give more flavor than *champignon*, but be sure to read the soaking instructions on the package carefully. Some need to soak for only ½ hour in tepid water, while others require 10 hours or longer in cold water. Also, remember that the weight will double or triple as the water is absorbed.

FOR 4 SERVINGS:

> *1 pound mushrooms*
> *Salted water, 2 tablespoons salt per quart water*
> *1 clove garlic, peeled*
> *⅓ cup olive oil*
> *2 tablespoons finely chopped parsley*
> *Pepper*
> *(Salt)*

1. Prepare the mushrooms by cutting off tough parts of the stems and any blemishes. Wash well under running water. Cut the mushrooms into pieces having an inch or so as the largest dimension. Wash again and then place in clean salted water to soak for ½ hour. Soaking in salted water is supposed to induce any worms to vacate the mushrooms.

2. Brown the garlic in a frying pan or saucepan containing the olive oil over medium heat, then remove and discard it. Allow the pan to cool a bit.

3. Replace the pan over medium heat. Add the parsley and the mushrooms and some pepper. Do not add salt, since the mushrooms will have absorbed some during soaking. Stir well, coating the mushrooms with the oil, then turn the heat down to low when the mushrooms have warmed. Whether you cook the mushrooms covered or uncovered will depend upon the type of mushroom. Some will absorb so much water during soaking that when all the water comes out during cooking it will seem that you have almost a mushroom soup. Others will absorb little water and should be covered during cooking. The plan should be not too much and not too little, until the mushrooms are fairly tender. When this point is reached, worry about the water. When finished, almost all the water

should have either been absorbed or boiled away, leaving the mushrooms in a thick sauce.

4. Correct the seasoning. Mushrooms so prepared may be served hot, tepid, or cold.

MELANSANE AI FERI
MELANZANE ALLA GRATICOLA
Broiled Eggplant

For this vegetable side dish it is necessary to choose the large round variety of eggplant.

These eggplants are those most often found in the United States. The recipe is exceptionally simple to prepare and the results pleasing.

FOR 4 SERVINGS:

> *A round eggplant 1 to 1½ pounds*
> *Salt and pepper*
> *Olive oil*

1. Wash but do not peel the eggplant. Cut it into slices about ⅓ inch thick, starting at the stem end and working down. You may wish to discard the ends, although they can also be cooked.

2. Place the eggplant slices on a platter and sprinkle them with salt and pepper. Pour some olive oil over the slices and then turn them. Repeat the salt, pepper, and olive oil routine on the second side and allow them to marinate for ½ hour, turning them once or twice and adding more olive oil as needed.

3. Broil the eggplant as you would a steak. They are better if charcoal-broiled, but unless you have a charcoal broiler with a cover, be careful. The eggplant absorbs a lot of oil and this will smoke and flame over an open charcoal fire.

4. Cook until nicely browned on both sides. Serve immediately, very hot, on warmed plates. If allowed to sit around the eggplant will become soggy.

MELANSANE A L'EBREA
MELANZANE ALLA MANIERA EBRAICA
Eggplant Venetian Jewish Style

Prepared this way, eggplant goes very well with either boiled or roasted meat.

If you cannot find eggplant 6 to 8 inches in length and 1 or 1½ inches in diameter, it is better not to try this recipe. If you use large round eggplants there will be too much waste.

FOR 4 SERVINGS:

> *1½ pounds eggplant as discussed above,*
>   *8 pieces plus or minus*
> *Salt*
> *Cooking oil, enough to fill a deep fryer or*
>   *saucepan ½ to ⅔ full*
> *3 cloves garlic, peeled*
> *½ cup wine vinegar, either white or red*

1. Wash the eggplant. Cut off a little from the stem end and split the eggplant in half lengthwise. Using a spoon, scrape out and discard the seeds. This should leave a shell with sides ¼ to ⅜ inch thick. Cut the eggplant lengthwise into strips ⅛ to ¼ inch wide. Sprinkle these strips with a little salt and place them out to dry, preferably in the sun. Even in the sun on a warm day it will take 4 or 5 hours for the strips to dry properly. Without sun allow another couple of hours.

2. Heat the oil to 375 degrees. If you do not have a thermometer test the oil by throwing in a small piece of eggplant from time to time. If it starts to sizzle immediately but not terribly violently the oil is approximately the right temperature.

3. Add the strips of eggplant a few at a time to the hot oil and cook them until slightly brown and fairly crisp. Remove them from the oil and drain on paper towels. Continue in this manner until all the eggplant is cooked.

4. Place the cooked eggplant strips in a dish with fairly high sides or in a ceramic bowl along with the peeled garlic cloves. Pour the vinegar over the eggplant. With a fork press down on the eggplant so that it lies flat in the dish and has a chance to absorb the vinegar. Marinate for at

east a couple of hours, occasionally repeating the process of pressing down with a fork. The eggplant need not be served the same day it is made, but if you plan to save it, remove the garlic. Store covered in the refrigerator. In addition to going well with boiled and roasted meat, it may also be served as an *antipasto*.

MELANSANE IN TECIA
MELANZANE IN TEGAME
Braised Eggplant

Eggplant prepared in this manner may be served as either a vegetable dish or as a light second course, but it is perhaps best as a snack accompanied by a piece of cold polenta *(page 221) or some good fresh bread.*

Allow at least 3½ hours to prepare this dish. There is not that much work involved, but there is a lot of waiting.

FOR 4 SERVINGS:

*1½ pounds eggplant, preferably those 6 to
    8 inches in length and having diameters
    of about 1½ inches
Salt
1 clove garlic, peeled
3 tablespoons butter
3 ounces olive oil
2 tablespoons finely chopped parsley
(Pepper)
(Water)*

1. Wash the eggplant and cut off the ends. Slice them lengthwise into strips about ¼ inch thick. For example, if the eggplant is 1½ inches in diameter, you will wind up with 6 strips ¼ inch thick and the length of the eggplant, 6 to 8 inches. Take a teaspoon and remove the seeds from the center of the slices. It is not necessary to get them all. Try to leave as much as possible of the meaty part of the white. Take the slices and cut them into 1-inch lengths. Place a layer of the slices on a platter and sprinkle on a little salt. Do not overdo it. Place another layer of eggplant on top and sprinkle again with a little salt. Continue this process until all the eggplant is on the platter. Allow it to absorb the salt for about an

hour. During this time turn the slices occasionally. Then put the eggplant on a cake rack to dry, again for about an hour. If after that time it still seems very soggy, press the pieces with a wooden spoon to remove as much liquid as possible. Better yet, take a handful at a time and wring it out with your hands, much as you would wring out a dish rag.

2. Brown the garlic in the butter and olive oil in a frying pan over medium heat, then discard it. Remove the pan from the fire for a few minutes to cool a bit.

3. Replace the pan over medium to low heat and add the parsley, eggplant, and a little pepper if you wish. Stir. When the eggplant pieces seem to be well coated with oil and butter, cover the pan and reduce the flame to low. After about 30 minutes correct the seasoning. During cooking stir often, particularly toward the end. Total cooking time should be about an hour. The finished dish should not be watery; however, it is easily burned, so it may be necessary to add a little bit of water from time to time.

4. Serve either hot or cold.

PEPERONADA
PEPERONI AL TEGAME
Braised Bell Peppers

So prepared, bell peppers may be served as a vegetable dish, an antipasto, *or as a sauce, the latter being especially appropriate when the meat is boiled but also good with roasted meat.*

Some people claim that the number of points on the end of the bell pepper opposite the stem will determine whether the pepper is sweet or hot. Other people, including our fruit man, say this is all nonsense.

Variations of this recipe call for the addition of eggplant, one cook using only the skin, another the interior, and a third using both. We give the most simple version: no eggplant.

FOR 6 SERVINGS:

2 pounds bell peppers, green, red, and yellow, if
    possible, to make a more interesting looking dish
1 large tomato
½ cup olive oil

1 large onion, chopped
2 tablespoons finely chopped parsley
Salt
(Water)

1. Remove the tough part from around the stems and quarter the peppers. Remove the seeds and cut the peppers into pieces, large or small, or mixed, as you wish.

2. Peel the tomato. This you may do easily by dipping it in a pan of boiling water for 15 seconds. Remove from the water and pull away the skin with a table knife. Another way is to hold the tomato over a high flame until the skin starts to wrinkle a bit. Proceed with a table knife as before. Cut the peeled tomato into several pieces and remove the seeds. Then chop the tomato. It need not be chopped finely.

3. Place the olive oil, peppers, onion, parsley, tomato, and some salt in a frying pan over fairly high heat. Cover the pan, but uncover and stir every 2 or 3 minutes until the mixture becomes serious about boiling. Then reduce the heat and cook covered for about an hour, stirring every few minutes. The mixture should be simmering gently. The peppers may need a bit of water to prevent them from sticking. On the other hand, if they become tender and are still watery, remove the cover, increase the flame, and boil off the excess liquid. The consistency should not be too watery.

4. Serve either hot or cold as a vegetable or a sauce. As an *antipasto* serve cold.

POMIDORO E SEGOLE IN TECIA
POMODORI E CIPOLLE IN TEGAME
Baked Tomatoes and Onions

This excellent vegetable dish may be served either with boiled or roasted foods, but when it turns out well and becomes pleasing, it can also be considered for a main course if the quantities are increased.

The portions below are for a vegetable course. They are ample but not as large as they might seem at first glance. The onions and tomatoes will shrink considerably during cooking.

FOR 4 SERVINGS:

4 medium-sized tomatoes
4 onions about the same size as the tomatoes
3 tablespoons finely chopped parsley
¼ cup grated Parmesan cheese
½ cup bread crumbs
Salt and pepper
(1 small clove garlic)
2 eggs, lightly beaten
Olive oil
Butter

1. Wash the tomatoes thoroughly and cut them in half across grain; that is, as you would cut an orange to squeeze it for juice. Remove the seeds from the tomatoes by holding them under running water and working into the cavities with a finger.

2. Peel the onions and cut them in half in the same way as the tomatoes.

3. In a mixing bowl combine parsley, grated cheese, bread crumbs, salt and pepper, and a little garlic if you like, squeezed through a garlic press or finely minced. Add about half of the beaten egg and mix well, using a fork. Add more egg, enough to make the mixture moist but not runny.

4. Divide the bread-crumb mixture among the onions and tomatoes making even layers on their cut surfaces. The layers should be about ¼ inch thick.

5. Coat the bottom and sides of a flameproof baking dish with olive oil. The dish must be large enough to hold the tomatoes and onions in a single layer; it must have a cover; and it must be suitable for use both on top of the stove and in the oven. Put the tomatoes and onions in the cooking vessel, bread-crumb side up. Dot them generously with butter.

6. Place the cooking vessel, covered, over low heat on top of the stove. Move the tomatoes and onions occasionally with a spatula to prevent them from sticking. Cook for 30 minutes.

7. While cooking, preheat the oven to 375 degrees.

8. Uncover the cooking vessel and place it in the preheated oven. Cook another 20 minutes. If after that time the bread crumbs have not browned, put the dish under the broiler for a couple of minutes. Spoon the juices over the vegetables.

9. Either serve immediately on a warmed platter or later, cold.

SPARASI DE BASSAN CONSI
SPARAGI DI BASSANO ALL'INSALATA
Bassano Asparagus "Salad"

This vegetable is very valued not only for its flavor but also for its diuretic quality and for that of its easy digestibility. Boiled, it may be served in various ways, but the most simple and best follows:

First of all the asparagus must be well scraped with a knife and a couple of inches of stalk cut off from the bottom. Wash with very cold water. The stalks are then placed in a pot in an upright position, tips up. Add water to a level about halfway up the stalks. Cover and bring to a boil. Add salt. The cooking time will depend upon the maturity of the asparagus, but should be a minimum of about 15 minutes. Test with a fork for tenderness or squeeze a stalk with the fingers to see if it gives.

So cooked, they should be well drained and placed on a warm platter. Sprinkle on some salt, pepper, olive oil, and vinegar or lemon juice and serve.

Bassano asparagus is white and plump, not often seen in America outside of cans. The recipes are equally good using green asparagus. Many claim that the green has a more pleasing flavor.

If a tall, slender pot is not available, use any large pot and loosely tie the asparagus with string to form a bundle which may stand on end.

The cooking time for thin green stalks may be somewhat less than the 15 minutes required for the plump Bassano type. After 10 or 12 minutes begin testing.

In Italy asparagus is generally eaten with the fingers, the last inch or so, which is usually a bit tough and stringy, being discarded. In the best restaurants the diners are provided with devices to hold the asparagus while they munch down the stalk. Knives and forks are not used.

FOR EACH SERVING:

Allow about ½ pound of asparagus for each person. The dressing should be four or five parts oil to one of vinegar or lemon juice.

TEGOLINE IN TECIA
FAGIOLINI IN TEGAME
Braised Green Beans

An excellent vegetable dish, but it may also be served as a light main course when accompanied by polenta *(page 221) or good fresh bread.*

The cooking time will depend upon the variety of bean and the age. They may take 15 minutes or less if young and tender and perhaps up to 30 minutes if old and tough. Whatever the situation with the bean, remember that cooking them as we do in this recipe will take longer than if they were to be simply boiled. Also, remember that Venetians like their vegetables well done by most American standards.

FOR 4 SERVINGS:

1¼ pounds green beans
3 tablespoons olive oil
2 ounces salt pork, finely minced or ground
2 tablespoons finely chopped parsley
¼ medium onion, chopped
2 cups water, boiling
Salt and pepper

1. Snap or cut the ends off the beans and pull away the strings if the beans are not a stringless variety. Do not cut up the beans; leave them whole. Wash well and then soak them in cold water for 15 minutes.

2. Place the olive oil and salt pork in a frying pan over a medium flame. Cook for 3 or 4 minutes or until any bits of meat in the salt pork are sizzling nicely.

3. Add the parsley and onion to the frying pan. Stir well while cooking the onion until it becomes translucent, 5 minutes or so.

4. Add the green beans, ½ cup of the boiling water, and some salt and pepper. Go gently with the salt since the salt pork will have given some to the beans already. Cover the pan and cook until the beans are tender when tested with a fork. During cooking check the beans every few minutes to see that they have enough liquid, adding more of the boiling water as needed. The end result should be tender beans coated with oil, but next to no water at all. If there is too much water, remove the cover, increase the flame, and boil off the excess.

5. Correct the seasoning and serve on warmed plates, or serve cool ater.

VERZE SOFEGAE
VERZE SOFFRITTE
Braised Savoy Cabbage

Although this may be served as a vegetable with almost any meat, it seems best with pork, particularly spareribs. It is a filling dish and we are fortunate that cabbage is in season during the cool weather when we have more desire to eat.

When served with spareribs the 2 are cooked together. The name of the dish in Venetian then becomes *verze sofegae co le costesine de porseo.* Use about 2 pounds of ribs for 4 servings as a main course.

The recipe is not at all difficult. The only trouble is with regard to the amount of liquid, which will determine the color of the cooked cabbage. The color in turn determines to some extent the flavor. The color should be a light brown, definitely more brown than tan, but not so brown as to have a burnt taste. The right amount of water is enough to produce steam but not enough that there are puddles of water in the pan. Plan on an hour and a half or longer for cooking.

FOR 4 SERVINGS:

2½ pounds savoy cabbage
5 tablespoons olive oil
3 ounces bacon, finely minced or ground
(2 pounds spareribs)
½ medium onion, chopped
Salt and pepper
(¼ cup water)

1. Remove and discard the first few outer savoy leaves. Continue removing the leaves and place them in a sink full of cold water. Wash well and shake off as much water as possible and then cut the savoy into strips about ¼ inch wide. Cut across the stem, not parallel to it.

2. Use a very large frying pan or casserole, or if need be a pot. It must have a cover. Place the olive oil and bacon (and the spareribs) in the

cooking vessel and put it over medium heat. When the bacon is sizzling nicely and looks as if it may start to brown, add the onion and a little salt and lots of pepper. When the onion becomes translucent, add the savoy and mix well. Cover, but uncover and stir after a couple of minutes. If the cabbage does not start to give up some liquids at this point, add about ¼ cup water to create a little steam in order to get the cabbage started. For the first hour keep covered except when stirring. You should stir every 10 minutes or so after the cabbage has wilted completely, but more often before that time. If after an hour there seems to be a lot of liquid, cook with the pan partially uncovered. If after 1½ hours you still have puddles of water, cook completely uncovered until the desired light brown color has been attained.

3. Serve immediately or place in a casserole or other ovenware and reheat later in a 300-degree oven. *Polenta* (page 221), is popular with this dish.

SUGO DE POMIDORO E SALSA
DE POMIDORO
CONSERVA DI POMODORO E SALSA
DI POMODORO
Tomato Sauces

Tomato in reasonable quantities is one of the greatest servants of the cook. Avoid, though, the temptation to use it in excess.

To the unpracticed eye *sugo de pomidoro* and *salsa de pomidoro* both are going to look about the same. The difference is that *salsa* has butter, salt, and pepper added. It is the *salsa* that is put on top of spaghetti and the *sugo* that is used in preparing other dishes. Besides being a spaghetti sauce, *salsa* may also be served with boiled or roasted meats, fried eggs, or most any dish where extra flavor and color might be desired.

Plum tomatoes are the variety that are used in making sauces. They are readily available in America in cans and sometimes even fresh. Unless fresh tomatoes are in season and especially good, there is no reason why one should not use the canned ones. In fact, good canned tomatoes are often better than the fresh and there is certainly a lot less work involved. Canned tomatoes normally come already peeled.

There are many qualities available in cans, some sweet and some more acid. Some experience and a knowing grocer will help determine which is most suited to your own personal taste.

A rough rule of thumb on quantities is that a pound of tomatoes will yield about a cup of sauce. It is better to make some extra, though, as some cans simply give less sauce than others. Leftover sauce will keep several days in a closed container in the refrigerator. It also freezes well, and a very useful system is to place the sauce in a plastic ice-cube tray so that a tablespoonful or two at a time may be removed without having to defrost large quantities.

It may seem stupid to make a large thing out of such a simple thing as tomato sauce, but when properly prepared it can make an ordinary pasta delicious or add the necessary something to an otherwise insipid dish.

Many of our recipes call for 2 or 3 tablespoonfuls of tomato sauce. If you do not have any homemade sauce in your refrigerator and do not have time to make some (or don't want to bother), there are some acceptable brands available at most supermarkets. Other possibilities are to dilute some tomato paste, or as it is often called, tomato concentrate. In a real pinch you may use tomato juice.

FOR ABOUT 1½ CUPS *sugo:*

3 tablespoons olive oil
(1 clove garlic, peeled)
1 small onion, chopped
1 medium carrot, diced
3 ribs celery, diced
1½ pounds fresh or canned plum tomatoes,
  coarsely chopped
1 or 2 fresh or dried basil leaves, or
  1 teaspoon ground dried basil

1. Use your largest frying pan. Place the pan containing the olive oil and garlic over medium heat. If you use garlic, brown it and then throw it away. Add the onion, carrot, and celery. Cook, stirring occasionally, until the onion becomes translucent, 5 minutes or so.

2. Some people insist that fresh tomatoes be peeled. If you wish to do so, drop them into boiling water for 15 seconds, drain, and peel. The skins should come off easily. Peeled, unpeeled, or canned, add the tomatoes and basil to the frying pan and stir. Cook, stirring frequently, until most of the

liquids have boiled away and the mixture, if cooked much longer, might stick to the bottom of the pan. This may take 15 minutes, ½ hour, or even longer depending upon the quality of the tomatoes and size of the pan. At any rate, when the mixture becomes thick enough that a cavity left by a spoon does not fill up readily with juice, you should be to the right point and should continue to the next step.

3. Pour the mixture onto a strainer over a saucepan. Stir with a wooden spoon and force as much of the sauce through the strainer as possible leaving behind seeds, skins, and other vegetables. Scrape the sauce from the bottom of the strainer into the saucepan. If the sauce seems too thin, place the saucepan over moderate heat and boil away some of the excess liquid, being extremely careful not to burn the sauce.

4. At this stage you have *sugo de pomidoro*. For *salsa de pomidoro*, proceed as follows:

Salsa de pomidoro:

> *3 or 4 parts* sugo, *above*
> *1 part butter*
> *Salt and pepper*

Heat the *sugo* and butter together in a saucepan and add salt and pepper to taste.

CROSTINI
Italian Croutons

Without crostini *certain soups are as lost as if the salt had been left out.*

The procedure for making *crostini* is extremely simple if you can find the right bread.

Italian or French bread having a diameter of 1½ to 2 inches is ideal. Cut it into ¼-inch or slightly thinner slices, allowing 4 per serving. Barely moisten the bottom of a frying pan with olive oil, place over very low heat, and add the bread slices. Turn them when very light brown on the bottom. When the second side has also turned to a very light brown, remove the *crostini* and place on paper towels until ready for use. The whole operation should take 15 minutes, more or less.

POLENTA
Italian Corn Meal Mush

Polenta is to the Venetian what potatoes are to the Irish, Germans, and Americans.

Basically, *polenta* is corn meal mush, but there seems to be a difference. Whether it is the grinding of the corn, the type of corn, the patience in preparation, or some other factor, *polenta* seems to taste better than mush. Perhaps it is only that *polenta* sounds better than mush.

Polenta is so commonly used in Venice that it is impossible to find a recipe. Everyone knows how to make it without measuring anything: boil the water, put in some salt, and add enough meal. And the Venetians are right, because this is the best way to make *polenta*. In the recipe below we give the ratio of water to meal as 3½ to 1. The problem is that with one package this ratio may work perfectly while a second package may need more or less water. So, it is best to do it the Venetian way, which is to say to eyeball it. Beating with a wire whip, slowly add *polenta* until a point is reached where there is danger of lumping. That is, when the meal hits the surface, were it not beaten immediately with the whip, it would form a lump. If you use too much *polenta*, you can add more water later, stirring it in a little at a time. If you have added too little *polenta*, cook it longer. It has been said that the two prerequisites for making *polenta* are a strong arm and a weak brain. To that we add a good eye.

Polenta is eaten with stews, game, cooked sausage, calf's liver Venetian style, and almost anything else where there might be some sauce to soak up.

Polenta may be eaten immediately after it is made, or it can be eaten cold. When cold it can be cut into slices and charcoal-broiled; or it can be fried using a special frying pan having ridges spaced about an inch apart, this to make it seem that it has been charcoal broiled.

The tools for making *polenta*, other than a strong arm and a weak brain, are a pot with sloping sides, a wooden paddle or spoon, and a circular piece of wood. Sloping sides on the pot make it easier to stir the *polenta* with the wooden paddle, and the board serves as a place to put the *polenta* when it is cooked, as a place for it to cool, and as a cutting board.

More about the board. The board normally has a handle and the handle a hole in it. The hole is there for two reasons: one, so that the

board may be hung up on a peg or nail, and two, a place to attach a string
The string is used to cut the *polenta* by drawing it down across the board
thereby slicing the *polenta*.

FOR 6 SERVINGS:

> *7 cups water*
> *2 tablespoons salt*
> *1 pound* polenta *or cornmeal*

1. Measure the water and salt into a 4-quart saucepan, one with
sloping sides if available. Place over a high flame and bring to a boil.

2. Reduce the flame to slightly above medium. While stirring the
water with a wire whip add the *polenta* very slowly. If added too quickly
lumps will form.

3. Stir the *polenta* with a wooden paddle every few minutes, folding
from the bottom onto the top. As the *polenta* cooks a crust will form on
the bottom of the pan and the sides as well. When ready, the *polenta*
should readily pull away from the crust when stirred. This should
happen after about 45 minutes. The longer you cook the *polenta* the better
it will be.

4. Remove the saucepan from the fire and in one swift motion invert
the pan over a wooden board, depositing the *polenta* in the center. Immediately fill the pan with cold water or it will become extremely difficult
to clean later. Soak the pan overnight.

5. The *polenta* if properly cooked should spread out onto the board
to a thickness of 1½ to 2 inches. It is traditional to cut a small slice from
one side of the *polenta* as soon as it has been placed on the board. The
reason for this is obscure, certainly can have little effect upon the outcome,
but it is the way it is done. Perhaps it is a libation to the *polenta* god.

6. Slice the *polenta* into strips an inch in width and 6 or 7 inches
long. Do this as it is served, not in advance.

7. Leftover *polenta* may be charcoaled or pan fried as explained above.
Or it may be eaten as is, cold.

RECIPES IN OTHER SECTIONS OF THE BOOK which are sometimes served as
contorni.

> Boiled Artichoke Hearts with Olive Oil and Salty Cheese (page 24)
> Better as an *antipasto* or a light lunch, but still good as a vegetable
> when served in small quantities.

Eggplant Casserole (page 104). Usually served as *minestra*, but good as a vegetable if the main course is not too heavy.

Stuffed Zucchini (page 191). Excellent as an economical main course, but good both as an *antipasto* and vegetable when served in moderation.

Asparagus with Hard-boiled Eggs (page 190). Extremely simple and good after a heavy first course.

Asparagus "Bull's Eye" (page 190). Same story as above except the eggs are fried.

Formagi
Formaggi
CHEESE

IN VENICE there is absolutely no cheese production and its consumption is dependent upon its importation from outside, either from the Veneto region itself or from other areas.

Venetians enjoy cheese as a condiment for *minestre*, as something to "change the mouth" after the main course, and not least of all as a preparation for the drinking of a good glass of wine.

Grana is the generic term for dry cheese suitable for grating. The most widely used is *parmigiano*, Parmesan cheese, sprinkled over soups, spaghetti, rice dishes, and often used in cooking. In wine shops it is also served in bite-size pieces to be nibbled at while one drinks his glass of wine. It is always hard enough to grate but often soft enough that it can be served as a table cheese. The harder the sharper seems to be the general rule.

Pecorino is so called because it is made from the milk of *pecore*, ewes. In its pure form it is quite sharp. It goes very well with pears, so much so that there is a proverb which says: *Al contadino non far sapere, quanto è buono il formaggio con le pere.* Very freely translated it means the peasants do not want it known how good a combination cheese and pears make. The story goes that this saying dates back to the days of large landowners when the crops were split between the peasants and the *padrone*. The idea was not to let the *padrone* know about cheese and pears so that the peasants could eat his share also.

Often *pecorino* is made from a mixture of ewes' milk and cows' milk; so made it is less sharp.

Typical quiet back canal scene.

225

Caprino, made from goats' milk, is quite sharp. It is eaten as a table cheese, often with a bit of olive oil poured over it. We prefer it straight.

Gorgonzola, one of the most famous Italian cheeses, comes in two strengths, *verde*, green, being sharper than *bianco*, white. The white, also called *dolce*, sweet, is softer as well as being milder. Both are table cheeses and among the best in the world.

Asiago, another table cheese, is sharp and hard, but not as hard as *parmigiano*.

Other popular sharp cheeses include *toscano* and *siciliano*, at best generic terms for Tuscan and Sicilian cheeses, and *provolone*.

Venetians also like sweet cheeses. *Emmental* and *gruviera* are Swiss types, the best qualities being imported. There are some pretty good imitations made in Italy.

Stracchino, various types of *ricotta*, and *mascherpone* are soft sweet cheeses. *Ricotta*, when mixed with cooked spinach makes an outstanding filling for *ravioli*. An interesting thing that is done with *mascherpone* is mixing it with cognac or rum and powdered sugar to form something between a cheese and a dessert. A half cup or more liquor and sugar to taste are added to a half pound of the cheese and it is slowly mixed until creamy and smooth. It is truly a delightful dish which even children like. The son of a friend of ours got into the *mascherpone* one day and really tied one on before anyone realized what had happened.

Speaking of children, here is something that they also like. Take a piece of hot *polenta* 2 by 4 inches by a little less than an inch thick and sprinkle on grated Parmesan cheese. Elderly people in convalescence also find this pleasing.

Another thing done with cheese that is somewhat unusual is to fry it. Use Swiss, or better, the famous Italian cheese *fontina*. Cut about a 4-ounce slice and fry it as you would an egg, but turning it and keeping it moving so that it does not stick. So prepared and served with a slice of bread it makes a nice quick lunch.

As little as we have said, it pretty well covers the cheese story in Venice. Although Venetians enjoy cheese, it is by no means a great thing in their lives. If cheese is there, they will eat a bite or two, but a meal for them is complete without it.

Dolci
PASTRY AND DESSERTS

VENETIANS ENJOY pastry and desserts but seldom trouble to make them at home. There are scores of pastry shops in Venice, most good and a few truly outstanding. Pastries are fairly expensive when bought outside, but not prohibitively so.

The recipes included are those that are traditionally made at home. Particularly important are those for *galani dolci* and for the two types of *fritole*, all three of which are eaten in surprisingly large quantities during carnival.

GALANI DOLCI

These sweets, simple but most tasty, are highly prized by Venetians.
Galani are difficult to describe and about all we can say is that they are a flat deep-fried pastry.

If you are lucky enough to have an egg beater with a pasta hook attachment, the recipe becomes relatively easy. The dough must be kneaded until the texture is uniform. Other important factors are to have the proper thickness of the dough and to have the oil at the right temperature. The latter two things are easily corrected when the cooking actually begins.

Women taking afternoon coffee and conversation in a typical square.

FOR 40 TO 50 GALANI:

4 cups sifted all-purpose flour
½ cup sugar
1½ teaspoons salt
¼ pound butter cut into small pieces
3 large eggs
Another 1 to 2 cups sifted all-purpose flour
Cooking oil
Powdered sugar

1. Place the 4 cups flour, the sugar, and the salt in a bowl. Mix thoroughly.

2. Allow the butter to become quite soft. Add it to the dry ingredients in the bowl and knead together until a mealy texture is attained.

3. Make a well in the center of the flour and add the eggs. They need not be beaten previously. Beat them with a fork while gradually pulling in a little flour from the sides of the well. When the ingredients are well mixed, add sufficient flour to produce a dough that can be kneaded without sticking to your hands.

4. Turn the dough onto a dusted. pastry board and knead until uniform, at least 5 minutes, better 10 or more. Allow the dough to rest while going on to the next step. The dough may be prepared in advance and stored in the refrigerator for a day, but the results will not be quite so good.

5. Fill a deep fryer or a saucepan half full with good cooking oil. Heat the oil to 400 degrees. More about the temperature later.

6. Take a piece of dough slightly larger than a golf ball and roll it out into a very thin sheet, much thinner than for a pie crust. Using a rotary cutting tool, preferably with a serrated cutting edge, cut the dough into squares, triangles, or any interesting shapes you may wish. The greatest dimension should be 4 or 5 inches since the *galani* will expand when cooking. A good idea at this point is to cut only 1 *galano* and cook it in order to check the thickness of the dough and the oil temperature. When added to the oil, the *galano* should start bubbling immediately but not violently. After 45 seconds or a few seconds longer, turn the *galano* with a fork. It should be a medium golden brown color. After another half minute the *galano* should be ready to remove from the oil. Place on paper towels to cool. Break it open to see if the dough is completely cooked. The *galano* should be crisp but not burnt. If the outside is golden but

the inside soggy, roll the dough out more thinly and try again. If the *galano* is pale, increase the oil temperature a little. Once the dough thickness and the oil temperature have been set, the *galani* may be made fairly quickly, 2 or 3 being cooked at a time. Continue rolling out and cooking the *galani* until all the dough is exhausted.

7. When the *galani* have cooled, dust them with powdered sugar. Some people prefer more sugar than others. *Galani* are eaten as a dessert or as a snack with a glass of medium sweet wine.

FRITOLE A LA VENEZIANA
FRITTELLE DOLCI
Venetian Fritters

These fritters are used very much in Venice during the period of carnival. They are a little heavy, but tasty, and, as do galani, *they go well with a good glass of medium sweet wine, either red or white.*

Fritole should be eaten the same day they are made for they become stale very quickly.

FOR ABOUT 3 DOZEN FRITTERS:

1¼ cups milk
¼ cup rice
½ teaspoon salt
¼ cup lukewarm water
1 ounce yeast (1½ cakes)
A pinch of sugar
3¼ cups sifted all-purpose flour
1 teaspoon salt
1 large egg
⅔ cup water
¼ cup strong liquor or liqueur, preferably
   rum or anisette
6 ounces seedless raisins
2 ounces pine seeds
2 ounces citron, cut into small pieces,
   ⅛ inch or smaller
Cooking oil
Powdered sugar or vanilla powdered sugar

1. Pour the milk into a small saucepan and bring it to a boil. Add the rice and ½ teaspoon salt. Cook over low heat for 30 minutes. Stir constantly toward the end of cooking so that the mixture does not burn. It should have a pasty consistency.

2. Disperse the yeast in the ¼ cup lukewarm water in a small bowl. Add a pinch of sugar and set aside. If the yeast is fresh, bubbles should begin to form immediately.

3. Put the sifted flour and the 1 teaspoon of salt in a large mixing bowl and add the rice-milk mixture prepared above. Mix with a wooden spoon. Add the egg and stir it in. It need not be beaten first. Still stirring, add the yeast-water mixture and an additional ⅔ cup water. Continue stirring until the lumps have disappeared and a very thick batter is attained. Bubbles should start to form within the batter. Add the liquor or liqueur, raisins, pine seeds, and citron. Mix everything very well. Cover the bowl with a damp cloth and place it in a warm spot, 80 degrees or so. Allow the batter to rise for about 3 hours.

4. Fill a deep fryer or a saucepan half full of good cooking oil. Heat the oil to 375 degrees. If you don't have a thermometer, test the temperature by dropping small pieces of bread into the oil. When they brown quickly, you are in the right temperature range.

5. Be careful not to burn yourself during the cooking of the fritters. Wet a spoon with cold water. Scoop up about 2 tablespoons of the batter, moisten a thumb with water, and cautiously push the batter off the spoon into the hot oil. Do this as close to the surface as possible in order to prevent splashing, but not so close as to burn your hand when the fritter bubbles upon contact with the hot oil. Cook the fritter until it has an even deep golden brown color, turning it once or twice during cooking. The fritter should be about 2 inches across. If larger or smaller, adjust the amount of batter accordingly for subsequent fritters. Remove the fritter from the oil and place it on a paper towel. Cut open this test fritter to make sure that it is cooked through. If so, proceed as described above for the remaining batter, cooking 4 or 5 fritters at a time. If not cooked through, try another test fritter, cooking it longer. If on longer cooking the fritter becomes too dark, reduce the oil temperature slightly. Place the cooked fritters on paper towels to cool.

6. When the fritters have cooled, roll them in powdered sugar and place on a platter. They may be served as a dessert or a snack.

FRITOLE CO LA SUCA
FRITTELLE ALLA ZUCCA
Pumpkin or Squash Fritters

One can also make fritters using pumpkin in place of rice.

Prepare these fritters in exactly the same manner as *fritole a la veneziana*, the preceding recipe, except for the first step.

FOR ABOUT 3 DOZEN FRITTERS:

¾ pound pumpkin or acorn squash
¾ cup water
2 teaspoons salt

1. Remove the seeds and peel the pumpkin or squash. Cut it into very small pieces.
2. Place the pumpkin or squash in a frying pan with ¾ cup water and the salt. Cover the pan and bring the liquid to a boil. Reduce the heat to a simmer and stirring occasionally cook until pulpy and reasonably smooth. This should take about 25 minutes. If it shows signs of sticking to the bottom of the pan, add a little more water and reduce the flame further.
3. Substitute this mixture for the rice-milk mixture in the preceding recipe.

CASTAGNE
Chestnuts

Chestnuts, joy of children and adults too, are best prepared in the autumn when they are fresh and sweet. When days are cold the chestnuts should be eaten very hot, the better to warm the stomach . . . and the hands as well!

There are three ways in which we prepare chestnuts: boiled, "peeled," and roasted.

CASTAGNE LESSAE
CASTAGNE LESSATE
Boiled Chestnuts

This is the simplest. Place the chestnuts in a saucepan and cover with water. Add a little salt and bring to a boil. Cook for 20 to 25 minutes and test one to see if cooked. Do this by cutting it in half with a sharp knife. The shell will still be tough. The meat should be tender but not mushy. Serve immediately, distributing sharp knives to the adults.

CASTAGNE PELAE
CASTAGNE PELATE
"Peeled" Chestnuts

This one requires patience and strong fingernails. With a sharp knife make several cuts through the outer shell of the chestnut. Peel away the shell leaving the inner shell intact, if possible. Place the peeled chestnuts in a saucepan and cover with cold water. Place over a high flame and when the water starts to boil add salt, a tablespoonful and a half per pound of chestnuts. Add also at this point a teaspoonful or even two, depending upon your taste, of fennel seeds. Cook for 15 minutes and test one, peeling away the inner shell first. Serve immediately, very hot.

CASTAGNE ROSTE
CASTAGNE ARROSTE
Roasted Chestnuts

The largest chestnuts are the ones usually roasted. Make a cut along the flat side of the chestnut, cutting against the grain, which is to say from side to side, not top to bottom. To do the cooking properly you need special equipment, an iron pan with holes in the bottom. This pan fits on top of a charcoal burner. Place the chestnuts in the pan over the fire and cook, turning frequently, until tender, 20 minutes more or less depending upon the fire. Test one to see if cooked. The shell should come away easily and the meat be tender but not dry. The shells should be charred but not burnt. It is easy to burn them cooking over charcoal, so be careful. Serve immediately, very hot.

Chestnuts may also be roasted in a conventional oven, but the results are not nearly so appetizing.

TORTA DE POMI
TORTA DI MELE
Apple "Pie" Venetian Style

This is definitely a home-style sweet, which is to say not very important or pretentious. It is indicated for large families, those with many little children.

This is a great favorite of Venetian children, so much so that an adult caught eating *torta de pomi* leaves himself open to jokes with regard to his mental age.

It is extremely simple to make, the result being a rather gooey glob of custard-like material with apples imbedded in it, all sitting on a somewhat soggy crust. When eaten it tends to stick to the teeth and the roof of the mouth, and it is rather sweet. No wonder children adore it!

Any apples may be used. The following recipe is for the Delicious variety. If the apples are green, greatly increase the amount of sugar.

FOR 6 TO 8 SERVINGS:

1½ cups sifted all-purpose flour
3 tablespoons sugar
1½ teaspoons salt
1 envelope dried yeast
1½ cups milk
2 ounces butter, warmed just enough to
   liquify it
¼ cup any sweet liqueur (Grand Marnier,
   Triple Sec, etc.)
4 good-sized apples, 1½ to 1¾ pounds
More butter
More flour
Another 3 tablespoons sugar

1. Put the sifted flour into a mixing bowl along with the sugar, salt, and dried yeast. Mix well and then all at once add the milk. Using an egg beater, beat until smooth. Add the melted butter, still beating, and then the liqueur. Let the batter rest while going on to the next steps.

2. Preheat the oven to 400 degrees.

3. Quarter and peel the apples. Remove the cores and slice the apples (it does not matter in which direction) very thinly, 1/16 to ⅛ inch thick.

4. Butter a pan 8" by 12" by 1½" or an 11- or 12-inch pie tin. Use a generous amount of butter. Dust the pan or pie tin with flour.

5. Place the apples in the pan or pie tin and level them out the best you can. Give the batter a last quick mix and pour over the apples. Sprinkle 3 tablespoons sugar evenly over the top. Pop the pan into the preheated oven and cook for an hour or slightly longer. When cooked the top should be golden brown and the "crust" starting to pull away from the sides of the pan. The center of the "pie" will still be somewhat runny but will set up as it cools.

6. Serve either warm or cold, but not hot.

ZAVAGION
ZABAIONE O ZABAGLIONE
Zabaglione

This dessert is easily made and does not require much time. It is quite flavorful and pleasing, particularly if accompanied by sugar cookies or bitter almond cookies.

The only trick with this recipe is to realize when the cooking is complete. If cooked too long, the egg yolks will solidify into lumps. At the first sign of anything resembling sticking to the bottom of the pan, remove from the heat and serve. The consistency should be that of a light, fluffy custard.

If you cannot find marsala wine you may substitute some other sweet wine or liqueur or even rum.

If possible use an electric beater, because the yolks and sugar must be extremely thoroughly beaten.

FOR EACH SERVING:

2 egg yolks
1½ tablespoons sugar
3 tablespoons good dry Marsala wine

1. Beat the eggs rapidly while slowly adding the sugar. Beat until the mixture has lost most of its yellow color and becomes rather white. Continue to beat while adding the wine.

2. The cooking may be done in a saucepan over a low flame, but it is safer to use a double boiler. Have the water boiling in the bottom part of the double boiler. Put the egg yolk mixture into the top part and stir constantly and vigorously with a wire whip. A wooden spoon may be used instead but the result will not be as fluffy.

3. Cook until the mixture just begins to attach itself to the bottom of the pan. Do not bring to a boil. Remove the top part of the double boiler and beat the zabaglione a few seconds longer with the whip.

4. Pour into warmed sherbert glasses and serve immediately. Or pour into cooled sherbert glasses, refrigerate, and serve later cold.

Fruti
Frutta
FRUIT

IF ONLY A FEW grapes or an orange or a half an apple, fruit at the end of a meal serves to freshen the mouth and aid the digestion.

Once upon a time in Venice one ate wonderful fruit grown on the nearby islands. The farmers there worked the ground and harvested the fruit at the peak of ripeness and in sailboats or boats that were rowed they brought it to the Rialto.

Unhappily, this has died out a little at a time because of high tides and floods and lack of farm labor. The young men no longer wish to work the land but would instead take jobs in the new factories and other places where they can more rapidly improve their station.

Take for example the Lido, the strip of land that protects us from the sea. Until 50 years ago there were only a few houses and hotels along the principal street, while the rest of the island was composed of orchards, vineyards, and vegetable farms. Now, very few fields remain, most having been filled with new houses, apartments, and hotels.

Perhaps we should not complain. It is true that we had marvelous fruit, but it is also true that the seasons were short. Today we find excellent fruit the year around, some of it coming from so far away that 50 years ago we would have thought it an impracticable dream. Excellent, yes—but not quite so good as if it were *nostrano*, ours.

Gondolas at the Molo, *near Piazza San Marco.*

Bibite in Genere
BEVERAGES

VENETIANS AS a group have the reputation for being among the heaviest drinkers in Italy and, in fact, they certainly consume their share and perhaps a bit more. They are great sippers, often starting in the morning before work and continuing right through the day, taking wine breaks instead of coffee breaks. As much as they drink, they cannot by any means be classified as "drinkers" in the derogatory sense. They enjoy drinking and the companionship that comes from sharing a bottle of wine.

VINI
Wines

Wine, of course, is the most popular drink throughout Italy, and Venice is no exception. Although there is no sizable production in the immediate vicinity, one does not have to search far to find many good wines.

FROM THE FRIULI ZONE:

Tokai and *pinot grigio* are often excellent dry white wines, sometimes quite strong.

Fireworks at Redentore, *July's big festival.*

FROM THE PIAVE:

Raboso, merlot, and *cabernet* are red wines, not outstanding, but very drinkable.

FROM THE VERONA ZONE:

Here we have both reds and whites. The best known red is *Valpolicella,* fairly light. Almost the same story and with a very similar name is *Valpantena.* Other reds are *Bardolino,* also fairly light, *Recioto,* sweet enough for desserts and sometimes sparkling, and *Amerone* from the same grape as *Recioto* but fermented further. It is dry and strong. The famous white wine from the zone is *Soave,* but there are also some very respectable *Tokai* wines.

FROM THE ALTO ADIGE AND TRENTINO:

Some excellent wines come from this troubled area, the most readily available of which are *Traminer, Riesling,* and *Terlano,* all three white. *Santa Magdalena* is a red of a certain distinction. *Sandbichler,* both red and white can be excellent. *Teroldego* is a red well thought of. Also some *spumanti,* Italian sparkling white wines, of good quality come from these areas.

It should be noted that the names given above are mostly generic and do not guarantee that a bottle bearing the name will be good. That depends upon the integrity of the man who finally bottles the wine.

The above mentioned are local in the sense that they are the best known that come from a reasonable distance. Venetians do not limit themselves to these but also drink wines from other regions, notably Tuscany and the Piedmont, the two most famous zones in Italy.

APERITIVI
Aperitifs

Before meals Venetians often take an *aperitivo* to stimulate the appetite. This can be simply a Bitter Campari, Select, Carpano Bitter, all with soda, or a Punt e Mes, or vermouth straight. There are numerous other possibilities. Aperitifs are generally taken without ice, but more often than not the bottle is refrigerated.

The above are simple *aperitivi.* Mixed *aperitivi* seem to be gaining in popularity. We give examples below.

Negroni—the most popular mixed *aperitivo* today in Italy:
⅓ part Bitter Campari
⅓ part sweet vermouth
⅓ part gin
(Ice)
(2 dashes Angostura Bitters)

Mix the ingredients and pour into a highball glass. Fill the glass with cold soda and decorate with an orange slice.

Americano—Originally the Italian idea of an American cocktail:

⅓ Bitter Campari
⅔ sweet vermouth
(2 dashes Angostura Bitters)

Mix the ingredients and pour into a highball glass. Fill with cold soda and add a lemon twist.

Spritz—Popular in Venice and unknown outside:

½ white wine
½ soda water
(1 tablespoon Select or Bitter Campari)

Serve in a highball glass without ice. Add a lemon twist.

Cavaliere's No. 24—Very popular with at least two Venetian residents.

1 part Bitter Campari
⅓ part cognac
1/6 part Bianco Sarti

Pour the ingredients into a cocktail glass. Top off with soda and add a lemon twist. If the weather is hot, add an ice cube.

The dry martini has made inroads in Venice, but to the thinking of most locals it still has a long way to go.

DIGESTIVI
Digestives

These are taken after meals, the excuse being to aid the digestion.

The most famous are Fernet Branca, Ramazzotti, Alpestre, *grappa*, *grappa alla ruta*, but there are dozens of others. In the last few years Scotch whisky on the rocks has steadily gained popularity while sweet liqueurs are taken less and less often.

In closing we have some thoughts to offer. Whatever you drink, try to make it help the meal. If the wine is bad it does more harm than good. It is better to drink a good red wine with fish than a bad white. A glass of good wine enhances, but a glass too many and it becomes meaningless. Therefore, do not drink so much before and during the meal that you lose the harmony between food and drink essential for deriving the greatest satisfaction from both.

With these thoughts in mind, we would like to finish with a Venetian proverb. Riempi el bicer col xe vodo, svodalo col xe pien; non lo lassar mai vodo, non lo lassar mai pien! *Fill the glass that is empty, empty the glass that is full; never leave it empty, never leave it full!*

INDEX

250 INDEX